Modern Skeletons in Postmodern Closets:
A Cultural Studies Alternative

KNOWLEDGE:
Disciplinarity and Beyond

SERIES EDITORS:

Ellen Messer-Davidow · David R. Shumway · David J. Sylvan

Modern Skeletons in Postmodern Closets: A Cultural Studies Alternative

James J. Sosnoski

UNIVERSITY PRESS OF VIRGINIA

Charlottesville and London

FOR GREGOR, JONATHAN, AND PATRICIA

who taught me the limits of arguments

THE UNIVERSITY PRESS OF VIRGINIA

Copyright © 1995 by the Rector and Visitors of the University of Virginia

First published 1995

Library of Congress Cataloging-in-Publicaton Data

Sosnoski, James J., 1938–
    Modern skeletons in postmodern closets : a cultural studies
alternative / James J. Sosnoski.
        p.   cm. — (knowledge, disciplinarity and beyond)
    Includes bibliographical references.
    ISBN 0-8139-1620-8 (alk. paper). — ISBN 0-8139-1621-6 (pbk. :
alk. paper)
    1. Postmodernism (Literature)   2. Criticism.   3. Culture — Study
and teaching.   I. Title.   II. Series.
PN6071.F17S67   1995
801'.95—dc20   95–24128
                                                                  CIP

Printed in the United States of America

CONTENTS

ACKNOWLEDGMENTS

Ellen Messer-Davidow and David Shumway have been exemplary editors. Ellen gave me a detailed reading of an early version of this book, and I am indebted to her for innumerable improvements. My debt to David goes back to the days when we cofounded the GRIP project (Group for Research on the Institutionalization and Professionalization of Literary Studies), which he now directs. The impassioned discussions on disciplinarity we had when he was my colleague at Miami University shaped this project, and since then he has provided me with continuous commentary. Gerald Graff's insightful reading of the manuscript led to many crucial revisions, and I am grateful for the time and energy he has generously given to my work. I owe a very special debt to Christopher Knight, a longtime colleague and friend, who persuaded me to publish these essays in book form. His careful readings of the manuscript at various stages of its development have had far-reaching effects on my views. I am deeply in David Downing's debt for his reading of the manuscript. The conversations I have had with him since the early days of the GRIP project have had considerable influence on my thinking, and working closely with him for several years has confirmed for me the view of collaboration I express in this book.

I have been privileged to work in a department in which my colleagues have been a tremendous resource. In particular I wish to thank Britton Harwood, Mary Jean Corbett, Fran Dolan, Laura Mandell, Susan Jarratt, Arthur Casciato, and Randolph Wadsworth. In addition, my understanding of institutional life has been enriched over the years by critical exchanges with GRIP members Steve Nimis, Paul Smith, Lisa Frank, Richard Ohmann, Evan Watkins, Jim Phelan, Jonathan Arac, Paul Bové, Burton Bledstein, Phyllis Franklin, Jeffrey Peck, and the late Henry

Schmidt. For many insightful conversations I am indebted as well to Don Bialostosky, Martha Woodmansee, Leroy Searle, Victor Vitanza, Ralph Cohen, and the late Jim Berlin. I am especially grateful to the students with whom I have collaborated on various related projects that have contributed to the analyses in this book—Takis Poulakis, Barbara Beisecker, Richard Barney, Katherine Borklund, Kim Gannon, Les Epstein, Terry Cooper, Rory Ong, Marian Schiachitano, Bob Broad, Holly Roberts, Dan Dawson, and Jim McFadden. I also wish to thank my chair, C. Barry Chabot, who supported this project in innumerable ways, encouraging me throughout the process.

Jonathan Lawrence has been a wonderfully helpful editor and the manuscript is much improved as the result of his sound advice. I owe many debts at the University Press of Virginia. Carol Mitchell has kept me aware of all deadlines with good humor. Mary Kathryn Hassett has given me a whole new perspective on publicity and marketing. And Nancy Essig has made crucial recommendations that have had an important impact on the book.

Without doubt my deepest debt is to Patricia Harkin, whose influence on my work is thorough and pervasive. Her several readings of the essays that make up this book have had such a profound effect on what I say that I think of her as my coauthor.

Prologue

his book was initially meant to be a theory of literary criticism. Like many other critics in the sixties, I believed that a theory of criticism was a theory of interpretation—applied epistemology. In the seventies I discovered Ralph Cohen's *Art of Discrimination* and took to heart his point that a theory of criticism should be a description of what critics actually do. Instead of searching for an appropriate method of interpretation, I studied what critics wrote.[1]

Influenced by the work of structuralists, semioticians, and philosophers of science, I conceived my project as an attempt to establish that literary study was a discipline based on canons of argumentation and criteria for judging the status of readings as knowledge. At the time, the applicability of Thomas Kuhn's *The Structure of Scientific Revolutions* to literary study was a hotly debated issue and provoked literary critics to read the work of Karl Popper, Imre Lakatos, Paul Feyerabend, and Stephen Toulmin. In this climate, I took as my point of departure the question, "Are readings of literary texts replicable?" I wondered if, given well-formed rules, several readers could describe a text in consistent ways. To test this hypothesis, I formed the Miami University Research Group Experiment (MURGE) with eight graduate students interested in discourse analysis; we undertook exhaustive analyses of the evidence critics of James Joyce's short story "Araby" used in their arguments.[2]

One result of our analyses increasingly troubled me—I was unable to account for the logical function of many sentences in "Araby" criticism. In our attempts to describe the logical structure of critical arguments, such sentences often proved quite embarrassing. They interfered with, obscured, mystified, or otherwise altered the logical flow of the arguments so much

1

that the essays we examined seemed more illogical than logical in their structure. In search of an explanation, I turned from logical to professional concerns and looked for traces of networks of critics, authorities, editors, and other forms of professionalism embedded in the essays. In this phase of the study, my attention fastened on relationships between the institution of, and the production of, criticism, and I scrutinized how textbooks and exams structured the critical practices of students trained by them. To focus my work, I studied one of the "Araby" critics whose career was exemplary, namely, Cleanth Brooks, who had not only collaborated on a series of textbooks that dominated literary criticism for two or three decades but had also written scholarly treatises and a history of criticism. Furthermore, he belonged to a network of theorists who inspired the New Critical movement, which dominated *Portrait* and "Araby" criticism from the fifties to the seventies.

At this juncture of the project, the more I studied critical arguments, the more they seemed like quarrels. Since many of my close friends were in the job market during this period, when I examined critical pronouncements I could not separate them from competition for rewards, stature, and power. In 1982, David Shumway, Steve Nimis, Jim Fanto, and I formed the Group for Research into the Institutionalization and Professionalization of Literary Studies (GRIP) to examine the effects of institutionalization on critical work. The papers I wrote as a member of this group are collected in this volume.

My study of literary *criticism,* which had begun as an attempt to build a model of interpretation, ended as an attempt to show how literary *critics* were molded by their training. The question I asked in the sixties, "What is literary criticism?" I reformulated in the seventies as "What do critics do?"; reframed in the eighties as "How are critics schooled?"; and rearticulate in the nineties as "What does criticism mask?" What first looked like a structure of the mind, then like a habit of mind, and later like a discursive formation, I now see as a disposition to disguise an intuitive mode of understanding as a logical enterprise. I moved from the view that literary criticism was a systematic, logical, and coherent discipline to the perception that it is an eclectic, analogical, and intuitive profession. Nonetheless, instead of being disappointed that literary study is not a particularly logical enterprise, I find myself appreciating how the illogic of criticism makes sense. But can a discipline be illogical? Is criticism intuitive? These questions motivate this work.

Modern Skeletons in Postmodern Closets responds to this dilemma: If we say literary study is a discipline, have we condemned ourselves to always trying to be one? In the chapters that follow, I offer a critique of disciplinarity as an ideal for scholars in the humanities and conclude that we need to develop an alternative way of describing ourselves. As David Shumway observes in *Creating American Civilization: A Genealogy of American Literature as an Academic Discipline,* we are formed by the ways we describe ourselves (2). In my view, continuing to give ourselves a disciplinary formation constrains what we do and commits us to institutional evaluations that put us at a serious disadvantage. In addition, it forces us to construe what we do in ways that are incongruous with recent and highly relevant theoretical developments. In a sentence, my thesis is that many skeletal forms of the very discipline that is the defining characteristic of the modern university can be found in the closets of critics who describe themselves as postmodern.

You might ask, as I do in the introductory chapter that follows: What skeletons?

What Skeletons?

Robert Pirsig's *Zen and the Art of Motorcycle Maintenance* is a narrative about a person trying to understand who he is by going back to where he used to live in order to recall who he was. Since he no longer believes what he did when he lived there, he is, in effect, a different person on his return. About to visit his old friends, the DeWeeses, he experiences himself as an imposter, and this brings to his mind a movie about a World War I spy. "In my memory," he writes, "is a movie about a World War I spy who studied the behavior of a captured German officer . . . for months until he could imitate every gesture and nuance of speech. Then he pretended to be the escaped officer in order to infiltrate the German Army command. I remember the tension and excitement as he faced his first test with the officer's old friends to learn if they would see through his imposture. Now I've some of the same feeling about DeWeese, who'll naturally presume I'm the person he once knew" (122). The memory of the film gives him the sensation of behaving like a spy. At the DeWeeses', he feels awkward because he cannot readily acquaint them with the person he has become. The scenario evokes comparable experiences for many readers. Being mistaken for the person you once were not only makes you feel like an imposter, it sometimes makes you act like an imposter.

Most of us at times allow others to assume we still are the person we once were. Returning home and being presented with the food we favored when growing up (in my case, kielbasa, a type of Polish sausage), we don't always explain that nowadays we avoid it. Or, when aroused in time for Sunday services, we don't necessarily explain that we no longer go to church. Such behavior seems appropriate. What middle-aged person would fault Pirsig's protagonist for not explaining to DeWeese who he now is and what his loyalties now are?

What we do in one context often contradicts who we say we are in another. For example, a person who for years has enjoyed listening to the opera on Saturday afternoons on his state-of-the-art sound system may not feel inconsistent in saying he is dubious about the use of technology in the arts while conversing about its application to literary studies. Were Pirsig's protagonist not so self-reflexive, he could have arrived at the DeWeese residence without sensing anything odd about the fact that his host might regard him as the person he once was. Indeed, in similar situations many of us would fall back into acting like the person we once were, rediscovering idioms we've forgotten, making gestures from which we have long since disassociated ourselves. We behave in these circumstances without any sense of self-contradiction.

The state of affairs I just described—being unaware that some of the motives we acquired in the past are inconsistent with our current beliefs—might be called "anachronistic." Until challenged, many such beliefs continue to govern our conduct. In relationships of intimacy, for instance, men who regard themselves as profeminist often are disconcerted to learn how many archaic sexist beliefs still govern their conduct. You might say such anachronistic beliefs are skeletons in the closets of their minds. Though we consciously amend beliefs that are challenged, many ingrained beliefs associated with those we've abandoned remain as they were. We all have such skeletons in our cognitive closets. Our mental residences may be remodeled continuously, but many of their private compartments escape renovation, going unnoticed until someone happens to open them. Tongue in cheek, we might say that literary critics have "archaic selves" (a phrase that both describes and illustrates the condition of being anachronistic).[1]

Though we have theoretical loyalties we abandon for others, there are occasions when we resume our older loyalties and thus our archaic theoretical persona. Some of us, for example, had deep loyalties to formalism, which we abandoned in sympathy with poststructuralist critiques. Nonetheless, on certain occasions we do not feel obliged to reveal our new loyalties. This is often a tactical matter. Conversing with New Critical colleagues does not require that we challenge their assumptions, so we usually don't in order to avoid unnecessary conflict.

Nowadays we readily admit that we present ourselves to our colleagues in the institution of criticism in strategic ways.[2] Erving Goffman describes such presentations of self quite succinctly in his *Strategic Interaction,* a sociological account of the calculative, gamelike aspects of interpersonal relations. In this volume he studies events whose outcomes depend not only on the players' awareness of their opponents' moves but also on the wit to use this awareness to their own advantage—drawing frequently from accounts of spying. In describing the attributes of good game players (which all spies are) he writes: "Perhaps the most important attribute of players is their *gameworthiness*," which includes "the intellectual proclivity to assess all possible courses of action and their consequences, and to do this from the point of view of all the contesting parties" (96). Many literary critics have this attribute. Addressing older colleagues, they use formalist idioms. Addressing younger colleagues, they use postmodern idioms. We hardly notice when we shift idioms. This seems judicious and harmless. However, we probably should not congratulate ourselves too earnestly for being unconsciously judicious. Though consistency may be the hobgoblin of petty minds, it is not always judicious to dismiss our inconsistencies as trivial matters.

In the ensuing chapters, I consider such anachronistic behavior from an institutional point of view as a strategic interaction. Since institutions inculcate beliefs, it often happens that persons work in institutions whose founding beliefs they no longer hold but whose instantiated practices they follow. I have in mind postmodern critics working in the modern American university (such as the professor I describe below whose deconstructive theory of language conflicts with his grading practices). This book delineates anachronistic theoretical assumptions embodied in institutionalized practices (such as exams) that still influence the conduct of some critics who nonetheless think of themselves as postmodern.

Critics who are called postmodern are usually thought to be critical of modern institutions. In this study I note that they often have skeletons of modernity in their critical closets that support rather than change modern establishments. Since criticism has been structured historically by argumentation, I focus my observations about such skeletons on critical debates, construing them as strategic interactions.

As a rhetorically inclined speech-act theorist might be prone to say, the efficacy of critical arguments depends on "felicity conditions." The discovery of skeletons in the closets of our mind is surely an infelicitous condition we would wish to remedy. This book reflects on this possibility.

Postmodern Critics Work in Modern Institutions of Criticism

In Laurence Veysey's account of their emergence, during the 1880s, universities were organized by departments understood as the "homes" of discrete disciplines of inquiry. Like other studies, literary scholarship was construed as a discipline whose hallmark was a particular species of argument embodying informal logic (usually following Aristotelian principles) as an index of the authenticity of its disciplinarity. Since that time, argument has been the accepted manner of establishing the merit of textual scholarship and critical interpretation.

On the other hand, according to Foucault's definition of them, modern institutions are dedicated to discipline in a more negative sense, and his view has inspired many critiques of modern institutions. In general, postmodern theorists resist the metanarratives their modern counterparts employ as the rationales for their inquiries. Postmodern critics often eschew strict methodologies, in contrast to advocates of discipline, who frequently promote such methodologies to stabilize the production of knowledge. Poststructuralist critics customarily regard formalism as a hierarchy of practices aimed at normalizing literature rather than attempts to be rigorous in critical analyses.

The tension between a disabling and an enabling sense of discipline is illustrated in a story a colleague at another university told me, one that has continued to haunt me. It seems that during a Ph.D. exam my colleague was chairing, the candidate was asked to define deconstruction. Believing this to be something of a "trick question," she responded that deconstruction should not be defined because, as Derrida has often noted, such terms continuously shift in their meanings. When the examiner countered her response by asking how it was then possible for Jeremy Hawthorn to include the term in his *Glossary of Contemporary Critical Theory,* the candidate, realizing that the line of questioning was a hostile one, was unsure how to reply to her inquisitor's interrogation. If she suggested that Hawthorn was wrong to try to define the term, she would open a Pandora's box of logical objections to deconstruction. Under normal circumstances she assiduously avoided such arguments, since the persons who usually posed logical quandaries about deconstructive theory seemed to her to have missed the point. (In her view, Derrida's philosophy of language was preferable to John Searle's.) On the other hand, if she suggested that putting terms in textbooks didn't stop their meaning from shifting, she would open a different but equally vexing Pandora's box. Taking this second direction would seem to suggest that deconstruction, which she had been advocating, undermined literary study as a discipline. Her examiners would rightly construe her as saying that, although terms from postmodern theory were institutionalized in textbooks and reference works in order to train students to be literary critics, their meanings nonetheless shifted in actual practice. This answer would leave her vulnerable to the objection that, if she were correct, then the authors of such textbooks were either disingenuous or foolish. Either way, she would be positioned as a proponent of destabilizing the discipline of literary study. Constrained by her circumstance—taking an exam—she found herself trying to guess what the correct move was supposed to be while simultaneously wondering if her adversarial examiner was out to checkmate her with his next move. Fortunately, she was saved by her dissertation director (and my narrator), who deftly suggested that she should not be held responsible for the incompatibilities between the institution of criticism and postmodern theory.

This story is not surprising. It is an instance of the sort of gamesmanship Goffman describes, which seems all too commonplace in the institution of criticism. It is hardly unusual for examiners to set rhetorical traps for degree candidates. Nor is it unusual for an examining committee to be comprised of professors whose views clash, thus making it difficult for candidates to avoid the pitfalls presented by questions directed at another professor more than at them. However, since I identified with her director, I was troubled by his response to the situation. On the one hand, he was acknowledging that there were incompatibilities between the postmodern theories he advised his candidate to study and the modern institution of criticism his colleague was bent on upholding; but, on the other hand, he was conducting an exam presupposing meanings stable enough to be construed as adequate, reliable, or correct answers. He seemed complicitous in the routine identification of stable meaning, despite his adherence to a theory of language that made such identifications dubious.

Stirred by the disparity between the role he had assigned himself (knight errant) in his narrative and the one I am tempted to give him (pawn), I began to ponder the various ways in which the modern university is inhospitable to postmodern critics (among whom I count myself). We have numerous skeletons of modernity in our closets simply because we routinely accept practices deeply ingrained in the American university system, which still is a modern institution. The chapters that follow concern the discrepancies between postmodern theory and its institutionalization as a disciplinary practice.

For many members of literature departments, to espouse a discipline of postmodern criticism is a contradiction in terms. Yet the modern institution of criticism, which is designed to create hierarchies of knowledge and knowers, continues to maintain itself despite the alleged takeover of postmodern thinkers. The account of the Ph.D. exam is an obvious example of the persistence of ranking or hierarchization, the hallmark of modern systems. Moreover, the grading practices that characterize modern institutions of learning survive even in literature departments, since the influential postmodern critics they employ give grades to their students and are "graded" by editors and reviewers for their "close readings."

Some critics who hold views associated with poststructuralist and postmodern thought believe that what the institution allows does not regulate what they do. My effort in this book is to persuade them that what they do fits surprisingly well into the grooves furnished by the institutions in which they work. At the same time, I try to persuade more traditionally oriented critics that even though Derrida, Foucault, or Lyotard bring into view the perplexities of our institutional practices, poststructuralist theory as such is not required to discern them. The field-coverage principle underlying our curricula, or the schools-and-movements principle underlying our histories of criticism, for instance, cannot be tossed aside as problems that affect only postmoderns. Such practices do not stand up to a close examination, no matter who conducts it. For some of us, however, they can be counted among the skeletons still closeted in our apparent postmodernity.

What Is a Postmodern Critic?

Postmodern critics addressing audiences dubious of "the postmodern experience" easily become rhetorically tongue-tied. If you avoid a postmodern vocabulary, you send the wrong signals. For instance, if you employ a traditional argument format, it goes contrary to the characteristic free play of postmodern discourse. On the other hand, if you give play to such *jouissance,* you are likely to forfeit any chance at persuading more traditional critics. The predicament I write about is the one I am in—working as a postmodern critic in a modern environment. But my predicament is not unlike that of a modern critic who has to work with postmodern colleagues. Calling ourselves by different names sometimes obscures the family ties of our frustrations.

In the profession of literary studies, as in life, we need names. "Are you a poststructuralist?" some of my colleagues ask, searching for a way of locating me in their frameworks. I usually answer, "Well, really, I'm more of a postmodern critic." As a name tag, this term conveys an allegiance; but, since anyone can wear it, the designation is not a reliable index of beliefs. I'd just as soon be called a "pomo crit" because that phrase has the ring of a sound bite and thus captures the spirit of tags more than "postmodern critic." Whereas "pomo" appropriately identifies an attitude, a fashion, or a style, "postmodern" misleadingly suggests a method, a procedure, or a weltanschauung. While convenient, names that purportedly identify schools of criticism are so superficial that they probably should be rephrased as sound bites, thus alerting us to the offhandedness of their use.

In this work, I ask critics who have allegiances to the traditions of modern disciplinary criticism to see themselves through the eyes of pomo critics; and, in turn, I ask pomo critics to see themselves as modern critics do. I construe my audience as critics who are skeptical of categories like modern and postmodern and therefore use them with caution. To encourage one's audience to be skeptical of the terms whose distinction one claims to be trenchant is a difficult rhetorical task. Nonetheless, anticipating the limits of a distinction in order to welcome a more heuristic one seems advisable.

I believe we are in a postmodern period to the extent that our culture has become an information technocracy dominated by the microchip. Many mainstream critics are skeptical of this perspective and even more unconvinced by definitions of postmodernity that attribute indeterminacy and self-referentiality to contemporaneous artifacts.[3] At the same time, they acknowledge that their institutions are responding to new technologies. Card catalogs are being replaced by computer terminals. Campus mail is now often e-mail. Texts are electronic. It's faster, easier, and more efficient to search a bibliographic database than its print equivalent. Information technology will soon be a pervasive feature of most university campuses. Whether you call such shifts in our cultural jetstream postmodern or a new phase of the modern is less important than understanding what storm fronts these fluctuations will create and how our present institutions can weather them.

From my perspective, the electronic revolution has already placed us in what can be called a postmodern condition. However, this state of affairs is not isomorphic to the contours of poststructuralist thought. Though modern academic institutions have been slow to adjust, partly owing to lack of funds, the economic winds that are carrying us from print environments to electronic ones have increased in velocity. Moreover, they have altered our production, reception, and distribution of texts. Sometimes, poststructuralist thought has been invoked to explain the differences in our atmosphere. Too often their explanation of the changes taking place reinforces the institutional behavior to which we are accustomed. Derrida, for instance, has been invoked in celebration of the nonlinearity of hypertexts by persons whose applications of them repeat the hierarchical structures of the print textbooks they intend to replace.[4]

The task I have undertaken in this book is to persuade all readers that justifying what we do as a discipline is not in everyone's best interest. To those readers who do not believe in the postmodern either as a cognitive style or as a period, I offer a critique of the disciplining of literary study. To postmodern readers I offer a caution about being undermined by the binarisms of modern institutions and a different emphasis—on analogy and intuition—than they would find in other postmodern writers. To readers who have not yet formed their views, I hope to offer an ecological view of the modes of understanding employed in the study of cultures.

One can read this book in the light of Gerald Graff's account of the profession of literary studies (see chapter 4). My early chapters foreground conflicts between modern and postmodern critics over the stability of interpretations in critical debates. My analysis complements and extends Graff's. It reveals a predicament common to literary critics of all schools— namely, that they work in institutions designed to house the sciences. But as Graff points out, we are often reluctant to face such predicaments as problems we share and all too often divide into separate camps to avoid addressing each other's concerns and thereby insulate ourselves from criticism. While modern critics see the failure of their endeavors to attract sufficient public support (especially financial) as a move away from the rigors of a genuine discipline, postmodern critics see the same failure as a fetishizing of rigor and discipline. One side wants to return to basic principles as a way of becoming more disciplined; the other wants to abandon principles but remain a discipline. At issue is the status of argumentation (the possibility of valid claims for interpretations). However, critics separate into different camps, where they argue with each other in their own terms, insulating themselves from the problematic relations their mode of argumentation has to other modes of understanding. Taking Graff's *Professing Literature* as my point of departure, I press the issue of debate further than he does in my discussions of analogies and by anticipating working in electronic educational environments (chapter 15).

There is another way of reading this book—as an attempt to reimagine what we do as critics. I contend that our institutional marriage with the sciences makes us imagine our modes of understanding to be coupled with logic. Modern critics have thought of their studies as a logical discipline (if not always a humane science) for the last century. That postmoderns characteristically invoke parallel standards of rigor and precision in claims for their work as a legitimate discipline allows me to name the skeleton in the postmodern closet "scientism." Because we locate ourselves within an array of conceptual contexts given to us by our teachers, we usually describe what we do in the terms we have inherited, only a few of which get challenged. As a consequence, we often entertain contradictory assumptions in our frameworks, as I pointed out above. Like Wittgenstein, we need to worry about "a one-sided diet" wherein "one nourishes one's thinking with only one kind of example" (*Philosophical Investigations* #593). Thus, as critics we might welcome comparisons with practitioners other than scientists. In this book, critics are perceived as storytellers; their arguments as narratives; their warrants, configurations. Rather than being seen as performing feats of logico-mathematical intelligence, they are perceived to perform tours de force of analogical and graphical intuition. From this perspective, literary critics are "configurers" who authorize themselves within an institution that privileges scientific discipline in ways that underestimate the power of the analogies that inform their work.

An Overview of What Follows

Modern Skeletons in Postmodern Closets is an account of the present state of literary arguments and a refiguring of the interpretation of literature as the study of culture (or, more precisely, as the critical formation of microcultures). It concerns the discrepancy between postmodern theory and its institutionalization as a disciplinary practice, and advocates a postdisciplinary form of cultural criticism. Considering that the study of cultures is inescapably a cultural production, then criticizing culture produces cultures. In this light, much of what follows can be understood as advocating a figural mode of understanding as an approach to culture building rather than as yet another conceptual approach to an object of investigation called culture. Since it is a person-oriented and collaborative effort to understand a collective cultural imagination rather than a text-oriented and individualistic effort to explain unique artifacts, I use the term *"configuring"* to designate this analogical mode of understanding, which is commonly called intuition.

I contend that some forms of cultural understanding, which are common to interpersonal understanding, are based in an analogous mode of insight we associate with intuition. To mark the difference between this mode and more familiar forms of understanding, I distinguish configurations (intuitive modes of understanding) from explanations and justifications. Configurations are highly interpersonal modes of understanding whose precondition is the narration of analogous experiences. They are forms of graphic understanding that rely principally on visualized resemblances. Take the configuration made familiar by the work of Donna Haraway—the cyborg. A cyborg is not an exact replica or even a simulacrum of a figure one might encounter; it is an image with respect to which many diverse experiences can be shaped into a recognizable pattern. Having read Haraway's description of her experience of cyborgs, her readers can then recognize cyborgs in their own experience. However, the resemblances on which such recognitions depend are too complex to specify in detail and can be articulated only in terms of a persistent shape given to specific experiences. This shaping is not a representation of the similarities among actual items in our experience. Rather, it is an image or archetype that reveals an analogy among experiences. The figure of the cyborg metaphorizes a type of cultural experience; it does not represent it. (Similarly, the archetype of the earth mother does not require that the women who may be recognized as earth mothers look alike; nonetheless, it is usually associated with a particular narrative pattern, a way of being in the world.) Literary critics use such forms of knowledge production when attending to archetypes, genres, metaphors, and other forms of analogical thinking. The traditional ideals of disciplinarity have required that we articulate these forms in abstract, nonvisual, and non-narrative significations. Even though the interpersonal relations that are the subject matter of literature require configurative modes of understanding, the study of literature requires impersonal conceptions of them. My thesis is that configural understanding is vital to the experience of culture but is often muted in arguments governed by disciplinary criteria.

Nonetheless, *Skeletons* is structured as an argument. In the light of my previous remarks this may appear to contradict my aims, so let me clarify my intentions. Academic audiences are accustomed to arguments. In order to support my claim that a particular form of argumentation is less appropriate for us than another, it seems legitimate to employ an argument about argumentation. From this point of view, *Skeletons* first argues that the type of argumentation that has characterized literary studies for a century simplifies the analogical modes of understanding commonly used in literary study by imposing on them logical formulations. The second part of the book then describes the analogical mode of understanding. To avoid a perplexing rhetorical difficulty, I call both the logical and analogical modes arguments. Thus, *Skeletons* argues that the traditional justificatory arguments used in literary studies distort the interpersonal mode of understanding required to comprehend culture and that configurations are less reductive.

Analogical modes of argumentation have usually been disparaged in disciplinary accounts of them. In their textbook on argumentation, *Web of Belief,* Quine and Ullian write that "some analogies that we use are notoriously weak. Perhaps a person hears a new voice and, noticing that the voice resembles that of an old friend, speculates that the voice's owner will be like the old friend in other significant ways. Such an analogy is shadowy, but we all tend at times to build on analogies that are no better. When a feature of a newly encountered person or object strikes a familiar chord it is often fairly instinctive to project to the new person or object what experience has associated with that feature" (59). When literary critics insightfully identify a work as an instance of a genre, they "build on analogies that are no better." Indeed, for this reason, generic criticism has been regarded as suspect in many quarters. Yet generic constructs are endemic to reading.

Given the low regard in which analogical warrants are held in disciplines, it has seemed advisable to avoid them in literary studies. This has not proved feasible. As I note throughout this study, literary critics are heavily indebted to analogies. For this reason, it seems appropriate to argue a case for them as a mode of argumentation, albeit not a mode that is on a continuum with arguments that depend on inferential warrants. In arguing my case, I rely on inferential warrants. This seems appropriate because I am not dealing with literary texts but with arguments used by literary critics. I try to show that the type of arguments literary critics use to justify their claims are, from a different angle of vision, more suspect than the analogical ones they avoid.

In chapter 2, "Changing Arguments," I take as my point of departure the difficulty of identifying an exemplary mode of critical argumentation for our time. I contrast the relative plausibility of regarding Cleanth Brooks's critical practices as an exemplary instance of New Criticism with the obvious impossibility of perceiving Paul de Man's as an exemplary instance of postmodern criticism. The belief that any one mode of critical argumentation, any metapractice, so to speak, should be put on a pedestal and used as a template for other critics is a modern, not a postmodern, notion. For this reason, training postmodern critics in an institution that requires measurable standards presents us with the mismatch between postmodern criticism and our institutional life. It is no longer feasible, if it ever was, to hope that one critical practice will dominate the field by refuting all its rivals.

I argue in chapter 3, "Disciplining," that the aspiration that a field-specific practice dominate is bound to the ideals of disciplinarity and to the search for an articulation of the discipline of literary study. After considering rationales for a discipline of literary studies, I turn in chapter 4, "Disciplined Isolation," to an examination of our century-long pursuit for a disciplinary rationale. Drawing from Gerald Graff's account of the history of modern literary criticism as a regime of patterned isolation that has resulted in a situation in which our work lacks "connectivity," I show how the criteria for a "strict" discipline, as delineated in Stephen Toulmin's *Human Understanding: The Collective Use and Evolution of Concepts,* produce patterned isolation. In particular, I link the ideals of disciplinarity with the field-coverage principle.

In chapter 5, "Shifting Status," I describe a short but typical literary interpretation of James Joyce's "Araby" in terms of the layout of its argumentative structure. Assuming that any claim for literary criticism as a "compact" discipline (Toulmin's term for a discipline in the strict sense) depends on the mode of argumentation attributed to its critical practices, I describe the traditional mode in detail. Noting how even the most obvious and rudimentary criteria for assessing the force of such literary arguments have shifted drastically since the sixties, I then raise the question of the validity of evidential criteria and grounds for refutation in traditional literary arguments.

I delineate three different modes of argumentation in chapter 6, "Explaining, Justifying, Configuring." In their publications, literary critics typically justify their warranting assumptions in order to produce evidence for their interpretations so they can meet the requirements for a discipline. This is often done by authorizing the warrants of a particular argument through the advocacy of a specific school of thought, such as deconstruction, Marxism, psychoanalysis, or New Historicism. Reflecting that such shifts in critical warrants have produced intense but not necessarily welcome interest in literary theory, I propose that justifications are not always the best form of argumentation for emerging cultural studies. In debates over the cultural value of artifacts, participants often do not share the same set of cultural experiences. Thus, configurations of experience that allow the disputants to recognize parallels in cultural experiences are appropriate premises for arguments about cultural values. Considering how widely configurations are used in literary studies, I make several observations in chapter 7, "Pretending to Refute," on the difficulties of finding any grounds for refutation in literary debates and remark that this might be taken as an index of the mismatch between justificatory arguments in literary studies and disciplinary ideals.

In the light of the instability of justificatory arguments about literature, I examine our examination practices in chapter 8. Noting that exams depend for their efficacy on a reliable mode of argumentation, I identify the six most common types of exams in literary studies. By offering examples of each, I show how difficult (if not impossible) it is to adjudicate answers to them. It appears that literary exams are conducted as tests of whether or not apprentice readers can mimic the reading practices of their teachers.

In chapter 9, "Constructing Intellectuality," I show how the procedures by which literature teachers question students reproduce the teachers' reading practices. After analyzing the exercises offered by Cleanth Brooks in his famous *An Approach to Literature*—the precursor to *Understanding Poetry, Understanding Fiction,* and *Understanding Drama*—I conclude that they are designed to regulate the habits of student readers and form them as disciples of New Criticism. It thus seems that what is apparent is also demonstrable: critical schools are the result of schooling. While obvious, this conclusion clarifies the sense in which literary criticism is a discipline. Although the discipline involved in "performance training" is surely legitimate, it does not match the ideals of disciplinarity associated with forms of knowledge production developed from methodological investigations into fields.

In chapter 10, "Academic Subjects," I contend that literary critics are made into subjects by the formation of discursive fields such as exams and textbook exercises. Texts are indeed "subjects" (often the idiom we use) in a more than casual sense. Rather than understanding literary texts as objects of investigation, it makes more sense—given the preceding analyses—to understand them as subjectivities materialized in discourse. In this sense, critics' subjectivities (their attitudes and self-enactments) are what is produced by criticism. Thus, if it is to be understood as the production of knowledge, what becomes known are particular subjectivities. Following this Foucauldian line of thinking, I go on to observe that criticism involves not only the formation of objects called a subject but also the formation of subjects called objective. Here I link objectivity to confessions of error produced by the examination process.

Having understood criticism to be a highly subjective practice, in chapter 11, "Truth Wars," I then wonder why critics attempt to refute each other. Since I earlier posed the question, "Can someone else's experience be refuted?" and answered "No," here I speculate that our formation as intellectuals in the institution of criticism is inseparable from our formation as masculinist critics. This seems to me infelicitous and leads me to conclude that we should begin to imagine postdisciplinary critical practices, abandoning our efforts to match our conduct against ideals of disciplinarity.

The last four chapters of the book describe a form of cultural studies based on configuring as the mode of argumentation. I begin in chapter 12, "Through a Postmodern Lens," by considering that the aims of literary study as traditionally articulated usually have a cultural dimension. In this section, literary studies are viewed in surprisingly familiar terms, thus illustrating how the perspective I offer matches what we already do. However, in my account, critical practices that are problematic from a disciplinary perspective appear in a very positive light from a postdisciplinary perspective. For instance, rather than decrying that our work incorporates value judgments, we can, in a postmodern era, celebrate this as one of the contributions we make to our cultures. Hence, we can legitimately define our aim as the study of the cultural formation of subjects, admitting that our practices, far from being objective, rely on the concurrent formation of subjectivities. Put more idiomatically, in studying cultural artifacts like literary texts, we create cultural values to which many persons wish to subscribe. That differing critics create different values which then must be negotiated through debate is not a defect of our practices but one of their aims. In sum, critics are engaged in the project of forming the culture.

Since the cultural criticism I advocate in these chapters depends on a specific mode of argumentation, namely, configuration, I show in chapter 13, "Alternative Cultures," how it can be understood as an argument. After describing thinking in analogies, I contrast this cognitive style to the analytic one, in which most critics have been trained. I then describe how literary criticism configures alternative cultural worlds in its interpretation of texts. From this perspective, reading is always a reading of cultures.

Having earlier criticized the quarrelsomeness of justificatory criticism, and in an effort to take into account the certainty that critics will disagree with each other, in chapter 14 I make a case for the protocol of "critical concurrence." Justificatory arguments have their force from their capacity to falsify or refute an existing claim. Though its goal is never reached, the ideal justificatory argument would result in consensus among the parties involved. All counterpositions would be falsified, thus identifying the surviving valid position. In literary criticism, however, few claims survive for long. The institution of criticism is constantly being reorganized, like a building perpetually in need of repair. This does provide work to be done but makes one worry that the time it takes to work *on* the building significantly reduces the time one has to do the work one hoped to use the building *for.* Any proposal for redesigning the institution of criticism has to take disagreement into account. It is foolish to assume that a consensus can be reached or a communality found that will control the spread of disagreement. Drawing on my earlier work "The Psycho-Politics of Error," I view disagreement positively, as something to be expected and welcomed in criticism. I suggest that, unlike the goal of a justificatory argument, the goal of criticism *not* be to eliminate disagreement. However, only agreement makes productive disagreement possible. I explore this paradox in the chapter.

In the concluding chapter, "Professing Literature in 2001," I try to show how the mode of argumentation I have been advocating suits the shift from print environments to electronic ones. Taking Gerald Graff's recommendation that we debate our differences as a positive approach to disagreement as well as an index of what we might hope for in this new environment, I speculate on what a university could look like in cyberspace. In doing so I describe the implications of the Cycles project in which David Downing and I are engaged. Various learning sites (classrooms, libraries, presses, and even headquarters of scholarly societies housing newsletters or journals) and the learning communities that inhabit them are linked through telecommunication into a single networked cycle of critical exchanges. Whereas in a print environment scholars might first propose certain ideas to students in a classroom, then present them for debate among their colleagues at a scholarly conference organized by the relevant professional society, and finally submit them in publishable form to a university press, the Cycles project turns this traditional pattern into an ongoing cycle of critical exchange in which the research conducted is presented in dialogical form and made available to other researchers without the time lag required of print processes. In sum, the Cycles project integrates the functions of a seminar, a textbook, a conference, a symposium, a newsletter, and a journal through scholarly correspondence conducted via electronic media, following a set of protocols that facilitate the ongoing dialogue by channeling it through various stages to its publication in a database.

The Cycles project is the positive outgrowth of the critique of disciplinarity I advance in the early chapters. It envisions an educational environment that is postdisciplinary. The criticisms that follow this introduction set the stage for imagining an exciting future for literary studies, one that we have already set about building.

Changing Arguments

CHAPTER 2

C ritics in every generation seem to ordain some of their fellow critics as ministers of their practices. Cleanth Brooks, for instance, is revered as the pastor of New Criticism. No less a historian of criticism than René Wellek called Brooks "the critic of critics." During the forties and fifties he was widely regarded as the most lucid and instructive close reader of literary texts. The readings he published in *Modern Poetry and the Tradition* (1939) and *The Well Wrought Urn* (1947) were considered outstanding instances of New Critical practice.

Similarly, Paul de Man seems to have been a touchstone for many critics in the late sixties and seventies. His work provided for admirers a consummate instance of the practice of deconstructive criticism. *Blindness and Insight* (1971) paralleled Brooks's *Modern Poetry and the Tradition* as an indicator of a significant shift in critical perspectives. Rhetoric took on an entirely new meaning. By the time *Allegories of Reading* was published (1979), figural language had become a byword. Following de Man's lead, countless critics focused on tropes, the trivium, and the relations between metaphor and metonymy in new and unfamiliar ways. He was *the* American interpreter of Derrida and poststructuralist thought. His work was heralded as "exemplary" in Frank Lentricchia's *After the New Criticism,* wherein he is spoken of as the foremost of "the fearsome Yale group," his name invoked in tones of respect and reverence by his colleagues (283).

Today, Paul de Man is no longer spoken of in tones of awe, and reverence for Cleanth Brooks has diminished. Indeed, for postmodern critics, the very idea that any one person (even Jacques Derrida or Michel Foucault or Jacques Lacan or Jean François Lyotard) could exemplify "the discipline" should no longer have any appeal. Yet the notion that literary study is *one* discipline, even if its "sublime master" (Paul Bové's phrase) is a neglected critic or one yet to be found, has hardly died out; and many poststructuralists, such as Paul de Man, regard Derrida as the harbinger of a new discipline. This notion, of course, would count for me as a skeleton in their closets.

Perhaps, given the tenor of our times, when literary critics often write about issues related to items in the news, we should look for a critic who can show us how our changing practices fit into our institutional life rather than look for a critic to exemplify our practices. We seem less to need another master interpreter than we need a plan for institutional survival. In this context, another figure stands out, Gerald Graff. His name now appears constantly in articles, books, even newspapers, and often in the *Chronicle of Higher Education.* He has appeared on *The Oprah Winfrey Show* to debate Allan Bloom. *Literature against Itself* became a clarion call for many critics who needed a defense counselor against the prosecutions of deconstructive critics. But it was his *Professing Literature* that established him as a crucial commentator on the profession of literary criticism. Since its publication, his essays and talks have appeared everywhere. And his recent book, *Beyond the Culture Wars,* is widely read and very influential.

Juxtaposed, the careers of these three widely known critics provide a crude barometer of change in the study of literature, particularly in the ascent and decline of their celebrity. The rise of Brooks's career signaled a shift from philological and historical methods to New Critical ones. In turn, as the title of Lentricchia's book *After the New Criticism* indicates, de Man's celebrity signaled a shift away from New Critical methods to poststructuralist ones. Graff's renown, by contrast, does not have the same implications as Brooks's or de Man's. While we can easily associate a particular interpretive strategy with Brooks (close formalist readings) or de Man (close deconstructive readings), we do not associate any method of reading with Graff. Nonetheless, Graff's career can be understood to signal a momentous shift in literary argumentation (see chapter 5). Since the distinction between a career that exemplifies the practice of a critical method and one that exemplifies the practice of critical argumentation is an unfamiliar one, it needs to be clarified before I can comment on the shift in literary celebrity from the former to the latter.

The significance of Brooks's career is bound up with a shift in the way critics read literary texts. His career marks the advent of New Criticism. Similarly, we associate de Man's career with a shift in the reading habits of American critics as well as with the advent of poststructuralism and deconstruction in particular. Graff's career reflects neither a shift in interpretive methods nor the advent of a new school of thought, yet he is as much, if not more of, a public celebrity (known by persons outside his field) as was either Brooks or de Man.[1] Brooks provided for his generation of critics a way of practicing reading to which everyone could respond. It was detailed, concrete, resonant, and practical. At a different time and placed differently in the university system, Graff provides a similarly concrete and detailed agenda for critics, one that is resonant and practical. However, unlike that of Brooks and de Man, Graff's fame signals a shift in the structure of literary argumentation. His lineage goes back to thinkers such as Wayne Booth, Ronald Crane, Richard Altick, Jacques Barzun, and Ronald McKerrow. Connecting Graff's work to Booth's and Crane's requires only that we note the attention in all three writers to argumentation, especially to the plurality of arguments and the problems associated with adjudicating among them.

Whereas Brooks and de Man provided methods of reading, Graff offers a set of critical protocols (though he does not use that term) for literary arguments. Methods are sets of procedures that ensure that a given task is done with appropriate systematicity; protocols are rubrics that enable interpersonal relationships. Brooks instructs us in critical methodology; Graff encourages us to conduct our arguments dialogically—that is, according to different protocols from those to which we have been accustomed.

Changes in protocols have surprising institutional consequences. Though they seem minor adjustments in the system, they can turn the system on its head over a period of time. For years I have been fascinated by one particular change in institutional protocol. In *Heritage and Promise: Denison 1831–1981,* G. Wallace Chessman and Wyndham M. Southgate identify a change in protocol that seemed quite modest yet paved the way for the transition of Denison from a religious college to a modern university. During the time it was a religious college, "chapel came every morning Monday through Friday, . . . and on Sunday at the Baptist church pew seats were even assigned" (31). However, during the period when the modern American university began to emerge, the "administration omitted mention of a mid-week prayer meeting from the catalogue and changed the words 'required to attend' to 'expected to attend' church twice each Sunday" (78). This modest change, from "required" to "expected," is a change in protocol. Intended not to offend the trustees, who "with long memories could detect a continued growth of 'unreligious tendencies'" (78), the change permitted the student body to alter their conduct irrevocably. Imagine, for instance, changing the rule back to "students are required to attend church twice each Sunday." Such a change would probably excite a riot, and this possibility alerts us to the significance of the original change.

I do not claim that this change in protocol in and by itself changed an institution from a predominantly religious college to a secular university. This would be a ridiculous claim. Rather, I suggest that profound changes are introduced into institutional structures as changes in protocols to allow for the gradual accommodation of much larger social and economic forces pressuring the institution. As we know, institutions are social structures that have powerful self-sustaining mechanisms built into them. These mechanisms are not, by and large, logical devices. We are all familiar with the nebulous sayings of brochures and other kinds of institutional prose, including, and especially, governance statements. Ambiguity, vagueness, and circumlocution in such statements have their purpose—they can be variously and unendingly reinterpreted to suit the circumstances and thus maintain the institution. Similarly, through a change in the description of a course or a program, administrators can make it appear that they are responding to the needs of the public without increasing the budget or hiring new staff. A Women's Studies or Comparative Literature program can be created by introducing a protocol of interdisciplinarity, so that faculty paid by different departments can be reassembled with almost no additional expense in a new program and just as quickly dispersed when the demand for it diminishes.

Institutional changes often take place through changes in protocols. This allows for a nondisruptive adjustment in the self-regulating system of the institution. Rather than explain why chapel services are no longer necessary, administrators can concede the point by announcing that chapel services are no longer "required," a modest and nondisruptive change that indicates attitudes have sufficiently shifted to make a break with tradition without jeopardizing the continuance of the institution. From this point of view—the identification of changes in protocols—Graff's proposals stand out from any of the others I have mentioned. When Graff advocates abandoning the field-coverage principle, he is not advocating replacing one method with another. In his analysis, the field-coverage principle is an administrative device rationalized as a disciplinary premise. In other words, Graff focuses on protocols. This is even clearer in his recommendation that we "teach the conflicts."

In his recent work, Graff elaborates protocols that allow critics to debate each other productively. Though his view is best known through the sound bite "teach the conflicts," his recommendation depends on a historical account as well as a theoretical analysis of literary argumentation. However unusual it may seem for a theorist of academic argumentation to discuss the attitudes of the parties involved, Graff's opinion has many precedents. In the section on "Research Methods" of the *Literary Research Guide* promulgated by the Modern Language Association, to take a significant example, James L. Harner notes that one of the most useful discussions in Jacques Barzun's and Henry F. Graff's *The Modern Researcher* is about "the researcher's virtues (accuracy, love of order, logic, honesty, self-awareness, imagination), verification, the establishment of dates, kinds of evidence, and bias"

(A14–15, #10). What Harner terms virtues I refer to as protocols, that is, the dispositions that govern negotiations and compacts among parties with diverging interests and that facilitate the settlement of difficult issues. Such matters are not customarily foregrounded. Protocols are not recognized as such.

Some readers may interpret Graff's protocol "teach the conflicts" as less than virtuous, as little more than an invitation to confront critical adversaries with their errors. In chapter 3 I show how Graff's recommendation is an invitation to build "critical communities" through critical concurrences. Rather than ask critics to change their methodologies, he entreats them to seek agreements among themselves despite the differences in their methods. Graff's advocacy of protocols rather than methods sets him apart from most other theorists of criticism.

It is difficult, however, to demonstrate the differences between disciplinary protocols of argumentation and the postdisciplinary ones Graff advocates. The difficulties are of two kinds: unfamiliarity and misrecognition. Contemporary literary critics do not devote much attention to argumentation in general and therefore are generally unfamiliar with its protocols. This leads to a state of affairs in which protocols (whether disciplinary or postdisciplinary) are not recognized as such. For instance, most critics would associate Graff with disciplinary argumentation and de Man with a postdisciplinary critique of argumentation. However, the opposite case pertains if you examine the protocols they recommend: Graff is far more postdisciplinary in his view of argumentation than is de Man, whose advocacy of disciplinarity is a modern skeleton buried within his poststructuralism. In what follows, I contrast de Man's views of the protocols of literary argumentation with Graff's.

De Man's Account of the Discipline of Literary Scholarship

By way of introducing his influential essay "The Resistance to Theory," de Man notes that it was written originally at the invitation of the MLA committee on "Research Activities" for their *Introduction to Scholarship in the Modern Languages and Literatures.*[2] It is, thus, a general account of scholarly work in literary fields and affords us a view of de Man's theory of literary research. Keeping in mind that the view de Man expounds in this essay is widely held, let's note the skeletons of the modern institution of criticism closeted in this essay, as well as the type of disciplinary argumentation it presupposes. Take the following passage: "Attention to the philological or rhetorical devices of language is not the same as aesthetic appreciation, although the latter can be a way of access to the former. Perhaps the most difficult thing for students and teachers of literature to realize is that their appreciation is measured by the analytical rigor of their own discourse about literature, a criterion that is not primarily or exclusively aesthetic. Yet it separates the sheep from the goats, the consumers from the professors of literature, the chit-chat of evaluation from actual perception" (*Resistance to Theory* 24).

In this passage, de Man advocates "analytical rigor" as a way of separating "the sheep from the goats," that is, professors from amateur chit-chatters. He advocates the analytical in his disposition toward linguistics (or, perhaps more accurately, philology). He writes, "Literary theory can be said to come into being when the approach to literary texts is no longer based on non-linguistic, that is to say historical and aesthetic, considerations" (7). And later, "Contemporary literary theory comes into its own in such events as the application of Saussurian linguistics to literary texts" (8). In these remarks we can discern a continuous concern about literary study as a "discipline," "an autonomous academic field" (21), albeit one that differs markedly from philosophic and scientific fields. It is a rigorous, methodological description of the "production and . . . reception of meaning and of value prior to their establishment . . . requir[ing] an autonomous discipline of critical investigation to consider its possibility and status" (7). De Man perceives theory as "a controlled reflection on the formation of method" (4) that requires "impersonal consistency" (6) and as "a relatively autonomous version of questions that also surface in a different context" (8). This linguistically oriented view of literary study presupposes a mode of rigorous argumentation governed by exacting methods of knowledge production.

Many postmodern critics subscribe to de Man's view. For them, also, literary study has "a subversive element of unpredictability" that makes it "something of a wild card in the serious game of the theoretical disciplines" (*Resistance to Theory* 8). It has aspects that are "inconceivable in the natural sciences and unmentionable in the social sciences" (11). De Man speaks for them when he writes, "Nothing can overcome the resistance to theory since theory *is* itself this resistance" (19). However, in the remarks I've quoted, de Man measures what literary critics do by comparison with scientists and wants to be a player in "the serious game of the theoretical disciplines." As I note in chapter 10, describing one's conduct by comparing it with someone else's prejudges the matter by the choice of the other term in the comparison. It is therefore desirable to compare the conduct of literary study with several widely differing modes of behavior, including nonacademic behavior.[3] Moreover, skeletons of modernism rattle a bit when de Man disparages the practical and emotional and assumes a refutational stance or uses modifiers such as "rightly," "truly," "genuine," and "rigorous" in his prose. These three "skeletons"—refutation, correctness, and detachment—deserve some attention:

1. *Refutation (or Disproving).*[4] In "The Return to Philology," de Man quarrels with an essay by Walter Jackson Bate over the status of theory in literary studies. There is little doubt that he believes his argument can refute Bate's. In general, de Man subscribes to a disciplinary theory of argumentation, according to which it is possible to refute or falsify claims. His critical conduct persistently operates in the mode of refutation. In "The Resistance to Theory," de Man speaks of "attacks," "overfacile opinion," and "crude misunderstandings." His antagonists are "always misinformed," and, memorably, he accuses his detractors of attacking "paper tigers." In the main, his essays attempt to refute the views of his opponents. Though he would be unlikely to speak of foundations or grounds on which his claims rest, he does insist there are confusions, misinformation, and other matters that allow him to refute his adversaries. This all seems in order, yet consider what the confusions and misunderstanding are about. The persons he designates as detractors of theory are "always misinformed" about "such terms as mimesis, fiction, reality, ideology, reference and for that matter, relevance" (10), and none of these objections can be said to be of "genuine rhetorical interest" (12). This proprietary view of terminology seems quite modernist. At the same time, I do not find de Man's discourse exceptional. Indeed, it seems commonplace. However, when I read such remarks, I hear the rattle of systematicity and logical consistency. The practice of refutation is one of the most puzzling skeletons in the postmodern closet.

2. *Correctness.* However understandable, the most disturbing phrases in de Man's remarks are ones such as "genuine rhetorical interest." When they occur near others such as "genuine semiology," I hear the bones of disciplinarity rattling. It appears that de Man believes in a correct way of reading, since he believes that "technically correct rhetorical readings may be boring, monotonous, predictable and unpleasant, but they are irrefutable" (19); and (judging from his presuppositions) he believes there are incorrect ways of reading as well. Like many other academics with poststructuralist views,[5] he believed in the possibility of adjudicating between correct and incorrect arguments even when the parties involved belonged to different schools of thought. For de Man, a deconstructive critic (like himself) could rightly correct a historical critic (like Bate), even when their arguments depend on disparate warrants. This belief is the noticeable skeleton in the postmodern closet—a trust in the appropriateness of ranking or grading critical views according to a scale of correctness.

3. *Detachment.* Scientific arguments are governed by protocols of disinterest and detachment to which we ordinarily refer as objectivity. De Man's "return to philology" is an index of his commitment to a detached, objective form of scholarship that is not entirely compatible with many aspects of a postmodern cultural studies that seeks to overcome the institutional restrictions on our ways of knowing. De Man countenances as appropriate

to literary studies only certain modes of understanding (rhetoric and philology), and these are invariably characterized as "detached." His lesser-known essay in the volume *Resistance to Theory,* "The Return to Philology," seems strikingly New Critical from a postmodern perspective. It advocates "an examination of the structure of language prior to the meaning it produces" (24). In de Man's view, the text is an object of investigation ("I have a tendency to put upon texts an inherent authority" [118]), and that investigation must be detached. Moreover, critics must detach themselves *from* themselves to be good critics. In de Man's remarks, the notion of detachment rattles very like the old bones of objectivity on the corpse of structuralism. The rattle is loudest when he writes that "the only teaching worthy of the name is scholarly, not personal" (4), and that texts have "an inherent authority" (118).

In contrast to de Man, Graff does not believe in detached, correct, refutable arguments. He has a much more postmodern theory of argumentation. This remark may surprise readers who associate Graff with the expression "teach the conflicts," which suggests that Graff proposes critical debates in which the conflicting parties arrive at a resolution of their differences by the victory of one critic over another. The slogan seems to support de Man's interest in refuting Bate. According to Graff, however, this view obscures his position by imposing an older view of argumentation on it. Though Graff wants us to recognize that critics are far more in conflict with each other than they appear to be in public documents and presentations, he does not believe that debating these issues will be resolved by means of refutation. Rather, he understands the resolution of critical conflicts to be a matter of negotiation. For him, it is not that some critical arguments are correct (rigorous and exact) and others are incorrect (ill-defined and misinformed) but that debates are events during which perspectives can be exchanged, concepts redefined, and claims adjusted. In de Man's view, powerful arguments can establish a standard, thus producing a school of thought that can be counted among the rigorous disciplines. In Graff's view, critical debates are a means of community building, forums wherein norms are continuously renegotiated. Whereas de Man's view of argumentation is exclusionary, Graff's is inclusionary. Whereas de Man's style of argumentation is assimilative and paradigmatic, Graff's is accommodative and historically contingent.

In advocating teaching the conflicts, Graff encourages the persons involved to be sympathetic to both sides of the issue, to look forward to developing positions that are not the simple-minded defeat of one side at the expense of the other. When teachers delineate opposing views of issues, Graff advises them to do so with energy and empathy.[6] This maneuver reminds us that in their societies debaters alternately take different sides of the issue. Such detachment has as its precondition empathy and differs substantively from the attitude characteristic of the "skeptical" tradition, in which persons are taught to demolish opposing views. Graff advocates listening to both sides. His protocol is *find what you agree with in the positions with which you disagree.* If this protocol were followed, it would change dramatically the institution of criticism, which is at present dependent on a skeptical or scientific protocol of falsifying positions that are anomalies in a paradigm. To put the issue more idiomatically, the skeptical protocols advise us to refute opposing schools of thought (see chapter 11). Since interpretations invariably differ, refutation is often the underlying goal of criticism. Refuting is a familiar critical habit, a disciplinary trait. This is not the point of view Graff takes in his recent work.

Graff conceives universities as *learning communities* in which students *collaborate* with their teachers on *cultural* problems that derive from *everyday experience.* These four emphases in his work can be considered protocols that have the capacity to resituate postmoderns in modern universities. In effect, Graff advises us to go "beyond the culture wars"—that is, to conduct ourselves in accord with the following protocols: (1) concur (rather than compete);[7] (2) collaborate (rather than segregate or individuate); (3) seek negotiated truces in critical, cultural conflicts; and (4) vacate our ivory tower. The crucial stratagem Graff advocates is bringing social conflicts into the classroom in a dialogical rather than a doctrinaire manner. In Graff's view, "there is always a background of agreement that makes disagreement possible, and through debate that area of agreement can be widened" (*Culture Wars* 45). Graff's recommendation about the status of conflict in our pedagogy has the same force as the change from "required" to "expected" in Denison's protocols for attendance at church services.

Graff's perspective, obtained no doubt in his excellent work on the history of literary studies as an institution, makes us realize that changes in the protocols of personal interactions have more far-reaching consequences than superficial changes in the impersonal content of curricula, programs, methods, and so forth. Though not often described in these terms, his proposals would change the protocols by which we work. Rather than a pedagogical protocol of conflict avoidance, he advises conflict negotiation when he encourages intellectuals to debate the issues underlying their conflicts.

Redesigning the Modern University

Graff's proposals for revitalizing the study of literature respect what has been going on in the work of literary scholars for decades. Rather than call for a revolution in literary studies, Graff says let's make the democratic process work for us, let's make an effort to restructure the institutional frameworks in which we work, let's remodel rather than tear down.

Some radical thinkers believe, with Foucault, that remodeling is little more than a capitulation to the institution because of the institution's capacity to assimilate new forms into its overriding structures. However, in the context of remodeling, repainting and redecorating rooms is quite superficial in comparison with creating doors and stairways where there were none. My position is that remodeling can be restructuring if what gets rebuilt are the "pathways" of the original structure.

Taking my architectural analogy a bit further, I suggest that some kinds of remodeling are superficial and others are structural. Obviously, if the remodeling only touches the surfaces of the rooms and corridors, it only makes the building look different without changing the ways persons interrelate. However, if you open a door between two rooms that were previously closed off from each other you alter the communication patterns among the persons inhabiting those rooms. For example, the shift from conventional classrooms to computer classrooms alters the relations between students and teachers because it gives students channels of interpersonal interaction they did not have (see chapter 15). Teachers in computer labs comment that the power relations in the situation change dramatically. The computer terminal is a door into another mode of interpersonal communication. The last seminar I taught, for instance, never met in a classroom because it was a teleseminar. I did not function in that virtual classroom in the way I do in the more conventional classrooms I have inhabited. Because the channel of communication altered my relation to the students, I could not (nor did I want to) communicate with them in the same way.

Since institutions are made up of interpersonal relations formed as contractual obligations, when key interpersonal relations are changed the institution itself changes. To take a simple example, if we rid universities of exams (a situation in which the interpersonal relation between a teacher and a student is mastery), the university as we know it would be a different sort of institution. I do not expect this to happen anytime in the near future, but it is important to realize that institutions do change. The modern university did emerge from a different sort of institution that at one time had no exams in the sense that we now think of them. We seem at present to be on the brink of change as universities shift from print environments to electronic ones. This shift provides us with an opportunity to change our modus operandi.

Disciplining

Most of us remember Sisyphus from Greek mythology as the figure who was condemned forever to push a huge rock up a hill, only to arrive close to the top, where the stone continuously slipped away and rolled back down to the bottom. But few remember that he was condemned to *always almost succeed* because he was something of a trickster figure. He caught Death, whom Zeus had sent to punish him, by surprise and chained him up; then later, after Death was loosed on him again, he got Hades to return him to life by a clever ruse, once again foiling Zeus. In this study, I wonder whether professors of literature, like Sisyphus, have been condemned to almost always be developing a discipline but never quite succeeding because some time ago we "tricked" administrators into believing we already were one. The trick of claiming to be a discipline depends on a sleight of mind that defines discipline in a way that fits what we do; and since the word is used in many senses, it is not difficult to speak of our work as a discipline.

The term "discipline" ranges in meaning from the conditions of scientific study to punishment: (1) a field of study or branch of knowledge; (2) training that develops self-control, character, or orderliness and efficiency; (3) the result of such training; (4) acceptance of or submission to authority and control; (5) a system of rules or methods; and (6) treatment that corrects or punishes.[1] On the one hand, discipline is a concept debated by philosophers of science in the tradition of Popper, Lakatos, Kuhn, Toulmin, and Feyerabend. On the other, discipline is a conception of power and punishment developed by historians who work in the tradition of Foucault.

Disciplines, as I understand them, are broadly based research programs designed to *control* the production of knowledge. A subject matter is identified. Various descriptions of it are advanced. These take the form of models, and thereby a subject matter is legitimized as a field of study. These models presuppose methods. If this model, then that method. By the exercise of the proper method, knowledge is reliably controlled. In the domain of literature, texts are described. Depending on the model of textuality advanced theoretically, they are centered or decentered. They exhibit or do not exhibit generic patterns. Their meanings are centripetal or centrifugal. They have levels or exist only at the surface. And so on and so forth. The varying models of literary texts presuppose methods of interpretation. If psychoanalysis, then depths. If formalism, then techniques. Each model is heuristic. It implies avenues of investigation and leads to new interpretations. This is the sense in which I understand the study of literature to aspire to be a discipline. I say aspire because in recent years competing schools of criticism with differing models and methods make the rationale of a discipline (control) implausible and the idea of an unending variety of disciplines (one splitting off from another) unwelcome. This is not a majority view.

Most critics of my acquaintance believe that the study of literature is a discipline—a set of practices that controls the production of a specific form of knowledge—and that if we shift our attention to the study of culture, our work should also be guided by disciplinary aims. However, few critics expect their colleagues to use terms consistently, much less to share the same conception of a common field and to investigate it with similar methods in exactingly systematic ways. Moreover, by scientific standards, the study of literature is an undisciplined set of practices that is out of control. Nonetheless, the American university system is designed to house disciplines, and literary critics must be able to show that their studies are legitimately quartered there. And so we try to show that we are one. Yet we must wonder if we can succeed, or whether, like Sisyphus, we will forever be trying to become a discipline. In this chapter, I first acknowledge that many of my colleagues, believing they have liberated themselves from or have solved this problem, think we are more like Prometheus than like Sisyphus. Then, I introduce Stephen Toulmin's distinction between a "compact" (scientific) discipline and a "would-be" discipline, which reveals that rationales commonly offered for literary study presuppose a more compact model of inquiry than literary critics employ in their practices. In conclusion, I recount some of the difficulties that make me take a different view of the matter than proponents of a literary discipline do. My fear is that we, like Sisyphus, will never be able to reach the goal of disciplinarity; and I am concerned, therefore, that the arbiters of discipline, like Zeus, will relegate us to the underworld of the university system.

Throughout this study, I borrow from the many critics who explore the issue of disciplinarity, especially those I mention below. The subsequent paragraphs should not be read as an attempt to refute their positions but rather to contrast my views with theirs.[2] With apologies for my obvious simplifications, I'd categorize the prevailing opinions about the status of literary study as a discipline in the following ways:

1. We are a discipline because we have every right to define what a discipline is (Barbara Herrnstein Smith).
2. We are an aggregate of conflicting disciplines (Gerald Graff).
3. We are a weak discipline, having less stature than the social sciences as a discipline (Gianni Vattimo).
4. We are implicitly interdisciplinary—one perspective in a plurality of disciplines whose perspectives converge (Wayne Booth).
5. We are a practical science (Louise Wetherbee Phelps).
6. We all should be transdisciplinary (Zavarzadeh and Morton).[3]
7. We have a disciplinary formation (David Shumway).

Each of these positions redefines the term "discipline" so that the work conducted in literature departments can fit in the university system. These redefinitions respond to a crucial problem we face: to justify our work in terms of institutional expectations. Hence we commit ourselves to showing that we are experts who are the only sound judges of what we do. If we fail to make this case to the satisfaction of legislators and administrators, we will be relegated to the status of service personnel, who do what is required to keep the system running. For example, university administrations pressured by legislators who wish to keep their constituencies happy tend to support literature departments in teaching language skills rather than literature. Our role in the university system is being reduced to preparing students to study the "real" disciplines. Remarking on the status of the teaching of writing in English departments, David Shumway notes that we provide skills necessary to the work of *other* disciplines (*Creating American Civilization* 100–101). To reverse this tendency we have to demonstrate that we are a legitimate study; critics undertake this task by defining a discipline in a way that makes our work legitimate. Above I distinguished seven typical strategies for linking what we do in literature departments to the legitimating criteria of disciplinarity. Though I cannot do these views justice by summarizing them in a paragraph or two, I think that, however inadequate, such summaries at least provide a glimpse of the background against which the motive for this study can best be discerned.

Without denying that at some point we need to show how our work fits the university system (which I take to be the intention of any redefinition of disciplinarity), I do not believe we do so without considering what members of literature departments actually do (see Evan Watkins's *Work Time*). Before we try to justify what we do, we need to worry whether what we do is done effectively. If we are committed to practices that are ineffective, justifying them in a new way does not make them more efficacious. Nor does changing them to get around obstacles in our way prove that something was wrong with the practices changed. It might be that the environment that allegedly promotes them actually prevents them from having their intended impact. However, admitting that we are ineffective presents us with the possibility that university administrators will take us at our word.

1. In the light of the rhetorical dilemma described in the previous paragraph, the position Barbara Herrnstein Smith takes in *Contingencies of Value* is very attractive. It might be described as "postmodern sophistry" (understanding the term in the positive valence current among contemporary rhetoricians).[4] Smith provides a more flexible view of English departments as departments of postmodern rhetoric than does Terry Eagleton (who makes the suggestion in the last chapter of *Literary Theory*). In her view, literary study is a discipline but not in any strict sense.

According to Smith, Toulmin's notion of a discipline is a "highly philosophized notion of what a discipline is. What I think of, when I think of a discipline, are the operations of an institution. I think of procedures of certification, procedures of recruitment, even the laws under which a college is established. They are not defined by 'paradigms.' Sometimes disciplines have defining problems and missions, but the articulation of a problem or mission can also be seen as a story that the practitioners tell about themselves" ("A Conversation" 155). Smith's view of a discipline, I would wager, accords with what most members of English departments think of when they think of what a discipline is. They probably would not call it a story they tell about themselves but would most likely prefer Smith's view to Toulmin's. Yet Smith's rhetorical solution leaves the ideal of disciplinarity lurking in the background. Meanwhile we waiver between competing with each other and concurring with each other. On the one hand, we argue *as if* we were arguing to refute each other. On the other, we tell each other stories about our commonalities. From my perspective, this view underestimates the influence modern institutions have on our work. It seems to say, "No matter how administrators evaluate us, we can do what we wish anyhow." By contrast, I believe universities control the practices they house by establishing hierarchies of rewards to encourage some and discourage others.

2. Graff's work suggests, on the other hand, that *we* can exercise control over what we do—and thus legitimate ourselves—by debating the issues involved in our work. However, he is quick to point out that the dialectics of inquiry he describes are constrained by the parameters institutions set for them. For him, the American university has become an aggregate of studies that, because of institutional constraints, are not well correlated to each other. He proposes that by debating the issues governing our studies

openly, we will not only be able to make their connectedness visible but also be able to participate in the intellectual communities that the rationale of disciplinarity authorizes. For Graff the problem is that the work of literary interpretation only appears to be a discipline because our relations to other disciplinary work are obscured. Were we better able to show how our work fits into the concerns of other disciplines within the university, the legitimacy of our studies would not be questioned. This is a useful clarification of the problem, if one assumes that our work does fit in. But I am less convinced than Graff that it does and hence more reluctant than he is to suggest that disciplinarity should continue to be a goal for cultural studies. Whereas Graff expects our critical debates to be conducted as justificatory arguments and thus fit in with disciplinary practices in other departments, I am concerned that this mode of argumentation will reinforce the very constraints from which he seeks to liberate us (see chapter 6).

3. In *The End of Modernity,* Vattimo offers us a conception of *pensiero debole*—"weak, or postfoundationalist thought"—to describe our contribution to the modern university system. In the introduction to that volume, Jon Snyder writes,

> Vattimo contends that the experience of infinite interpretability has led to "the weakening of the cogent force of reality" because it has made "all that is given [by metaphysics] as real, necessary, peremptory and true" into simply another interpretive possibility among a plethora of such possibilities. . . . [T]he formerly "strong" categories of thought— such as truth, Being and logic—have indeed consequently been 'weakened,' for they have been turned into a potentially *fictional* experience, that is, an experience about which we can never unequivocally say, "it is true." (xxii)

Vattimo believes we should accept this "fictionalized experience of reality which is also our only possibility for freedom" (29), but he is apparently not concerned that such a view does not match up well with other conceptions of the production of knowledge in the university. In my view, Vattimo's terminology alone automatically places us in a position of institutional inferiority and symptomatically shows how any comparison of our work to disciplinary work leaves us at a disadvantage.

4. The disciplinary pluralism implied by Wayne Booth's *Critical Understanding* breaks down the artificial barriers of departmentalization by offering a theory of perspectivism, in which the work of different disciplines complements each other. It is an appealing position, more open-ended than the hard-line pluralism of Ronald Crane. Still, I hesitate to embrace a pluralism of disciplines, because it brings with it a modernistic tendency to integrate the various *objects* of investigation. In "Interdisciplinarity and Authority in American Studies," David Shumway offers an excellent critique

of the idea that we can integrate disciplinary objects, pointing out that attempts to integrate existing disciplines usually result in the creation of a new discipline with its own disciplinary object. From my postmodern perspective, so to speak, Booth's perspectivism construes subjects as if they were objects and presupposes a detached, impersonal, supradisciplinary perspective.

5. Another kind of redefinition of discipline is undertaken by Louise Wetherbee Phelps in her *Composition as a Human Science*. On the grounds that we have a right to describe our own enterprise, she argues that we can define what we do as a discipline—not a scientific one in the usual sense of the term, but nonetheless a discipline because it has the character of a discipline: an inexhaustible topic, a connection with the intellectual life of the culture, principles that distinguish it from other studies, a moral imperative, methods that complement others, incentives, modes of dissemination, and, finally, an ironic self-reflexivity (ix–x, 44). Phelps contends that studies that are personal can be construed as human sciences and retain their disciplinary character without capitulating to the scientism with which our work has previously been infested. For her, "theory is autobiography," and thus what we do can be theorized as a discipline, as it has been in the work of Gadamer, Dewey, and Freire. She seeks a practical wisdom out of which a praxis can emerge. Her efforts, which she characterizes as the embedding of theory as a new form of writing in a metatheoretical framework (ix–xi), seems to involve us in more conceptual apparatus than necessary. While sympathetic to her endeavor, I find that the terminological scaffolding she assembles in order to speak of practical wisdom would neither provide theoretical links to other disciplines nor make our work more accessible to public spheres.

6. The transdisciplinary stance Mas'ud Zavarzadeh and Donald Morton take in *Texts for Change: Theory/Pedagogy/Politics* addresses the problem of disciplinarity as a problem of ideology. The wrong sort of discipline is in place, and they present us with a better model. Rather than produce interpretive essays that ensure the illusion of a unitary subject, we should produce critiques that interrogate the very conditions of our own knowledge, emphasizing "the institutional arrangements of knowledge." Transdisciplinarity is a "*trans-gressive* space in which configurations of knowledge are displayed as ultimately power-related" (10). Such an endeavor can reveal how we are disciplined, but as Morton and Zavarzadeh conceive it, their project reinscribes us in disciplinarity. Replacing the study of texts with the study of theory is not in itself a counterdisciplinary move, for it replicates the disciplinary conventions of argument. Furthermore, unrelenting critique is confrontational. Critique—"not to be confused with criticism" (6)—has negative results, a limiting condition. It tells us what not to do but not what to do. As critiques become more and more massive,

their accumulated weight becomes itself an obstacle. Proverbially, critique becomes a matter of beating a dead horse; there is neither care for what the criticism under attack did well nor purposefulness in continuing to punish it for faults it cannot correct. Moreover, substantive criticisms of the historical development of literary studies as a discipline are already in place. It is time to consider how disciplinarity has embedded itself in postmodern alternatives to it like theirs and to suggest further alternatives.

7. I find myself most drawn to Ellen Messer-Davidow's and David Shumway's delineation of disciplinarity. They have gathered in several collections of essays a sampling of divergent views on the ways the ideal of disciplinarity has influenced virtually every aspect of university study, from accounting to gay studies.[5] Their introductions to these collections provide a cogent overview of the various perspectives and remind us of the complexity of the issues involved. In "Disciplinarity: An Introduction," they provide a very helpful overview of disciplinarity as a historical project. In the introduction to *Knowledges* (with David Sylvan), they point out that "if disciplines are such by virtue of a historically contingent, adventitious coherence of dispersed elements, then to study that coherence is necessarily to begin questioning portrayals of disciplines as seamless, progressive, or naturally 'about' certain topics. In studying disciplinarity, one defamiliarizes disciplines; one distances oneself from them and problematizes their very existence" (3). Their efforts to show how heterogeneous are the conceptions of discipline that circulate among practitioners is very instructive. I find it quite salutary that they are not troubled by the conflicting views of disciplinarity they trace but rather see this state of affairs as unexceptional. At the same time, I am more troubled than they are by the constraints our quest for disciplinarity imposes on our practices.

Shumway's work treats discipline as a historically contingent formation, and his intention is to thereby deprivilege disciplinarity. At the same time, he defines disciplinarity in such a way that literary studies can still be considered an instance of it. As I read him, Shumway identifies in *Creating American Civilization* five conditions that make a study a discipline: (1) a disciplinary object, (2) a well-defined set of discursive practices that (3) give form to its production of knowledge, (4) a supporting apparatus for the distribution of its researches, and (5) a way of transmitting its accumulation of knowledge to students (149–52). I am mostly concerned with the first three conditions and comment below on Shumway's account of them in his *Creating American Civilization,* where he investigates how American literature became a subdiscipline within the discipline of English literary study.

The sine qua non of a discipline for Shumway is the construction of a language for a specific practice, a disciplinary object (1–3). Literature is just such an object of study. American literature's object is a selection of "writings produced in this country" known as "American Literature" and subject to "prior evaluation" owing to its status within the culture (1). It is studied through a well-defined set of discursive practices shared by the persons devoted to the study of the disciplinary object. These are "methods and procedures" that allow for the production of knowledge (152). The knowledge produced is a "body of statements" (152) with a specific form (97). This delineation of literary study as a discipline seems to me quite accurate, but it is an account of what we *say* we *do*. My reservation is related to the rhetorical dilemma I mentioned above—the terms we use to describe our work may be chosen because they are the passwords that admit us into the vestibule of disciplinarity. Or, perhaps more to the point, we may confess that we are a discipline because that admission allows us to take communion in the cathedral of learning known as the American university system. What would we say if we were not under this constraint? Though some critics would describe their work as disciplined, others would not.

It is not my intention in this study to refute the accounts mentioned above. Each seems descriptive and each brings out a different dimension of our commitment to belonging within the university system. What I wish to provide is an alternative way of describing what we do. I offer an alternative to the accounts of our disciplinary formation Shumway, Messer-Davidow, Graff, and Phelps provide because their accounts reinscribe the power of disciplinarity. Working in a disciplinary regime has disadvantages we do not discuss for fear we will not be supported by a university system that seems to require us to be disciplined. And yet our silence will not in the long run protect us, if indeed it ever did. How much longer should we subscribe to a conception of knowledge production that assumes a hierarchy in which our modes of understanding are devalued by comparison with science?

My approach to this difficult problem is to take a careful look at argumentation in literary study, since it is, in Shumway's articulation, a representation of the logical procedures we follow, the form disciplinarity imposes on our "production of knowledge," part of the disciplinary "*apparati*" (the essay format our forums have over the years preferred), and the basis of literary training (transmission). In sum, argumentation is intrinsic to almost every aspect of our work. That our work has a logical form of argumentation that allows us to call ourselves a discipline is the issue I examine in this study. In my view, disciplinarity—a condition wherein control over the production of knowledge is gained by training in methods—is an unsuitable ideal for the emerging cultural studies, particularly because it has shown itself to be a dubious rationale for literary studies.

A Dubious Rationale

The conviction that research, whether scientific or humanistic, should be fundamentally disciplinary has been a part of the conventional wisdom of the academy for about a century.[6] In *Professing Literature,* Gerald Graff reports that in 1895 Martin Wright Sampson, after conceding that "'English literature is only chatter about Shelley,'" warned his readers that "until instructors 'draw the line between the liking for reading and the understanding of literature,' they will make themselves 'ridiculous in the eyes of those who see into the heart of things'" (122–23). Twenty years later, I. A. Richards echoed Sampson's warning as a motive for writing *The Principles of Literary Criticism* (6). The assumption that liking literature is personal and that analyzing it is a disciplined, impersonal matter has governed the institutionalization of literary study for a century and is the defining characteristic of modern literary criticism.[7] It is rooted in the development of the professions during the last half of the nineteenth century. In the 1890s, when the prestige of a research program depended on its disciplinarity, humanists modeled their inquiries on the success scientists had in organizing their studies as disciplines. As the century turned, literary study developed a philological character. Soon afterward, a historical method for research overshadowed the philological one. By midcentury, a formal method of interpreting texts, ushered in by New Critics, dominated literary study. Not too long after the publication of Thomas Kuhn's *The Structure of Scientific Revolutions* (1965), many humanists, influenced by his theory, believed that literary studies was in a pre-paradigm stage of development but would soon achieve the status of a rigorous discipline. Yet as we near the twenty-first century, few believe it has. While professionalization and its attendant disciplinarity have produced the powerful academic institution we call the sciences, the humanities have lost professional power during this century. (This circumstance provokes the question, Are disciplinary goals suitable for the studies traditionally called the humanities?) Academic studies seem to acquire institutional clout to the extent that they become disciplines (discrete fields of academic study explained by methods specific to them).

Writing in the tradition of Karl Popper and Thomas Kuhn, Stephen Toulmin raises the question, "How, then, do diffuse and would-be disciplines differ from compact ones; and what conditions must be satisfied before a disciplinary activity can actually set out on the historical path of a genuine discipline?" (*Human Understanding* 379). He then sets parameters on answering his question: "We can best answer these questions by recalling the conditions required for the development of a compact, well-structured discipline, and then considering the various possible ways in which a potential discipline may fail to satisfy them" (379). Having set these parameters, he then answers his question by defining the "disciplinary" aspects of an inquiry in contrast to the "professional" aspects of an inquiry:

> A compact discipline, then, has five connected features. (1) The activities involved are organized around and directed towards a specific and realistic set of agreed collective ideals. (2) These collective ideals impose corresponding demands on all who commit themselves to the professional pursuit of the activities concerned. (3) The resulting discussions provide disciplinary loci for the production of "reasons" in the context of justificatory arguments whose function is to show how far procedural innovations measure up to these collective demands, and so improve the current repertory of concepts or techniques. (4) For this purpose, professional forums are developed, within which recognized "reason-producing" procedures are employed to justify the collective acceptance of novel procedures. (5) Finally, the same collective ideals determine the criteria of adequacy by appeal to which the arguments produced in support of those innovations are judged. (379)

Toulmin's account of a compact discipline represents the strict view of a discipline.[8] Literary study, as he notes, cannot be regarded as a discipline in the same sense that, say, chemistry can (see *An Introduction to Reasoning,* chapter 15). Most literary scholars would agree and admit that theirs is a "diffuse and would-be discipline." Nonetheless, they often endeavor to make it more compact. Traditional critics, for instance, claim their work is solidly based on canons of argumentation. These criteria count as disciplinary for traditional critics in a weaker (but parallel) sense of the term than Toulmin's (which remains distinct from the Foucauldian sense of "discipline").

With respect to their work, traditional critics stress the enabling aspects of discipline rather than the disabling ones. The work done by professional literary critics, for the most part, is the composition of arguments and long-standing canons of argumentation that provide disciplinary standards for literary studies, giving it legitimacy within the American university system. The attitude that typifies a modern critic is that arguments are rational discussions, not power relations, and have few if any disabling effects. For such critics any claim to disciplinarity must be warranted in the possibility of rigorous argumentation, that is, in the possibility of establishing textual facts, registering valid claims about texts, identifying errors in critical judgment, and proving other claims false. In short, the incarnate spirit of the tradition of modern critical discourse is a principled disciplinarity.

However, literary arguments do not have the same logical force as scientific arguments. They are not predictive, replicable, or falsifiable. Although literary arguments embody a kind of logic, literary study cannot achieve the ideals of a compact discipline. In this light, we do ourselves a disservice in calling ourselves a humanistic *discipline* because we must always appear a failed discipline.

For the institution of criticism to be regarded as a discipline (whether potential or actual), at least three of the conditions Toulmin elaborates should pertain: (1) that it have its own proper object of study, (2) that it be broken down into fields for specialists, and (3) that it conduct legitimate research (that is, research according to "justificatory arguments" [*Human Understanding* 379]). In the last several decades, the appropriateness of these three rationales of disciplinarity for literary studies has been challenged.

1. *A Proper Object of Study.* We are all familiar with the difficulties in defining "literature," the term we ordinarily use to designate our proper object of study. Probably the most notorious failure was the attempt of the Russian formalists to define "literariness." As a consequence, the traditional boundaries of literature have been successfully challenged. It is now commonplace to encounter opposition to any form of canonization. That great works of literature can be identified is no longer a profession-wide belief. Long-standing canonical lists of great works have largely been revised to include works previously neglected for political and social rather than disciplinary reasons. Moreover, distinctions between autobiography and fictional works such as bildungsroman have eroded. Feminists have reintroduced diaries, letters, and journals into the curriculum. Tidy generic distinctions no longer hold much sway. Detective stories, science fiction, and romances, once relegated to the shelves of nonacademic bookstores, now are taught with increasing frequency in universities. Films, advertisements, and even shopping malls are regarded as texts. In sum, the object "literature" lacks even minimal definition.

2. *Specialized Fields.* If literary study lacks a proper object, it of necessity must lack coherent fields of specialization. There are more specialties in literature than can be enumerated, since the object has no limits.

Specialization is a necessary element of disciplinarity. Disciplinarity is tightly bound to the social organization of expertise as professions. Professionals have legal control over an expertise. This power is legitimized by conceptual control over a particular research specialization. The authority of modern professional literary critics is based on specialized research fields such as the nineteenth-century romantic poets, the early-eighteenth-century novelists, the French medieval romance, and so on. Critics have demarcated these fields as sets of texts in particular historical relation to each other, but these fields are justifiable only if texts are, in some sense, loci of facts. In the last twenty years, however, what can be determined as factual about literary texts has been narrowed to their most trivial features. The elements that once seemed to be a matter of discovery now seem better described as a matter of invention. Scholarly agreements are now more likely to be explained in terms of interpretive communities than in terms of neutral evidence. In place of what once seemed as concrete and objective as stones and trees and other landmarks we now have a myriad of features, none of which is perceptible without a particular theoretical lens. Such reunderstanding of what was once construed as the factual basis of literary scholarship has considerable consequences for the conduct of research. Literary scholars no longer seem in control of a field and thus lack legitimacy as experts. In place of disinterested knowledge we now have political, social, and cultural debate. Literary scholars rarely *discover* cultural universals, immutable truths about the human condition, and eternal values; they most often preserve or challenge prevailing cultural norms, beliefs, and ideologies.

It now appears that literary scholars are experts only in the sense that lawyers, politicians, and ministers of religion are experts, that is, to the extent that they are in command of a set of techniques for the manipulation of discursive environments. This is far removed from the ideal of a compact discipline and calls into question another rationale for disciplinarity—the legitimation of research.

3. *Legitimate Research Programs.* Every discipline has a theoretical base to legitimate the conduct of research—what Toulmin in *Human Understanding* calls "reasons" or "warrants" that are used in "justificatory arguments" (379). It is not possible to have a discipline without having a theory of its subject matter to warrant arguments about it. It should therefore seem curious that we have recently witnessed a sharp outcry against literary theory. Such outcries, however, are not unusual. Modern literary scholars have a long antitheoretical history. Many of them have announced that their practices do not require the esoteric and jargon-ridden theoretical pronouncements rival critics sometimes make, a statement sometimes infelicitously equated to the statement that the study of literature does not require theories. I will not take up such confusions here[9] because the point I wish to make is that literary studies, far from operating within a specific, agreed-upon research paradigm (a logically coherent set of theorems), operates with a very wide range of theoretical assumptions. Further, these theorems vary from attempts to minimize theory to attempts to link literary theory with the theoretical bases of other disciplines.[10] Within this spectrum a variety of conceptually incompatible theorems inform an even larger variety of practices. Even during its heyday, New Criticism exhibited little theoretical uniformity. Procedures of close reading were widely disseminated in textbooks, but the resulting eclectic practices, which often get lumped together as "close readings," cannot be characterized as "normal science."

The institution of literary criticism was formed with the expectation that critics would meet the conditions required of a discipline. But historically, literary criticism has never matched these ideal conditions. Although many critics now admit this, they still understand literary criticism to be anchored in its methodologies, which legitimate the resulting research. Under close inspection, this position is untenable.[11]

Literary critics avoid using the term "methods," preferring instead to speak of "approaches." The substitution was introduced by Cleanth Brooks and Robert Penn Warren in *An Approach to Literature* in a climate wherein a search for a more scientific approach to criticism was being encouraged by theorists such as John Crowe Ransom (see chapter 9). In such endeavors, critics typically focus on selected texts, which they designate as literature and then interrogate through a series of questions—the answers to which they assume will yield viable interpretations. The questions that make up their practice are derived from abstract, theoretical models of texts, and their sustained application to specific literary works results in a distinctive type of reading usually identified with some school of interpretation: close reading with New Criticism, psychoanalytic readings with Freudian or Lacanian criticism, and so on. The questions Brooks and Warren asked were not always the questions Northrop Frye, Ronald Crane, or Kenneth Burke asked. Consequently, different approaches get identified and named— Marxism, New Historicism, deconstruction, postcolonialism. A number of handbooks of such approaches are routinely published, and many historians of literary criticism use the "schools and approaches" framework as a means of organizing their discussion of critical networks. In his *Republic of Letters,* Grant Webster gives an account of the rise of this movement. In my view, critical approaches are intended to parallel scientific methods and foster a tendency to describe practices in terms of procedures. In the "Theories Need Not Be Methods" chapter of *Token Professionals and Master Critics* I show how they are related to our attempts to describe our work as a discipline. Some critics think of cultural studies as one of many approaches to literature. In my view, attempts to make our work appear to follow disciplinary ideals by describing critical practices as "approaches" is debilitating for three reasons: (1) approaches simplify, (2) approaches proliferate, and (3) interpretive approaches produce circular arguments.

1. Approaches tend to simplify the complexities critics seek in texts. Gerald Graff acknowledges the need in literary studies for the simplification of procedures and vocabularies, but also notes that "'Complicating' and 'problematizing' are the characteristic activity of the academy, which takes things that ostensibly, from the common sense point of view, seem simple and uncontroversial—a literary classic, a war, an election, an epidemic, a comic strip—and shows that they are complex, problematic, less stable and self-evident than we thought" (*Culture Wars* 102). Far from complicating and problematizing, approaches *intentionally* reduce practices to procedures (What good is a method whose steps are too complex to fol-

low?). Since reading and writing are astonishingly complex and ineluctably personal activities, they are difficult to reduce to methods. This has spawned extensive borrowing from studies already institutionalized as disciplines whose aims do not require that the complexity of reading acts be preserved, notably linguistics, psychology (both analytic and cognitive), anthropology, sociology, history, and especially philosophy. The results are notorious. No one approach can be privileged. Thus, all the borrowed warrants from other disciplines survive. But in the process, a hodgepodge of interpretive claims get authorized as if they were textual "facts."

2. Literary criticism is a melting pot of interpretive methods—our approaches-oriented training procedures ensure that they proliferate. But the well-known proliferation of approaches to literature (the *Encyclopedia of Contemporary Literary Theory,* 1993, lists forty-seven) is not a hallmark of disciplinarity. Further, the eclectic mix our melting pot produces has not in turn produced more prestige for critics working in a university system regulated by disciplinary ideals. Nor does it make sense to become more ruthlessly reductive by collapsing the number of current approaches into fewer canonical ones. The aim of gaining control over a subject matter, which is the justification of methodology, seems injudicious in the case of literature. The heart of the problem is our tendency to equate theory with method.[12] Our premise has been that if there is a field to be studied, then an appropriate method should be applied. This is the rationale for a discipline in the strict or compact sense. The proliferation of approaches in our studies, however, may suggest little more than a plurality of professional networks. That they constitute a range of interpretive communities would be a difficult case to establish and a project more likely to arrive at the conclusion that each reader has a unique method of reading and thus constitutes a discrete field of inquiry.

3. In scientific disciplines the formal reports that present the results of methodological investigations are structured as arguments. In literary studies the results of critical readings are reported in arguments wherein the approaches used to read texts become the justificatory warrants used to demonstrate claims, a rather circular but unavoidable kind of argumentation.[13] Methods of reading become theories of reading, which are reduced to theorems to justify readings. Literary arguments presuppose that if readers read texts as the critics do, then readers will agree with the critics. This is indubitable. However, as I note in chapter 10, such techniques produce subjectivities rather than objective judgments. Hence our work usually appears subjective in the light of disciplines that require objectivity.

While it is true that few critics advocate methods, many hold the position that criticism should display continuity, share theoretical notions, reflect a collective intellectual ambition, conform to specific procedures of reading, and follow well-defined criteria for evidence. Such articulations (easy to find in the MLA's guides to research) reveal a desire to turn literary criticism into a discipline. These critics often work diligently to describe what we do in terms that do not restrict what we do and yet allow us to call our work a discipline. In this chapter I have suggested that the ideals of disciplinarity do not suit literary study, a claim I hope to sustain in the chapters that follow. I contend that, despite the unsuitability of disciplinary ideals for our work, the institutional power of such ideals leads literary critics to construe what they do as a discipline. Recently, however, Gerald Graff has called our attention to the patterned isolation characteristic of our institutional lives. In the next chapter I show how his analysis of our profession is significantly related to my concerns about disciplinarity.

Disciplined Isolation

CHAPTER 4

Information is useful unless there is too much to use. It piles up in stacks of old newspapers and magazines, or in layers of memos filling your office mailbox as rapidly as junk mail does at home, or in rows of e-mail messages that grow like weeds. To avoid being overwhelmed, we throw information out, discard it, put it in wooden, plastic, or electronic wastebaskets. But occasionally what is to others disposable information is to us indispensable. Of the many catalogs, the Land's End one survives. Of the many memos, the one on the departmental film series gets taped to the door. Of the many coupons, the one for a free second pizza gets saved under the magnet on the refrigerator. Information has to touch our lives before it becomes significant. If we studied our choices of information, we would see the patterns in our lives. In the previous chapter I remarked that discipline *patterns* our work by making it a function of the university system. In this chapter I take a closer look at the resulting "patterned isolation" and the ways in which being informed by discipline commits us to piling up information in ways that isolate us from other inquirers, both within and without the university.

Since 1985, when he edited *Criticism in the University* with Reginald Gibbons, Gerald Graff has identified several problems that are aspects of the general problem of patterned isolation in the study of literature: (1) the field-coverage problem, (2) the cafeteria-counter curriculum problem, (3) the unconnectivity problem, and (4) the public-relations problem. In my view, these are the manifestations of our pursuit of the ideal of disciplinarity.

Graff's solution to these interrelated problems is "teach the conflicts." In the preface to *Criticism in the University,* his and Gibbons's remarks foreshadow this well-known recommendation for revitalizing the study of literature. Proposition 7 states, "The university is like a family in which the parents hide their disagreement from the children" (12). Proposition 6 is more specific: "The organization of the university now prevents these conflicts from becoming visible and educationally functional" (12). In "The University and the Prevention of Culture," Graff remarks that "no proposal for reform will go far unless it sets its sights on abridging the structural isolation of individuals, groups, and departments that now prevents the possibility of an intellectual community of debate" (79). Since the American university is organized as a city of disciplines, each housed in a separate department, it is not difficult to discern in this pattern an isolationism that, I will argue, buttresses Graff's charge against the academy.

The Field-Coverage Problem and Disciplinarity

Graff's criticism of the field-coverage system we use to organize our labors emerges from his work on the history of literary study. He delineates "the field-coverage model of departmental organization" in "Taking Cover in Coverage" and in "The Humanist Myth" (chapter 1 in *Professing Literature*). It is a bureaucratic principle "which has conceived literature departments as aggregates arranged to cover an array of historical and generic literary fields" (*Professing Literature* 7). In Graff's analysis, the field-coverage principle is an effective institutional structuring precept, but its very effectiveness as a bureaucratic instrument creates harmful effects in literary studies—incoherent curricula, fragmented inquires, and unconnected learning.

Graff notes that "the field-coverage principle accompanied the modernization and professionalization of education of the 1870s and 1880s when schools and colleges organized themselves into departments corresponding to what were deemed to be the major subjects and research fields" (*Professing Literature* 6). From the perspective of this study, the field-coverage principle is directly related to the mode of disciplinarity, which has infused modern literary criticism for a century. (In the first section of chapter 10 I link the concept of a field of inquiry to the ideals of disciplinarity, which provide the organizational structure of the modern university.) As we have already seen, Toulmin's requirement for a compact discipline is that the study in question identify its own proper object. We orient ourselves around conceptions of historical periods, genres, and other organizing fields as our proper objects in order to fit the disciplinary organization of the modern university system. There are other ways of organizing our work.

Responding to the problems associated with our patterned isolation, Graff, for instance, recommends that literary study rethink itself as cultural study, a recommendation I support (see chapter 12). This makes excellent sense as a response to the problem of field coverage. In a disciplinary orientation, literary scholars construe the proper object of their work to be texts belonging to historical periods. However, the globalization of communication as the Internet spreads and the collapse of textual boundaries in the wake of postmodern theory lend credence to Graff's recommendation. The advent of the culture wars, precipitated by recent interest in multiculturalism (stirred no doubt by globalization), makes the study of culture a sensible emendation of traditional literary study. In addition, recent theoretical reconsiderations of texts as webs of intertexts without apparent borders also make culture (understood as a web of textuality) a more accurate focus for our work than the text as an object bordered by covers. Texts are now typically understood to be films, buildings, gestures, and so on. Thus, our cultural habitat is a sensible focus for work. In chapters 12 through 15 of this book I take up this issue in detail, so let us turn our attention to Graff's description of the programs literature departments offer.

The Cafeteria-Counter Curriculum Problem and Information Retrieval

In *Beyond the Culture Wars,* Graff continues to pursue the problem of field coverage, adding to his analysis that the literary studies curriculum has no "common denominator," that it is "a mere cafeteria counter of professorial research interests" (128). This cafeteria-counter approach to literary study, wherein students are presented with an array of courses that are not in any way obviously related but that may be purchased to satisfy the requirements of their degrees, is the result of the infinitely expandable aspect of the field-coverage principle. "In the coverage model," Graff points out, "innovation even of a threatening kind could be welcomed by simply *adding* another unit to the aggregate of fields to be covered" (*Professing Literature* 7). The resulting aggregate does not, as the notion of disciplinarity implies, automatically reassemble itself into a coherent map of the field allegedly covered. It remains an aggregate.

In this study I offer a reason for the haphazard character of curricular expansion that complements Graff's. In his view, the aggregate of research interests that make up the cafeteria counter of courses will not fall into place as a coherent picture of the field unless the differences among the courses are debated by their instructors. I agree but note that the cafeteria-counter curriculum is an effect of our quest for disciplinarity. The coverage principle ensures that apprentices in a discipline are in possession of the established opinion in a given field. This need to cover "the best that has been thought and said" in a field has a side effect—a tendency to base our programs on the acquisition of information. Whether this side effect is deleterious in the sciences I have no way of knowing, but I can testify to its deleterious effects in English departments. Though we celebrate the uniqueness of literary works, we do so by establishing relative uniformity in our reading practices and by avoiding eccentric interpretations. In the main, our programs depend on the acquisition of specific methodological, technical, and historical information (within an established range of options). Students learn conceptions of texts, genres, techniques, periods, themes, and so on. On the foundation of these concepts we build schools of criticism. Our system of training has as its precondition the acquisition of information pertinent to the discipline of literary interpretation. Our students digest enormous amounts of information about appropriate ways of reading texts. Graff's account of the cafeteria-counter curriculum is, I believe, the tip of the proverbial iceberg. What lies beneath the surface is a mountain of information.

Information is usually understood to be discrete bits of unrelated data; knowledge, on the other hand, is usually understood as data that can be related to an inquiry. As Theodore Roszak remarks in *The Cult of Information*, information was not much valued prior to World War II because "most people thought about information in those days [as] disjointed matters of fact that came in discrete little bundles" (3). Recently, the term "information" has been used in ways that overlap with the term "knowledge." Still, the word "information" retains the sense of discrete, unrelated bits that are exchanged, even if only as electronic impulses. In most usages, whether technical or commonsensical, information suggests fragments that make discrete sense but that become knowledge (connected) only when related to other bits of information and given significance as the answer to an inquiry.

Returning to the narrower context of literary studies with this distinction in mind, we should note that field-oriented or disciplinary pedagogy (most familiar to us as the lecture) inescapably turns knowledge of literature into information about literature. In this scheme, students can be examined on the contents of specific fields as if they were piecing together a puzzle presented to them in fragments meant to be unified through their hard work—as if, when successful, they would be rewarded with an accurate image of the whole field that the puzzle creators cut into pieces for the students' edification. In the light of postmodern theory, this practice is self-defeating because the persons working on the puzzle shape each piece as they go along, each in his or her own way. When such pieces are regarded as information, they remain fragmented. What gets covered is not a coherent picture of something that can be called literature, as if it were already pictured on the box from which its pieces were drawn.

But why should literature be considered a unified field? Critical inquiry is often inspired by conflict. Take, for instance, Graff's reading of Conrad's *Heart of Darkness,* which initially clashed with the Nigerian novelist Chinua Achebe's reading (discussed at length in "Taking Cover in Coverage" and *Culture Wars*). Their conflicting readings, as Graff observes, are not mere matters of idiosyncratic interpretations; they raise social issues—in this case, about Conrad's colonialism. Such conflicts inspire other readers to engage in the careful interpretation of the texts involved. In literary arguments these texts are not treated as pieces of information that fit together into a larger puzzle called literature. Nor are textual forms treated as discrete bits that fit into a larger whole called *the* theme of the text. In the sort of cultural studies Graff advocates in his example, neither texts nor their component parts are treated as information. They are occasions for inquiry. To illustrate my point, consider introducing the information that many of Conrad's sentences have the form of indirect discourse into the dialogue between Graff and Achebe. This information would appear to be a strangely random fact arbitrarily introduced unless it could be related to some issue in the conversation on which it shed some light.

Outside their relation to cultural conflicts, interpretations tend to be logical puzzles. As a result, when their conflicting claims go unnegotiated they produce only information about the readers involved rather than provoke inquiries into social problems. This effect (the cafeteria counter) is palpable when the literature of our cultural past is being studied. For instance, to most students of literature, Chaucer's relation to the church hierarchy of his day is mostly a matter of information that is required in order to understand certain interpretations of the *Canterbury Tales.* Unlike the dialogue between Graff and Achebe over the interpretation of Conrad's *Heart of Darkness,* discussions of Chaucer's view of the church are likely to have little bearing on the lives of most contemporary readers as a social issue. Hence his view of the church has the status of historical information. However, had Chaucer's characterization of the rape victim in "The Wife of Bath's Tale" been the subject matter in Graff's classroom, Chaucer's view of women would likely become more than information. (Whether the class's construction of Chaucer's view could count as knowledge in a disciplinary regime is an issue we must postpone until chapters 6 and 7.)

Although Graff does not make a distinction between interpretations learned as information and those that become part of an inquiry, he does distinguish between presenting students with interpretations *outside* the context of debate and *within* it. In my experience, student reactions to *Fatal Attraction* call for this distinction. After watching the film, most of my students rejected feminist interpretations that single out the misogynistic characterization of Alex Forrest (played by Glenn Close). They regarded them as academic, that is, as instances of looking for hidden meanings, as if we were filling our counters with consumer choices that they have no interest in consuming (see chapter 4 of *Culture Wars*). However, when presented with the original context of such criticisms—Adrian Lynne's remaking the end of the film to suit market analyses—and when shown the horror-film techniques used to do so, the class entered a different dimension of analysis. At first students treated the feminist interpretations as information, that is, as data with little or no bearing on their lives. Such interpretations typify what teachers do—search for hidden meanings. Subsequently, when students began to feel duped, began to feel like the subjects of market engineering, then lively debates about the cultural impact of the film ensued.

I am not suggesting that lively debates do not occur when it is a question of close readings of texts independent of their cultural contexts. This does happen. I am distinguishing between such debates and ones occasioned by the perception of a problem within one's own culture.[1] In the first case the issues are academic; in the second they are public. In the first case texts are presented as puzzles in interpretation for students to solve; in the second they are presented as the textuality that informs the beliefs they have acquired from their culture. The difference is that, in the first scenario, interpretations are perceived as bits of information students have to learn for whatever test is likely to imposed upon them; in the second, interpretations of the film devolve around constructions of the cultural significance of the film relevant to their views of it. In the second scenario students find themselves to be members of the culture of which the film is a part rather than subjects about to be tested on the intrinsic meaning of a text their teachers interpret (often enough against the grain of student experience).

When cultural problems are treated conceptually in an academic setting, understanding is converted to information that can be purchased and consumed in preparation for exams. Grading tends to convert understanding into consumable information. Technocracy spawns this tendency to quantify the qualitative, to simplify the complex, and to mechanize the processes involved. Earlier in our cultural history, few would have valued information over knowledge gained through argumentation or over understanding derived from experience, but the cultural status of information has increased dramatically. Quizzes that test the retrieval of unrelated information are popular national shows, and trivial pursuits are major international tournaments.

Displacing general understanding with commonplace information is one of the signposts of technocracies. After decades of specialization, the general knowledge of the populace constricts into narrower and narrower specialties. One becomes knowledgeable only in a tiny domain and relies on fellow experts for information (reported knowledge) about other domains. For instance, unable (and therefore increasingly unwilling to make the effort) to understand the operation of VCRs, we tend to rely on the information accompanying them telling us which buttons to push to make them work, trusting the experts who built them. The contrast I draw between information and understanding has its application on the plane of events we regard as self-education. Instead of understanding how computers accomplish what they do, we find ourselves (for the most part) content to use them on the basis of the information given in the accompanying manuals and often only on the most accessible levels. If the buttons or keys change (or even if they are relocated), we find ourselves unable to function because we cannot extrapolate from our experiences to analogous situations.[2] We perceive parts as discrete bits or pieces rather than in relation to each other.

From the foregoing we can see how our cafeteria-counter curriculum matches the tendencies in our culture. Furthermore, it has to be said that not all of our students are bothered by it. That many accept and some (those who want to test well) prefer acquiring information to struggling for understanding does not negate Graff's analysis. If anything, it makes it all the more telling. Defining debate as a setting in which several persons are pursuing the same inquiry dialogically, let's explore its potential for reversing the cafeteria-counter curricula's to replace understanding with information.

Before we undertake this exploration, however, we should review our suppositions. Our main premise is that understanding is governed by inquiry. As its corollary we take it to be axiomatic that once the quest for understanding is achieved, questing for it is no longer necessary. Thus, understanding can be treated cafeteria style as information, as an established set of facts. Further, we can stipulate that the most salient characteristic of information is that it can be stored and retrieved.

Unfortunately, information is, in principle, ungoverned. Facts are routinely stored in arbitrary categories (e.g., alphanumeric) in order to function as information. Imagine, for example, printing all of the answers to a questionnaire without first contextualizing them by querying the database in order to retrieve only those facts relevant to what you wish to know. Were the database huge, the result would be unintelligible, a pure information glut, one bit after another in agonizingly repetitious fashion—like being condemned to search a phone book without intending to call anyone, just reading name after name, address after address. It is only *querying* the database that makes it a source of knowledge rather than information. However, for knowledge to be searched and retrieved, it has to be converted into information. This is the sort of information processing students conduct when they study for exams.[3]

Contemporary students of my acquaintance often wish to master the definitions of the key concepts of major theorists outside the context of any inquiry whatsoever—collecting tools of all sorts just in case they might come in handy. Some are delighted to discover that terminology can be learned in shorthand fashion from glossaries without even having to read the theorists being studied. Indeed, innumerable glossaries and anthologies have come on the market to provide us with information about every theoretical tremor in our academic terrain. Nor is this orientation toward faster and faster retrieval of information about theory surprising.

In literature departments, to meet the perceived need to study a new but very large field, theory is treated as information. The burgeoning industry this perception generates has a distinctive media orientation based on the marketing of concepts.[4] Consonant with the information age in which we now live, the theory industry is an affiliate of the news industry, which can treat inquiry only as information (about inquirers or the results of their inquiries) because it is inescapably a *representation* of an inquiry, not the inquiry itself. So when inquiries become news, they become information because news has to be stored and transported before it can be retrieved and edited for marketable consumption. Though not the only capability of the media, information retrieval is its most conspicuous one. Hence the ways inquiries are formatted as news must be factored into accounts of news about academic inquiries. In the news media, for instance, the only professors teaching at Duke seem to be radical, poststructuralist theorists. Synopses of their views are evidently newsworthy. What is not newsworthy is the complexity of their inquiries. The format of news is abbreviation and categorization.

To Graff's analysis of the cafeteria-counter problem, I add several amendments. First, I make a distinction between modern and postmodern that he does not employ (see chapter 12). We cannot disregard the impact of the information age on our work. Reminding ourselves that we live in a postmodern information age while we work in modern institutions seems an appropriate instance of self-reflexivity. Second, the theory industry (with Duke construed as its most recent factory) has greatly contributed to the expanding cafeteria-counter curriculum. Third, understanding, which is largely narrative in character, must be reduced to factual information in order to be stored and retrieved. In the process, experience is reduced to a conception of itself. Literature, which is about cultural experiences rather than about themes or ideas, is as difficult to codify as we are. Nonetheless, academic mechanisms (like exams) designed to maintain a body of disciplinary knowledge that can be stored and retrieved as sharable (nondebatable) information pressure literary scholars to produce information uncontaminated by debate.[5] Granting that information tends to be stored in arbitrary patterns that give it a cafeteria-counter structure, the tendency to avoid collaboration (I prefer this term to "debate")[6] deserves separate analysis. In what follows, I argue that the unconnectivity of our field-specific endeavors points to the irony that the standardization and normalization germane to disciplines encourages individuation at the expense of collaboration in cultural studies.

The Unconnectivity Problem and Individualized Uniformity

Departments no longer house single disciplines; they group studies, which are often difficult to relate to each other, in somewhat arbitrary gatherings motivated by budgetary considerations and quixotic historical conjunctures. It would be ludicrous to believe that critical inquiries are interrelated by dint of being housed in the same department—nowadays English departments house the study of American television, spaghetti westerns, and postcolonial African writings. In recent years, many literature departments (and especially English departments) have found it increasingly difficult to identify a subject matter they have in common, much less a coherent methodology they uniformly employ. The tendency to split up and form a new program or department, what Graff calls "patterned isolation," reached a budgetary standstill in the 1970s. Subsequently, departments have been sheltering increasingly disparate inquiries. Subject matters burgeon. Canons expand. Methods proliferate. But the aftereffects of patterned isolation remain. Autonomy now seems to apply to every research endeavor. It is as though every individual has a proper subject matter and a correspondingly unique method, almost as though every critic could be viewed as the *Chronicle of Higher Education* views Harold Bloom—a "one-man department."[7] Consequently, it is difficult to connect what one person is doing in a classroom with what others do in their classrooms within the same department, much less with experts in other departments. Once again, my explanation of this phenomenon complements Graff's. For him the villain is an institutional bureaucracy that cannot control its ability to expand; for me the villain is an institutional bureaucracy that cannot enforce standardization.

For Graff, the modern university, through its elective system, fosters differences of opinion and belief, whereas its predecessor institution, the religious college, fostered uniformity and orthodoxy. The villain for Graff is the expendability of the field-coverage principle. He cites Gary Waller's notion of the "park bench principle of curricular change" to illustrate how the field-coverage principle functions in the modern university: "When a powerful newcomer shows up, everyone on the bench shuffles over just a little to make room for the latest arrival. Occasionally, if things get a little crowded, the one at the end falls off—Anglo-Saxon, perhaps, or philology" (*Culture Wars* 133).[8] To make way for each new field added, an undersubscribed field disappears from the program—"a victim of numbers," as bench players in sporting fields often say to explain their demise.

Though I agree that the modern university has a quota system dictated by budgetary parameters, in my analysis it requires uniformity and is, from a different perspective, relatively intolerant of difference. In *Token Professionals and Master Critics: A Critique of Orthodoxy in Literary Studies,* I argue (as its subtitle implies) that institutions regulate themselves by requiring practices that reinforce their founding principles and hence entail uniformity. Differences at microlevels (e.g., New Criticism and deconstruction) can be seen to be quite uniform at higher levels of generality (e.g., formalism, ahistoricism). Institutions depend on practices of uniformity at levels much more general than the level at which a given critical practice functions. In other words, modern institutions depend for their efficacy on comprehensive standards. Thus, standardization is a process with pervasive effects on the professional conduct of members of the institution.

Though the individuals who practice a given discipline are likely to differ considerably from one another, their membership in a discipline commits them to a contractual obligation to relate their work to the work of colleagues. However diverse a department might be in its personalities, its members are obliged to coordinate their efforts. Departmental committee work invariably has this aim. The undergraduate and graduate committees usually work hard to establish cogent programs that transmit their discipline beyond the walls of the rooms in which their deliberations take place. To teach freshman composition or a graduate course in literary theory is not an invitation to ride a personal hobbyhorse. Persons who do not assign their students themes or who offer their students idiosyncratic speculations are usually reprimanded and asked to conform to standard practices or depart.

The hallmark of the modern institution housing various disciplines is individualization at the price of uniformity (Graff and I analyze different sides of the institutional enigma of individualized uniformity). The modern university is organized by departments separately funded in order to ensure their autonomy. Yet owing to credentialing procedures, universities require standardization. Hence the tendency intrinsic to the inquiries housed in universities is toward the uniformity of practices. Each discipline, while autonomous, encourages widespread standards. Standardization ensures expertise. Its self-regulating mechanisms are exams on the objects under investigation as well as the methods employed to further their investigation. As the investigations deepen, the practitioners become increasingly expert in them, developing exacting vocabularies that move further and further from ordinary language usage.[9] Candidates for the profession of a discipline are thus expected to master the idioms of inquiry, since these are derived from methods unique to the mode of investigation. Following norms individuates by grading the candidates who fail to follow them.

I examine such normalization in chapters 8, 9, and 10. In each of these chapters, the exam (structured by argumentation) is understood to be the cardinal institutional practice. It is the principal means of standardization. In the modern university, critics cannot abandon the practice of examining candidates in their fields. Hence they cannot abandon standardizing critical practices. It is the standardization of modes of inquiry that allegedly ensures coherence and connectivity in the curricula according to which students are to be schooled in a discipline. However, the disciplinary system operates well only when competing schools of thought can be falsified through argumentation. In the absence of falsification, schools and methods proliferate as rapidly as inquirers develop innovative researches.

Though it is true that the "park bench principle" maintains a quota of fields in the modern university, few administrators would offer it as the rationale behind their implementation of disciplinary programs. Nevertheless, in the humanities, where an instructor's methods cannot be falsified (strictly speaking), it is difficult to defend the removal of courses. Instead, administrators simply offer budgetary constraints as rationales for dropping courses and programs.[10]

By my account, the problem of infinitely expanding curricula is endemic to the modern university, which requires disciplinary uniformity in its practitioners. Rather than creating a situation in which ten persons study ten different cultures, it requires a situation in which ten persons study the same field in the same way. Thus, if ten cultures are to be studied, either the ten persons must study all ten cultures with the same proper methodology, or the ten persons are each in different fields studying ten different objects proper to them. The modern university funnels the multiform interests of a heterogeneous population into the uniform homogeny of a single method or field. Thus, if too many fields are to be covered, the situation taxes the organizational resources of the modern institution. At the overload point, the curriculum becomes a cafeteria counter. At the same time, I would add, our situation is such that not only are there more than ten fields to be studied, there are more than ten methods with which they can be approached. This multiplies the problem and makes it increasingly difficult to relate one field, method, or study to another.

To solve this multiplication problem, Graff proposes a cultural studies agenda that brings the culture wars into the classroom and commits us to debating them in nonspecialist terms accessible to the general public. He asks, How can we organize the overwhelming body of cultural materials that have, by accretion, become our subject matter? His solution—bringing the culture wars into the classroom—seems at first an exacerbation of the problem. Yet he is not advocating that all cultures must be represented there; he proposes only that specific problems with various cultures (webs of textuality) be debated. Not all texts of all cultures, but those that are the subject of public concern.[11] In sum, Graff proposes to introduce connections among the studies to which students are subjected by relating them to the context of current cultural experiences.

This recommendation goes against the grain of disciplinarity. Rather than have the specialist identify the problematic, Graff proposes, in effect, that we allow the media to identify problems with which we should be concerned. This brings us to the relation between what we do and how the public might benefit from it. In considering this problematic relation, we might ask, Can amateurs become members of disciplinary schools of thought?

The Public-Relations Problem and the Jargon Experts Use

In my reading of his work, Graff views the general public as our students. Both what we say in the classroom and publish outside of it is made publicly available. Unfortunately, our publications are often inaccessible to the public, a feature of our work Graff would like to change. Nonetheless, we do make it *public.* For him, the walls of the classroom are not its boundaries. Moreover, our most immediate contact with the general public, Graff implies, is at the classroom site, since most students are part of a more public sphere beyond the university campus (*Culture Wars* 103, 142).[12] So, in principle, our relation to students is, in most if not all respects, the same one we have to the public. In practice, students are our apprentices and the public our benefactor. What would bringing these relationships closer together, as Graff recommends, commit us to? At the very least, as the political correctness debates have indicated, we need to make our inquiries meaningful to wider audiences.

In "Hidden Meaning, or, Disliking Books at an Early Age" (chapter 4 of *Culture Wars*), Graff gives an autobiographical account of his introduction to literature. He recounts how his dislike of books dominated his early education, how he found the teachers' remarks unintelligible and constrictive, thus identifying himself with many contemporary students. The turning point for him occurred when he was a junior in college and his instructor spoke about the critical controversy surrounding the ending of *Huck Finn.* This controversy divided the class into critical camps and inspired Graff to study both the novel and its critics with newfound enthusiasm. This anecdote is a parable about teaching the conflicts.

The public, represented in the anecdote by Graff-as-a-student, becomes involved in literary research at the moment it becomes an issue *for them.* At that moment, when they find that they have internalized the controversy as an inner conflict, they are engaged. Later in *Beyond the Culture Wars,* Graff offers another anecdote, this time about his own class. In the second story, students in Graff's class become engaged in Conrad's *Heart of Darkness* when they internalize the conflict between traditional critical readings of the novella and Achebe's postcolonial reading of it as imperialist fiction. Over his career, we see Graff rethinking his audience. In his first book, *Poetic Statement and Critical Dogma,* he writes with academic specialists in mind; in his most recent book, he writes for nonspecialists.

In *Beyond the Culture Wars,* Graff also goes beyond the classroom in his rethinking of the literary specialist:

> From 1900 to 1990 the rhetoric of college catalogs, presidential ora-
> tory, and fund-raising and recruitment propaganda has stressed that the
> college or university is firmly committed to both the preservation of the
> old and the encouragement of the new. In fact, however, the old and
> the new clashed, resulting in a dramatic split between two kinds of aca-
> demic humanists, the research professional dedicated to the production
> of new knowledge for an audience of other professionals and the general-
> ist man of letters dedicated to teaching rather than research and to pro-
> moting the spirit of the humanities among the public at large. (131)

His proposals seem to imply that these two groups should merge, that the public at large be included in our research endeavors or interpretive communities, that is, in our "schools of thought." He does not press for an end to research specialization but rather recommends that we make more of an effort to consider the public as our legitimate audience and, perhaps, our legitimate collaborators as well—especially when the public is represented in our classrooms by our students.

I agree with Graff that the walls of the classroom are not its boundaries, though my view of this situation is influenced by Kenneth Burke, who gives a somewhat different spin to the matter. Burke's explanation of the situation Graff describes in his account of teaching *Heart of Darkness* is that readers in general identify with the conflict in the fiction if it symbolizes for them a dramatic conflict that can be related to their own experiences, however analogously (*Rhetoric of Religion* 543–47). We might say that readers become engaged with the literature they are reading when they recognize their own experience, either directly or indirectly. Thus, when that recognition is challenged they are aroused. The situation is quite common, for example, in study of *Fatal Attraction.* Women students often do not identify with the Glenn Close character (the other woman). If they do not, they are likely to identify with the Anne Archer character (the wife). Their position in classroom debates about the cultural significance of the film hinges on these identifications. Women who identify with the wife are just as annoyed as any man in the class with feminists who defend "the other woman." In one sense or another the film configures their experiences. Either they see their parents and find themselves emotionally engaged by the

compelling portrait of the child in the film, or they see themselves at one
or another point in the sexual triangle. Or they desire as women to be
careerists and partly identify with Alex Forrest and are infuriated with
Adrian Lynne's use of her psychological disorder. In any event, it is the
recognition of the experiences represented in the film as analogous to one's
own that precipitates engagement with the film.[13]

The public's experience of the cultural artifacts we study, understandably, hinges on whether they recognize the experiences represented in the
texts at issue. This condition, the perception of an analogy to one's own
experience, applies to any reader, however professional. Yet disciplinarity
rules out such analogical or configural understanding as too subjective, personal, and self-interested. In effect, disciplinarity requires that we remain
experts and refine our terminologies in ways that so objectify the materials
we study as to render them unrecognizable to the general public. Our academic descriptions of our readings alienate the public, in my view, because
they picture experiences in terms quite remote from ordinary descriptions.
Our analyses have the look and feel of pictures in an encyclopedia—illustrations of concepts. At the root of our public-relations problem is a specialized vocabulary designed to give us credibility as specialists and maintain our status in the university system. Once again, as throughout this
chapter, the ideal of disciplinarity is the culprit.

I find more to criticize about the ideals of disciplinarity than does Graff.
In this and the previous chapter, I have offered reasons why disciplinarity
is a dubious rationale for literary study. What alternatives do we have? As
I suggest in chapter 14, the negotiation of a culture war would be nearly
impossible outside a context in which the disagreeing parties concur that
the same problem exists in their varying cultural experiences of it. The first
step toward negotiation is the recognition that they are identifying the
same problem. In arguments between couples, for instance, negotiation is
usually stymied when the partners cannot concur that the same problem
exists. In such instances, each person frames the experience differently and
neither can recognize the other's description of events, usually assigning a
villainous role to the partner in one's life history. Unless persons concur
that they are speaking about the same cultural experience and agree on a
mutually recognizable configuration of the problem, their differences will
persist. As Graff notes, disagreements presuppose agreement as their background.

"It is self-defeating," Graff writes, "to think of disagreement as an im-
passe" (*Culture Wars* 43). I agree but add that the protocol he recommends
by implication—*find what you agree with in the positions with which you
disagree*—goes against the grain of disciplinary training, in which arguments are solved by refutation, the hallmark of disciplinarity.[14] The differing ways in which the specific experiences are framed cannot be negoti-

ated as long as the participants try to refute all other parties or insist that their method falsifies all others. In the last analysis, unless a mutual recognition of the cultural experience at stake occurs, the persons involved will never get beyond the ships-passing-in-the-night stage of the disagreement.

Persons from differing intellectual traditions frame similar experiences in diverse ways. If persons involved in the interpretation of an experience enter a discussion with the attitude that they have a better conceptual framework than anyone else in the discussion, they will be predisposed to refute everyone else in the group. Such contentiousness is likely to sharpen everyone's conceptual tools but not likely to facilitate the negotiation. It makes more sense to enter discussions expecting to shed differences in conceptual frameworks in order to advance the discussion. Hence allegiance to the exact definitions of theoretical concepts seems ill-advised. But once again, we run head-on into a disciplinary attitude that suggests that the conceptual map or paradigm of the field being studied is to be maintained unless it can be falsified. In sum, disciplinarity forces us to defend our conceptual terrain and to dismiss analogical impulses capable of mediating our differences.

This study concerns the ways in which a late-nineteenth-century preoccupation with discipline in the modern sense remains built into the institution of criticism as the habitual way of doing things. I critique the link between modern disciplinarity and the institution of criticism because I believe it warps our endeavors. I favor abandoning the notion of disciplinarity in the way we speak about ourselves. It invokes comparisons with the sciences. We should stop gauging our own efforts by comparison with the successes of the sciences, as has been our history. Instead, we should forge a new rhetoric to articulate our endeavors, one that paints a more balanced picture of understanding literature. Let's not be afraid to speak of analogy and graphic criticism and discuss what we are doing as "configural" (see chapter 6).

Though critics may disassociate themselves from the sciences, they are nonetheless contaminated by the residue of scientific methods remaining in their practices as a result of the way literary study has been institutionalized. I contend that the study of cultures is institutionally misbegotten and still suffers from an inbred residue of scientism. This is an ecological study of literary criticism. It notes how the disciplinary atmosphere we breathe has adversely affected our development and works toward a more balanced environment.

Shifting Status

CHAPTER 5

Forgetting is easy enough, but not remembering is even easier. Events of your own life are easily forgotten, but events before your time are hard to remember. You can recall what you have forgotten after some effort, but it is often impossible to bring back to mind what you've tried to teach yourself to remember, and you resort to looking it up. Wars, for example. I have very vague memories of World War II, vague ones of the Korean War, and vivid ones of the Vietnam War, all of which took place during my lifetime. I tend to omit World War I from the list, and I have no clear sense of when the Spanish-American War took place or how long it lasted, since these wars occurred before I was born. For better or worse, critics remember the state of literary studies similarly in terms of their personal histories.

Critics who entered literary study in the late fifties and early sixties saw its practitioners shift their intentions from efforts to become a discipline in the compact, or strong, sense Toulmin delineates to a benign neglect of the issue. By the seventies critics were content to think of their work as a discipline in the loose, or weak, sense because the debates between the scholars and the critics no longer had much resonance. Thus critics who entered the profession in the early seventies and later, when courses in Anglo-Saxon, history of the language, and textual scholarship were no longer required, did not experience the conflict between scholars and critics that began early in the century and persisted until the mid-sixties.[1] Instead, they are more likely to have experienced the conflict between traditional and deconstructive critics.[2]

However, when our memories are refreshed by reading histories of our profession such as Gerald Graff's *Professing Literature,* the debates between the scholars and critics as well as the earlier ones between the generalists and the investigators (also known as researchers or scholars) can be seen, in surprising ways, to inform the debates between contemporary critics who regard themselves as traditional and poststructuralist critics who regard themselves as avant-garde. From an institutional perspective, all of these debates can be construed as the same one, differing mostly in its historical contexts. The generalists complained that the research scholars were too scientific. Then the critics, hoping to supplant the scholars, not only complained that the generalists were vague but also that the scholars embraced the wrong sort of science. Still later, poststructuralist critics complained that both the New Critical formalists and the exacting structuralist critics were too centered, structured, and systematic (i.e., too scientific). In all of these debates, which span the history of the institutionalization of literary studies, we can discern a persistent conflict within the halls of Arts and Science colleges. As the arts were institutionalized in universities predisposed to benefit scientific study, critics wavered between construing their practices as scientific and objective and construing them as artistic and personal. The persistent issue has been, Should criticism be a rigorous and objective discipline? During the course of these critical debates, the status of critical arguments has shifted.[3]

Graff's career, which bridges both the period of the scholars versus critics debates and the period of the traditional versus poststructuralist criticism debates, is an instance of the shift in the status of argumentation. His earliest book, *Poetic Statement and Critical Dogma,* addresses the question, If literature does not contain true statements about the world, how can critics argue that it interprets our experiences of that world? By arguing that poetry makes true statements about the world, he seems to elevate argument to the status of art. In *Literature against Itself,* Graff discredits "the myth of the postmodern breakthrough" (31). In its first chapter he writes, "This is a book about our ways of talking about literature—how they got started, why they have taken the turn they have taken recently, where they go wrong, and what we can do about setting them right. More broadly it is about certain contradictions in the languages of the humanities—the terms (or 'paradigms') in which we do our thinking in and about humanistic activities." The next sentence adds, "It is also a book about the social context of literature and criticism—how both literature and our ways of talking about it have been conditioned by social pressures and how they have in turn influenced social life" (1).

This social subtext of *Literature against Itself* was mostly neglected by reviewers and readers, who focused largely on Graff's arguments against poststructuralist critics such as de Man and Derrida. Graff's next book— *Criticism in the University,* which he coedited with Reginald Gibbons—focuses entirely on the social and historical context of criticism and is a prelude to *Professing Literature,* in which the social (in the sense of institutional) aspects of criticism are given far more prominence than in any comparable history of criticism. Graff's subsequent book, *Beyond the Culture Wars,* is entirely invested in the social context of the study of literature. What I focus on in Graff's career is the movement away from treating criticism as a discourse that can be corrected by attention to its discursive contradictions and toward treating criticism as a mode of social negotiation. *Beyond the Culture Wars* directly reflects this shift. Though Graff is often attacked for reintroducing disciplinarity in the strong sense back into literary studies, in his more recent work his assumption that conflict and controversy are not likely to be resolved by refutation does not support this view.

A case can be made that Graff's career is exemplary of the condition of criticism for critics of my generation (having entered the profession in the late sixties), who were trained in the modern institution of criticism but have practiced largely in a postmodern institution.[4] By the fifties, New Criticism had established itself as the mode of modern criticism. Northrop Frye first broke the hold of New Criticism on English departments, and E. D. Hirsch made the first major counterattack against it. The symposium on "the languages of criticism" at Johns Hopkins University in 1966, which introduced poststructuralism to critics working in this country, was for many the beginning of the end of modern criticism. However, our academic institutions have not adjusted to the shift. They keep trying to neutralize it and assimilate it. Thus in many places we have modern institutions hosting postmodern critics.

In this chapter I first describe literary arguments that conform to Toulmin's view of the disciplinary uses of arguments. Then I look at these arguments from a postmodern perspective, noting how what seemed just a few years ago the obvious and natural way of doing criticism no longer seems either obvious or natural. However, in the spirit of Wittgenstein's *Philosophical Investigations,* I would emphasize that it is "of the essence of our investigation that we do not seek to learn anything *new* by it" (#89). Rather, in these observations I hope merely to defamiliarize the mode of literary argumentation we readily take for granted.

Arguments as Social Practices

One way of describing the shifting status of argument during the last thirty years is mentioned in Charles Arthur Willard's *Argumentation and the Social Grounds of Knowledge,* namely, as a shift from the tendency to treat arguments "as an applied logic" (16) to treating them as one of our most important "communication practices" (15). In describing this shift, Willard suggests that instead of judging "how far arguments fall short of ideals" that we have "let logicians hand us" as "legitimating concepts" that "defined our work" (16), we are now inclined to view our rationality in terms of communication practices. He notes how these practices are aspects of social activities that have been variously described as "'communities of discourse' (McKerrow), 'rhetorical communities' (Farrell), 'domains of objectivity' (Foucault), 'social relationships' (G. J. McCall et al.), 'speech communities' (Hymes), 'disciplines or rational enterprises' (Toulmin), 'social frameworks' (Goffman), and—to use traditional sociological labels— 'organizations,' 'reference groups,' 'collective mentalities,' and 'shared frameworks of assumptions' (Filmer et al.; Turner)" (10).

Willard goes on to say that "the things which pass muster as knowledge do so because of argument practices; every field's design characteristics for what shall count as knowledge stem from its explicit or implicit theory of argumentation" (19). Borrowing from Toulmin's notion of an argument field, he maintains that we can "think of a field as a constellation of practices organized around one of a few dominant assumptions" (10).

Thinking of a field as a constellation of practices might be confusing when applied to literature (where fields are thought of as historical constructs), for it suggests that in literary study every field is doubly constituted—as a historical entity and as a methodological one. Yet this double sense of a field seems appropriate. Literary critics usually focus their work on historical periods, but the approaches they bring to their historical fields constitute specific texts within them as argument fields. Thus we not only have to distinguish between historical fields but also between the ways they are constituted by the various schools of thought. Since every historical field is also demarcated by argument fields, the proliferation of methods has provoked a disciplinary nightmare.[5]

This analysis would seem to imply that communication among literary critics working in different fields is quite difficult. That would be true only if we maintained a logical view of argumentation. Willard, setting aside this traditional way of viewing arguments, sees them as social communication practices that allow us to move among various fields. This is possible because fields, in his view, are more accurately described as "traditions of activity" than as logical constructs (11).[6] This is quite resonant with the shift in Graff's work to which I have called attention. It is a shift from thinking of critical discourse as stand-alone arguments (which Willard dubs "the solitary thinker view" [5]) to thinking of it as a dialogue or debate. "Argument studies," Willard writes, "thus may be plausibly said to be fruitful ways of understanding the similarities and differences across the fields" (13). As Willard's justification of his analysis presupposes, we often think of arguments as independent of their social contexts. In what follows I try to give a balanced picture of literary arguments, describing them both as constitutive of fields of inquiry and as forms of communication. I begin with the most salient feature of any argument, evidence.

The Role of Argument in Literary Study

Why do critics quote the texts they interpret? And why is it that critics not only quote the texts they interpret but also summarize them and refer to them by invoking easily recognized textual landmarks? Textual references, summaries, and quotations all function in critical discourse as evidence. Their absence would be more notable than their presence. No matter to which school of thought critics subscribe, nearly all of them (including deconstructive critics) offer textual support for their interpretive claims. This humdrum feature of criticism suggests that critics use the format of an argument when they publish their interpretations. In short, arguments seem to be fundamental to critical work. For solitary thinkers to make stand-alone arguments seems to be the natural and obvious way of doing criticism.

Let's start with what is apparently common sense for modern critics. *Criticism is what critics do,* assuming that critics are those persons who have been designated critics by their appearance in bibliographies of criticism.[7] How can we describe their activities? What work do critics do? Nearly all critics

1. *read* some text
2. *discuss formally and in public* the texts they read
3. *make sense* of texts regarded by other readers as difficult to understand
4. *make claims* about how other readers should make sense of texts
5. *make comparisons* among texts, especially those similar to the ones they are reading
6. *generalize* about texts, periods, and so on
7. *give evidence for* their readings
8. *try to justify* their readings
9. *seek agreement* with other critics about how texts should or should not be read

This seems a sensible, if rather general, description of what critics do. The various activities named on the list, however, are interrelated. It is difficult to describe their interrelations, because the activities often appear to be random if not chaotic. Nonetheless, some activities subsume others. Hence it is possible to delineate them in a more or less orderly pattern commonly called "argumentation." It hardly seems to say anything new to remark that critics argue in public about how to read literary texts with other readers of those texts. This description of critical activity corresponds rather well to Toulmin's widely accepted delineation of the practice of argumentation.[8]

By this account, it seems obvious (even "natural") that arguments are indispensable elements of modern literary study, a conclusion anyone might reach by merely watching what critics do.[9] Nor is this an accident of history. Until quite recently, the critics who have worked in the modern American university, which took its shape shortly after the turn of the century, were trained in a common form of argumentation. It is structured by an informal logic first articulated by Aristotle, in which claims are supported by evidence and therefore can be verified. It is requisite in this tradition for critics to discriminate between correct and incorrect readings. For example, in Holman's *Handbook to Literature*, the most widely used of its kind, we read of argumentation that "its purpose is to convince a reader or hearer by establishing the truth or falsity of a proposition" (42).

Traditional argumentation has long-standing protocols. Most literary students trained in it have been formed by its scholasticism. Dissertations, for example, follow a pattern reminiscent of the treatises of medieval theologians. "Most rhetoricians recognized five parts for the usual argumentative discourse: *exordium, narratio, confirmatio* or *probatio, refutatio,* and *peroratio*" (Corbett 303). Before a traditional critic proves his or her own case (*confirmatio*), he or she gives the history of preceding arguments (*narratio*) and afterward refutes the likely objections (*refutatio*). Traditional papers, if only in the first footnote, still begin with reviews of the scholarship, much of which is falsified in order to set the stage for the author's view. Footnotes, many of which, as Stephen Nimis points out, have no logical relationship to the argument they footnote,[10] are usually formulaic gestures toward verification (*confirmatio*) or refutation (*refutatio*).

Literary study, many would say, has no place in the university system unless it can produce knowledge. When literary claims are not supported by evidence, they are difficult to defend as knowledge in any strictly disciplinary sense.[11] Thus the preeminent rationale for literary study is its disciplinarity. And disciplinarity, at least in the sense of a study capable of producing reliable knowledge, depends for its efficacy on a credible mode of argumentation. As I mentioned above, in this study I take as my point of departure Toulmin's view of argument as the foundation of any discipline because it is the most commonly cited theory of argumentation in literary study.

In Toulmin's theory of argumentation as set forth in *The Uses of Argument*, every sound argument has the following structure: Given x, if y, then z. This is a less formal rendering of the classic structure of the syllogism: Given that $x = y$, if $y = z$, then $x = z$. In Toulmin's account, given a particular set of facts, presuming an acceptable warrant, a specific inference or conclusion can then be drawn legitimately. His scheme is familiar to students as a diagram:

$$\text{Given set of facts } x \longrightarrow \text{we must infer} \longrightarrow \text{conclusion } z$$
$$\text{If we assume}$$
$$\text{Warrant } y$$

A literary argument, in Toulmin's terms, can be described as one in which a text like James Joyce's "Araby" together with its intertexts and contexts are the data from which conclusions are derived by inferences warranted by various generalizations about texts and their relations. To concretize this rather abstract formulation, let's look at a short argument from "Araby" criticism—John Freimarck's "'Araby': A Quest for Meaning."[12]

> The story of a young boy journeying to Araby in hope of winning the favor of an idealized girl immediately raises echoes of the Grail Quest story-pattern! Indeed, several actions and images in "Araby" common to basic versions of the Quest suggest this theme stimulated Joyce's imagination in ordering his modern material, and of course the reader who recognizes them is tempted to look for clues. Yet even in the case of Joyce such a reader can rest assured that it is not as important to scrutinize what goes into a story as to assess what comes out.
>
> In "Araby" a boy ignores the reality of his bleak, winter surroundings and allows the word "Araby" to suggest the exciting summer world of romance. But, if it is a land of spices he dreams of, classical writers note that the richest part of Araby was infested with snakes. The very title of the story is the first of several images promising the apocalyptic world of romance, but containing the demonic.
>
> In a world hostile to romance, Mangan's sister is the object of the boy's "confused adoration." By the time his lady speaks, his naive crush has led to the heroic bearing of her image like a chalice through market streets, and worship in a chapel-like room where the boy presses his hands together and murmurs "O love! O love!" Hearing she longs to go to Araby, but cannot, he promises to return with a gift if he should make the trip. Imprisoned on the other side of the railing before the house, turning the silver bracelet "round and round her wrist," the girl is the supplicant woman. The quest and marriage theme is strengthened when "she held one of the [railing] spikes, bowing her head towards me." In some versions of the Quest, the knight may marry or sleep with the maiden who carries the grail or bleeding lance. In any case, no favor is lightly given; the journey preempts his thoughts and the everyday world is denied: "I had hardly any patience with the serious work of life."
>
> The boy's confusion is something he causes himself. The girl's brown dress suggests she may not be the true lady, and the boy's love is itself suspect. The image he conjures up includes the border of her slip; and lying on the floor, prostrating himself before her, peeking under the drawn shade, the boy is a voyeur. He is already doomed to failure because he does not have the chaste mind and body essential to the quest. This is emphasized shortly before he leaves for the bazaar. After going

upstairs (a position of relative height) he receives the traditional vision, seeing "nothing but the brown figure cast by my imagination," a figure complete with the petticoat showing. Not only is the vision imagined, rather than beheld, but it is not even pure.

Finally the boy begins his journey, leaving the house to the strains of "The Arab's Farewell to His Steed." The deserted train takes the place of a horse, passing through the waste land of "ruinous houses" and crossing the body of water, a river, on its way to Araby.

Araby, the building with the "magical name," is likened to a church; this, and the attendant at the door link it to the magic castle which the knight approaches in the evening. Inside, the young boy examines vases and flowered tea-sets, grail-like containers. Approaching the two men and the woman, he is deterred by their attitude and the trivia of their conversation. In the grail castle the knight's success depends on his asking the right question concerning the grail which is carried past him. The woman questions the boy: "I looked humbly at the great jars [grails] that stood like eastern guards [the cherub at the East wall of Eden?] at either side of the dark entrance to the stall and murmured: 'No thank you.'" The wrong answer has been given and the boy asks no questions. The lights go out. When the knight does not ask the correct question in the castle it disappears and he wakes up at the edge of a cliff by the ocean, or in a manure wagon being driven through a town where people insult him because of his failure to heal the land. Here the boy realizes his journey is over and feels humiliated. His failure brings an increase in knowledge, which, continuing the story's ironic counterpoint to Romance, does not bring hope or felicity.

To press these parallels further is possible, but to do so would be to pass the point of diminishing critical returns. The problem is one of perspective which, in *Dubliners,* involves always keeping in mind the fact that the main impact of the story is on the naturalistic level, the faithfulness to the detail of Irish family life. It may be more to this level that Joyce's notion of paralysis really refers than to any other. The continual wonder is how Joyce can introduce so intricate and faithful a Quest story-pattern and yet subdue it to the naturalistic one we read at face value. The myth element enriches the story, but we are never really on the quest for the grail—we are in Dublin all the time with the psychologically accurate story of the growth of a romantic boy awakening to his sexuality, idealizing Mangan's sister and encountering frustration in the process. (366–68)

This essay develops an argument that can be analyzed in Toulmin's terms. The framing argument (within which microarguments are subsumed) is discernible. Having quoted, summarized, and referred to various passages in "Araby" as his evidence, Freimarck then reads the story in the light of the Grail-quest pattern of romance. He "makes sense" of passages that otherwise might seem obtuse by pointing out that Joyce's story is, in part, patterned after the Grail romances.

Given facts like sentences containing the expressions "chalice" and "journey," and that "The wrong answer has been given and the boy asks no questions," etc.;

If we assume that the genre of the Grail-quest romances provides generic expectations of ironic failure leading to self-understanding;

Then we must infer that the boy's "failure brings an increase in knowledge," even though the text does not make it explicit.

Other readers, who may have wondered how specific details of the text fit together, now have an answer. Difficulties with Joyce's text are resolved by the warranting assumption that the story it narrates is an analogue to other stories to which Joyce from time to time alludes in order to enrich the associations his text affords the reader.

Freimarck's essay is a typical literary argument, if a rather conventional one. Questions readers have about difficulties in texts are answered by claims that the text should be read with a particular interpretive strategy in mind; the answers are justified or warranted by invoking critical concepts, for example, "theme," "quest," "romance," and so on, which are rule-like generalizations about texts.

At the microstructural level, literary arguments are a complex of arguments chained to each other in varying ways. However, we ordinarily summarize arguments by describing their macrostructure, a generalizable framing argument that we remember, outline, or summarize as I did above. Freimarck's mode of argumentation corresponds roughly to the classical rhetorical notions of arrangement (*exordium, narratio, confirmatio, refutatio,* and *peroratio*). It attests to long-standing canons of argumentation in literary study.

Critical Schools and Literary Warrants

In literary arguments, warrants play a powerful role. They assemble aspects of the text being read as evidence. For example, it seems likely that no reader would have interpreted the jars in "Araby" as the Grail had they not been apprised of the stratagem of reading "Araby" as an analogue to Grail-quest stories, the generic conception of texts that warrants Freimarck's argument. Similarly, when the boy remains silent, many other explanations can be given for his silence than that he failed to ask the key question, just as his literary precursor, Perceval, failed to ask the Grail question. That the boy does not return to the Grail castle and ask the question on a second visit does not appear to disturb Freimarck's reading. Nonetheless, other readers—less interested in the irony to which Freimarck points—might find this assumption too questionable. Some critics disdain generic warrants as fervently as others disdain psychoanalytic ones.

Many critical battles, indeed, are waged over the warranting assumptions of rival critics with competing interpretations of texts. In examining such critical wars, it seems obvious that critics schooled in different assumptions about literary texts are disposed to quarrel with each other.[13] The most recent battles have as their combatants critics like Freimarck, who search for centripetal patterns in texts, struggling against followers of Derrida and de Man, who perceive centrifugal patterns. When the name-calling begins, the names of contending schools are tossed about to identify interpretive strategies.

The fate of literary criticism as a discipline, I am inclined to believe, depends on the outcome of the current battle between postmodern forces and traditional ones. If, as many postmodern critics assert, critical claims cannot be definitively adjudicated because texts are not repositories of facts but intersections of meaning that lack centeredness and therefore cannot be regarded as determinate, then to maintain that literary criticism is a discipline in any compact sense becomes problematic. If disciplinarity is the fundamental rationale of literary study, what happens if literary disputes prove irresolvable? The most puzzling thing to me is that there are no apparent consequences. Barbara Herrnstein Smith put the matter quite forcefully in an interview. When asked about her view of literary study as a discipline, she said, "What I think of, when I think of a discipline, are the operations of an institution," glossing this remark by adding, "I think of procedures of certification, procedures of recruitment, even the laws under which a college is established" ("A Conversation" 155). To me this suggests Foucault's sense of discipline rather than Toulmin's. In Smith's view, critical schools are cognitive styles. Literary warrants are preferences readers have in their styles of reading. Critical schools are schools of taste and preference. Her reaction is characteristic of many contemporary critics, especially those who believe we live in a postmodern era.

What Is Obvious Is Rarely Transparent

Sometimes experiences seem obvious because we are accustomed to speaking about them from a particular point of view and in a particular idiom. In this section I call into question the obviousness of what I said in the section above entitled "The Role of Argument in Literary Study." Because our history as critics makes certain aspects of our work seem obvious, some of the commonplaces on which traditional accounts of our activities rely need to be seen as less than transparent.

It appears obvious that "Araby" critics have *read* Joyce's story. But, of course, the interrelated acts of attention, selection, and comparison that critics perform while reading are not transparent. So much has been said in the last decade about the activity of reading that the activities presupposed by the term are no longer available to common sense. During the seventies, the work of Stanley Fish, Wolfgang Iser, David Bleich, Norman Holland, and many others, not to mention a renaissance of interest in thinkers like Louise Rosenblatt, revealed a myriad of assumptions about what happens while one reads. In the nineties it is no longer obvious what a critic might mean by the term "reading." Does he or she refer to a transaction, a transmission, or an interaction? Is he or she assuming an informed, super, competent, communal reader, or subject, position? Moreover, what happens in private is not always made public. Since a critic in his or her public persona professes a specialized discipline, it does not seem far-fetched to guess that personal experiences get left out of the public discussion. But should they? Are feminist critics who discuss their personal experiences of literature mistaken in doing so? In sum, what is meant by the term "reading" now depends on what school of thought is invoked.

Not only is the most elemental act of criticism no longer taken for granted, but, as I will suggest in the next several chapters, the possibility of "grounding" the discipline of criticism in the rigors of argumentation is fiercely contested. Nowadays, appeals to logic, evidence, facts, data, reason, and other aspects of traditional argumentation are often greeted with disdain. Today many critics admit that their claims are not always conclusions drawn from rule-governed inferences entailing truth or falsity (which is their logical function in most theories of argument) but often intuitive judgments or, as I refer to them in the next chapter, configurations. Moreover, critical assertions cannot typically be regarded as statements of fact, because they are not about objects but about states of affairs.[14] It thus seems appropriate to describe critical assertions as "judgments" not necessarily warranted by evidence—inferences from the "facts" of the text. Traditionally, *critics quote, summarize, or refer to the texts they read* to support their assertions. However, today this is merely evidence that critics have read a text in a particular way.

It is generally believed that literary criticism has a social function that goes beyond the solitary, private activity of reading. Critics used to assume that *offering evidence for critical claims implies an aim of seeking agreement.* Critics, it was readily assumed, sought to get other critics to believe what they believe. This was thought to be the social function of criticism. And indeed, most critics still believe that criticism is a form of persuasion. But nowadays critics ask themselves what they are hoping to persuade other readers of. Many reject the notion, once current, that critics persuade the public of the "nature" (the universal truths) of their culture. Thus the purpose of literary study was thought to be the accumulation of knowledge about "our" culture so that it could be handed down to those who wish to become members. Today critics wonder whether the persons in charge of this enterprise know what *the* culture is. Do they know its nature, its essence? Do they know its eternal verities, its universal truths? What counts as critical knowledge?

Although for years I was reluctant to accept the view that literary studies, as a discipline, was founded on acquired tastes rather than on reasoning, I now find this view increasingly difficult to contest. Moreover, I find it perplexing to assess the role of arguments in literary studies.[15] Critics who do not much believe in their arguments *as arguments* continue to argue. The question is, why? This brings us to the subject of the next chapter, which discusses the differing rationales for arguments.

Explaining, Justifying, Configuring

CHAPTER 6

David Lodge's *Nice Work* takes as its dramatic focus the relevance to the general public of work in English departments. Its plot is a variation of the changing-places story. When the British government declares 1986 "Industry Year," the ambitious vice-chancellor of Rummidge University initiates an "Industry Year Shadow Scheme" in which faculty shadow their counterparts in the business world. Philip Sallow, the chair of the English department, designates Robyn Penrose, an untenurable junior faculty member, the URFAIYS (University of Rummidge Faculty of Arts Industry Year Shadow) of Vic Wilcox, the managing director of an engineering firm that manufactures castings for the automobile industry. Robyn has published a dissertation entitled *The Industrious Muse: Narrativity and Contradiction in the Industrial Novel.* She is an ardent postmodern feminist who has never been inside a factory. Her counterpart is a conservative businessman who is trying to survive in hard times under the duress of an imminent hostile takeover of his factory as well as the growing likelihood of his dismissal by the conglomerate taking over.

As the novel progresses, Robyn and Vic argue about the racist treatment of workers, the appalling working conditions in the factory, the monotonous factory routines, the pornographic materials pasted on the factory walls, a sexist calendar promotion. In each argument Robyn's premises are drawn from her academic study and Vic's are drawn from years of hands-on experience. Both are influenced by each other's arguments. As a consequence of their exchanges, Vic decides to make several changes in the factory routine. Their growing respect for each other (fostered of course by the heightening sexual attraction between them) is dramatized by Robyn's waning commitment to her academic colleague and lover, Charles.

70

Robyn's steadily growing sympathy for Vic's point of view peaks in a delightful scene wherein Charles joins her for a working weekend at her flat. As the scene opens, he is reading a book on deconstruction. When Robyn asks him if it is any good, Charles notes that it has an especially fine explanation of Lacan's remark, "I think where I am not, therefore I am where I think not. . . . I am not, wherever I am the plaything of my thought; I think of what I am whenever I don't think I am thinking" (*Nice Work*, 122). He and Robyn then get into an argument about Lacan's use of the distinction between metonymy and metaphor. In the course of their argument, Robyn observes that Vic has a metonymic rather than a metaphorical vision. Her point is that his factory can be better understood if it is represented by metaphors—"The place is like hell"—than by metonymies—"dirt, noise, heat and so on" (123). This remark reflects her recent experiences of factory life. When Robyn first drove to Pringles, "somewhere on the other side of the city: the dark side of Rummidge" (63), she felt the district was "so like the satanic mills of the early Industrial Revolution" (81). When finally inside the factory, "To Robyn's eye it resembled nothing so much as a medieval painting of hell" (86). Charles does not seem to comprehend her point, so Robyn translates her metaphor into a concept: "I just told you: hell. Alienation, if you want to put it in Marxist terms" (123). Their abstract argument about ideas is a counterpoint to the arguments Robyn earlier had with Vic. These nonacademic exchanges, by contrast, are about lives rather than texts, and they have consequences in the real world rather than on academic discourse about it.

In Lodge's account, Charles is characterized as a typical academic, who understands metonymic premises best, by contrast to Robyn, who frequently understands matters through metaphoric premises. Literary and artistic configurations inform Robyn's understanding of the industrial revolution. The novels she had studied configure for her the events she witnesses. It is a bit ironic, therefore, that Vic—the hard-nosed industrialist—is eventually persuaded by Robyn, whereas Charles—her academic colleague—dismisses her argument. For Charles, abstract concepts like "alienation" justify inferences from other, equally abstract concepts like "industrialization." By contrast, Robyn uses the configurations borrowed from fictions about industrialization to understand her own experience of industry. On the one hand we have an argument warranted by the concept of alienation, and on the other by medieval depictions of hell. Robyn trusts the latter as much as the former. Charles is most at home with premises derived from theoretical frameworks like Lacan's or Derrida's. He is uncomfortable with Robyn's metaphoric delineation of her experience. Lodge locates Robyn on the side of the metaphoric and both men on the side of the metonymic, though Vic is more pliant than Charles. This is hardly an accidental alignment. Lodge has a stake in the outcome of their arguments, having structured his theoretical work around an attempt to apply and extend what Roman Jakobson says about metaphor and metonymy to the analysis and interpretation of literary texts.[1]

As his fiction suggests, Lodge's theorizing can be further extended to the analysis of argumentation. On the one hand, literary critics typically employ informal logic based on inferential warrants in their arguments. Inferential logic (if *p*, then *q*) can be characterized as metonymic because it is linear or syntagmatic. On the other hand, literary critics not only violate the principles of informal logic in their arguments, they also invoke experience in highly *ana*logical ways as a means of persuasion, much as Robyn does. (I once heard Hugh Kenner give a talk at a Joyce conference in which his premise was that the Circe chapter of *Ulysses* had to be understood *as if it were* a tape recording.) Though from a terminological perspective I prefer "justification" to "metonymy" and "configuration" to "metaphor," Lodge's view that contrasting cognitive orientations permeate literary studies seems to me accurate. It also seems reasonable to employ more than one mode of argumentation.

The efficacy of arguments depends on their contexts. When Robyn translates one type of argument into the other by changing their warrants (replacing hell with alienation), she recognizes that the expectations of her different audiences require different modes of argumentation, different formulations to establish the same claim. Addressing Charles, the terms of her argument are quite abstract. Addressing Vic, they are quite concrete. From this motif, we might infer that Lodge implies that we should be concrete rather than abstract when addressing the general public. Robyn got Vic to see the factories through her eyes rather than his own; she didn't convert him to postmodern theory. This seems a sensible pedagogy.

Are Literary Arguments Explanations, Justifications, or Configurations?

Since disciplinary arguments tend to organize themselves around abstract concepts, critics treat the experiences configured in literary texts *as concepts.* Abstracted from the depiction of experience, conceptions of human behavior are sometimes presented as generalizations about universal human experience. This was rather common in the formative decades of modern criticism. In *Contemporary American Criticism* (1926), James Cloyd Bowman identifies this practice as the underlying method of literary criticism as such when he remarks that it "may not inexactly be described as the statement of the concrete in terms of the abstract. It is its function to discern and characterize the abstract qualities informing the concrete expression of the artist" (83–84). Bowman goes on to say that although art is the expression of personality, the critic "disengages" from those expressions the "true objects of his contemplation," namely, "the multifarious elements of truth, beauty, goodness, and their approximates and antipodes" (84).

The rationale for this view of the function of criticism was known as humanism, the idea that literature made its audiences more humane because it promulgated truths about the human condition. Laurence Veysey writes that "the hope of illustrating the truths of liberal culture" led to the invention of "the survey course for undergraduates in 'Western civilization'" (207), whose counterparts are survey courses in literature. In *Some Principles of Literary Criticism* (1911), C. T. Winchester argues that "the distinguishing, defining mark of literature" was that it contained "truths of undoubted value" (41). This humanistic view of literary criticism thrived earlier in the century, but it was still in place when I was in graduate school in the early sixties. It was quite common to hold the view that scientists did not need to look back into their history, because older scientific laws were falsified, whereas humanists, by contrast, could still read the classics and derive "universal truths."

Ironically, by disengaging the universal from the particular and thus freeing texts from their historicity, modernist critics offer arguments that allegedly can stand alone—that is, can be written without seeking corroboration from persons who have experienced the feelings, emotions, thoughts, deeds, and words that embody the experience. Since the truths are universal, they apply to everyone, and thus arguments about them can address anyone without taking into account the particularities of one's condition. Differences in experience are irrelevant. Universal truths can be perceived universally.

Though few critics nowadays assume their conceptual arguments are likely to convey universal truths, most do not doubt that literary arguments can stand alone. It is another instance wherein a practice that has been institutionalized survives despite the circumstance that its justification is no longer believed. Unfortunately, such practices, even when emptied of their original motivation, still have institutional effects. The patterned isolation about which Graff speaks is mirrored in the stand-alone argument. Such alleged single-author discourse, as I mentioned in the previous chapter, is aptly characterized by Charles Arthur Willard in his *Argumentation and the Social Grounds of Knowledge* as "the solitary thinker view."

We might ask, at this point, why it is that, if critics are dependent on discourse communities, they nonetheless maintain the fiction of single authorship.[2] No matter how you view it, the concept of the single-author argument seems quite inappropriate to literary criticism; yet it survives. Recent discussions of discourse communities (Foucault on the "author"; commentaries on authorization; Erving Goffman on "footing") all have disabused us of the notion that a literary argument can stand alone. Why, then, does this notion persist? The likely answer is because it has a long history, going back to Aristotle.[3] We have inherited a tradition of argumentation that assumes a universal audience addressed by a solitary thinker. I believe this to be another instance in which a postmodern ethos is constrained by a modern practice that has come to be taken for granted. In this chapter I juxtapose two modern modes of argumentation with one that has been disparaged by the advocates of disciplinarity—argument by analogy. The latter type of argument is appropriate to many postmodern concerns, especially if the audience of literary critics includes nonspecialists—a point Lodge's fiction dramatizes.

I distinguish between three different kinds of arguments: explanations, justifications, and configurations. Because it explains why an event occurred and gives evidence demonstrating how the event occurred, I designate the first type of argument an explanation. Such arguments are characteristic of compact disciplines, which are capable of explanatory power or predictability. These arguments work from premises that are established scientific laws. They are scientific formulations and can be as expressed as formulae. In contrast, justifications or justificatory arguments do not offer explanations. They work from premises that have to be justified for their audiences and are not laws but more like ad hoc principles or rules adopted to accomplish a specific goal. These arguments are characteristic of the "softer" disciplines, such as social sciences. Stephen Toulmin offers meteorological arguments that forecast the weather and legal arguments as examples of justifications. By contrast to explanations and justifications, configurations are appeals to the experience of an audience. They operate by offering the audience virtual experiences with which they can identify. A familiar instance would be an argument that describes a horrible event and then (via the emotional identification its audience forms with the persons involved) appeals, "Would you want this to happen to you?" Political campaigns use configurations (Bush's famous TV ad that portrayed convicted prisoners leaving jail is a notorious instance). I propose that many literary arguments are best described as configurations rather than as justifications or explanations. This is not, however, the customary view.

Literary critics often speak of explaining the text. And, of course, the expressions "explication" and *"explication de texte"* are well-known terms for literary analysis. However, by the use of explanation in the narrow sense defined above (discourses that have predictive force and operate from established laws), literary arguments are not explanations.[4] I choose to avoid the term "explanation" when speaking of literary analysis because it seems counterintuitive to talk about explaining texts when they produce so many conflicting interpretations. It certainly seems more appropriate to speak of such theoretical warrants as justifications, for they do justify interpretations. Moreover, modern critics construe their endeavors in many ways that parallel the social sciences. Psychoanalytic, anthropological, sociological, and linguistic theories are often employed in literary arguments. Hence it seems appropriate to speak of their employment in literary arguments as justifications of interpretation, especially when they encode themselves through their implied audiences as this or that school of thought. At the same time, it is not inappropriate (though it is not commonplace) to speak of literary arguments as configurations, for they describe the experience of reading the text to their audiences in ways their authors believe are likely to be analogous to the reading experiences of those audiences. It can be said that literary arguments persuade their audiences by offering them virtual readings of the texts in question. When I read a stunning argument about a text I have previously read, I virtually reread that text through the description of it offered me, sometimes abandoning the implications of my actual reading. Literary arguments are, in these instances, addressed to persons who, because they have read or will read the texts in question, can appreciate the virtual experience induced by the argument. When criticism encodes a particular school of thought, it appeals to like-minded readers. The arguments are not valid for everyone, only for those who are capable of the virtual experience of the text in question because they have had analogous experiences.[5] In cases where the experience of the audience differs from the virtual experience proposed by the reading, persuasion is impossible. If I claim, for instance, that reading is like dreaming, I am not claiming that this experience is valid for everyone but appealing to persons who have had reading experiences analogous to mine. Though most literary arguments are constructed as arguments that are valid for everyone, many are persuasive only to the extent that their audiences have had reading experiences analogous to the ones the argument presupposes. That some readers did not have such experiences does not invalidate the agreement among other readers that they did. Interpretive strategies are not universal.

It might be helpful at this juncture to take up some examples. First, we can say that explanations are not good characterizations of literary arguments and therefore need not be exemplified. The mode of argumentation that Toulmin calls justificatory is exemplified by John Freimarck's "'Araby': A Quest for Meaning," from which I quoted in chapter 5. Indeed, the traditional mode of argumentation in literary studies is justificatory. This pertains to both modern and postmodern critics. Paul de Man's mode of argumentation does not differ from Walter Jackson Bate's or John Freimarck's. They use the same type of warrants—metonymic or justificatory—to establish that their claims can be inferred from the evidence they offer. Freimarck quotes "Araby" to establish his point. De Man and Bate argue from similar kinds of textual evidence. That their warrants must be justified is clear from the circumstances of the two arguments. Many readers of "Araby" would not accept Freimarck's premise that the story is an analogue to the Grail-quest romances, so he has to justify it (and he does so) before he can make his interpretive claim. The argument between de Man and Bate is not about the interpretation of a specific text but about the justification for their differing warranting assumptions. Bate rejects as nihilistic the theory of meaning to which de Man, following Derrida, subscribes. De Man defends it as a form of close reading in the tradition of Bate's Harvard colleague, Reuben Brower.

The mode of argumentation I call configuration is exemplified by Gerald Graff's account of his debate with the Nigerian novelist Chinua Achebe over Conrad's *Heart of Darkness* (discussed at length in "Taking Cover in Coverage" and *Culture Wars*). Achebe's reading provided Graff with a new configuration of the experiences in the text. In other words, Graff saw the text through Achebe's experience of it. As Graff indicates, he found it "harder to take for granted that Conrad's outlook and my own were the natural and normal one" (*Culture Wars* 29), and this provoked him to raise the question with his students, "Is literature a realm of universal experience that transcends politics?" (31). In my choice of Freimarck and Graff as examples, I wish to suggest two implications. First, as Lodge seemed to imply in *Nice Work,* configurations may be more appropriate than justifications in addressing the general public. Second, configurations may be more appropriate to cultural studies, where the differences among readers need to be respected while they are being negotiated. Cultural criticism frequently concerns argument situations in which the experiences of one of the participants are not readily available to the other.

The Audiences of Literary Arguments

In "Argumentation, Speaker, and Audience," chapter 2 of *The Realm of Rhetoric,* Chaim Perelman distinguishes among three discourses in a way that parallels the distinctions I offered above. His categories are discourses that (1) demonstrate, (2) convince, and (3) persuade. He asks, "What distinguishes argumentation from formally correct demonstration?" (9). He answers that demonstrations depend on axioms, which are not "topics of debate," whereas arguments need to "justify their choice of axioms" (9). The latter involve settling disputes through negotiations that seek consent (10–11). Such arguments do not rely solely on reasoning and often aim at inciting action and changing attitudes (12–13).

He then distinguishes between two types of audiences presupposed by arguments—"discourses which are addressed to a few and those which are valid for everyone" (17). He writes,

> The distinction between discourses which are addressed to a few and those which are valid for everyone allows us to better understand how

persuasive discourse differs from discourse that attempts to be convincing. Instead of thinking that persuasion is addressed to the imagination, sentiment, or a person's unthinking reactions, while the convincing discourse appeals to reason; instead of opposing one to the other as
subjective to objective, we can characterize them in a more technical
and exact way by saying that discourse addressed to a specific audience
aims to persuade, while discourse addressed to the universal audience
aims to convince. (17–18)

I focus on Perelman's tactic of looking at the implied audience of a discourse in order to underscore my earlier observation—that literary critics
have been informed by a tradition of argumentation that addresses a universal audience. In his view, a convincing argument assumes a universal
that does not depend for its efficacy on the experiences of its audience. No
matter what their experience is, the argument can stand alone and still
induce conviction. Modern literary arguments assume that no matter what
the reader's experience of the text may be, the argument can be convincing
because the text has a determinate meaning. Such arguments, as Perelman
notes, are often wedded to "appeals to reason" rather than "imagination,
sentiment, or a person's unthinking reactions," that is, to the opposition
between objective and subjective. The distinction Perelman introduces between a universal audience and an audience of only a few adds an important
consideration. In his account, some discourses are construed as "valid for
everyone"; others are not.

The terms of Perelman's distinctions reveal the assumptions about argumentation that we have inherited from the modern formation of our work
as a discipline. An explanation (Perelman's "demonstration") presupposes
an audience of specialists who have agreed on the premises involved in the
argument, but its conclusions are valid for everyone. This seems most characteristic of arguments in the hard sciences, which, in Toulmin's terms, are
compact disciplines. A justification presupposes an audience for whom the
warranting assumptions in the argument need to be justified. Such arguments are aimed at audiences for whom the relevant school of thought must
be identified and the assumptions defined or linked to acceptable authorities in order to be convincing, but their conclusions are still construed as
valid for everyone. They are characteristic of the social sciences. In psychological arguments it matters considerably whether the argument is warranted by the theories of Sigmund Freud or C. G. Jung or Jerome Bruner
or Aaron Beck. Modern critics regard literary arguments as justifications
in order to locate them within the parameters of disciplinary argumentation. From the point of view I assume, de Man, Bate, and Freimarck are
text-oriented critics who claim that meaning can be derived from the "authority of the text," and each addresses his claim to a purported "universal
reader." These critics presume that any reader, no matter what his or her

experience, can and should derive the same meanings from the text that they do.

De Man's implied readers, peer experts, are also Freimarck's and Bate's. By addressing an audience of peer experts (even if they belong to different schools of thought), these writers assume a "universal audience" in Perelman's sense of the term *to the extent that* they regard their inferences as valid for everyone (in de Man's case, this conception is a skeleton in his postmodern closet). (Note: Using Perelman's distinction between a universal audience and a particular audience introduces an ambiguity into the discussion when it turns to schools of thought. Though it is obvious that the members of a school of thought are surely particular audiences, arguments addressed to peer experts fall into the category of universal when a writer regards his or her school of thought as the only legitimate one. Implied audiences remain universal when the arguers assume that any right-thinking individual would be capable of understanding their discourse. Such arguments presuppose validity for everyone because they also presuppose that some individuals are wrong in their choice of warranting assumptions, in their choice of a critical school.)

One of the features of justificatory arguments is a technical vocabulary. What distinguishes Graff's recent position (e.g., his discussion of his debate with Achebe) from de Man's and Freimarck's is his conception of the audience of criticism as the students in his class, whom he sees as part of a wider audience—the general public. Though his audience is broader than peer experts, Graff does not universalize it. He takes note of their differences in race, gender, and creed where possible, as well as of their differences from academic professors. His implied readers are not other specialists, nor are his idioms arcane.

Although we know that de Man spoke to specific students in his classes, it appears likely (judging from the way he and his students describe his pedagogy) that his implied audience, even when speaking in a classroom, was *the* student, that is, a universal audience rather than the specific students who sat in front of him. Teachers commonly address an amorphous, general student body in their lectures. Moreover, their warrants usually qualify as axioms that need to be justified, so their arguments can be considered candidates for the designation "justification."

At this juncture, another question flares up: If a theoretical premise justifies an interpretive claim, what justifies the premise? In literary criticism, the theoretical premises that authorize an argument are most often borrowed from another discipline. Their authority is usually due to the stature a particular figure has in that other discipline. Since thinkers such as Freud and Lévi-Strauss have achieved authority in their own discipline before literary critics borrow upon their premises, their success invites the formation of a literary-critical movement devoted to their new way of thinking.

Members of that movement can then authorize themselves by invoking the theories already authorized elsewhere.[6] However, it must also be noted that the theory wars we witness from time to time in our journals testify to the resistance critics of one school have to the work of critics of other schools. The plurality of critical schools testifies to the difficulties any one has in calling any other's premises into question with sufficient force to silence any new approach. In the next chapter I take up these difficulties.

Robyn Penrose could not have explained factory life to Vic Wilcox. She was not an economist or sociologist. If she had tried to justify her views by quoting Derrida or Althusser, as her friend Charles does, it would also have been ineffective. She reaches Vic by configuring factory life for him in a way that is analogous to the way she experiences it. She does not pretend to refute Vic.

Pretending to Refute

On page two of the "Tempo" section of the July 18, 1994, *Chicago Tribune* there is an article entitled "The Twisting of Melville and Twain: Peter Shaw Rescues the Classics from Politically Correct Revisions." It is accompanied by a photograph of the chairman of the National Association of Scholars, whose caption reads, "Peter Shaw refutes the idea that there are secret meanings entirely at odds with every impression that you get from the story. 'Whether male or female,' Shaw noted, 'these critics meticulously labor to replace common-sense interpretations of the classics with "ironical" readings.'" The *Tribune* staff writer, John Blades, did not mention that Shaw was engaging in a long-standing debate among literary critics, one that goes back more than a few years. A decade ago, J. Hillis Miller and M. H. Abrams did a lecture tour of American universities in which they debated the merits of deconstruction. One of their stops was Miami University in Oxford, Ohio, where I taught at the time. Since we were having the same debate among ourselves, it was rather strange to witness its staging. It seemed rather obvious to the audience that neither speaker would ever convince his opponent but that as long as the tour lasted they would continue to debate in much the same terms. This poses an interesting question: What would it take for a traditional, modern critic such as M. H. Abrams or Walter Jackson Bate to refute the warrants of a deconstructive critic such as J. Hillis Miller or Paul de Man, or vice versa? In terms of the distinctions I made in the previous chapter, it seems that their debate could only be resolved by one critic convincing the other that his interpretative strategy was predicated on a fallacious premise. In other words, only by refuting Derrida and other theorists could Abrams or Bate convince Miller or de Man. Alternately, Miller and de Man would have to refute Abram's and Bate's warrants.

As the public debate between Abrams and Miller testified, though refuting is thought to be a widespread practice, it is not. Sometimes the discourses that get called refutations are little more than dismissals, ad hominem slanders, or exercises in liberal pluralism.[1] From a logical point of view, for instance, it is not possible to refute the idea that "there are secret meanings entirely at odds with every impression you get from the story."

Technically speaking, a refutation is a counterargument.[2] Thus we might say that refutations are dialogical in character. However, this would be somewhat misleading. In speech situations, especially those we think of as debates (Abrams/Miller), refutations are offered as rebuttals of the previous speaker's argument or they anticipate an argument and hence have a dialogical character. In written discourse, a refutation often lumps its opponents into a camp—"politically correct critics." Disputes frequently take place in the absence of the author being refuted. Neither of these last two instances deserves the designation "dialogical."[3] The term "refute" is often used as a synonym for "disagree with." This is certainly the way the *Tribune* staff writer is using the word. Similarly, it is more accurate to describe the alleged debate I witnessed between Abrams and Miller as a disagreement than as a debate. Though some of their dialogue had the form of a rebuttal, it did not function as one but seemed merely like a statement clarifying a point of disagreement. That the two critics appeared simultaneously and took turns speaking did not make the event a debate, even though it had the appearance of one. In this study I use the term "refutation" in its technical sense—as a rebuttal, that is, an argument intended to establish a claim that a previous argument is illogical. Disagreements are usually counterclaims, position statements, and clarifications that are little more than shouting matches: you may believe p, but I believe q. A refutation attempts to show the illogic of the chain of reasoning from which a given claim is adduced. This cannot be staged. In the case of Miller and Abrams, their apparent debate was, in its effects on the audience, a stage for their disagreement.

Since the Miller/Abrams disagreement had the appearance of a debate, it seems appropriate to consider in a bit more detail what it would take for a critic of one school to refute a critic from a different school. Taking the distinctions between explanations, justifications, and configurations I developed in the previous chapter, it follows that refutations cannot occur in the last type. As I argue below, configurations cannot be refuted. So for our purposes, let's use the term "falsifications" to name successful counterarguments in the domain of explanations and "refutations" to name successful counterarguments in the domain of justifications. Of justifications, Perelman notes that "a convincing discourse is one whose premises are universalizable, that is, acceptable in principle to all the members of the universal audience" (18). What would make a premise universalizable? It would have to be persistently reliable—a rule or axiom that produces approximately the same results over and over. In the matter of reading, it could be an interpretive strategy that reliably produced quite similar readings of a text in a broad spectrum of readers. Put concretely, it would have to be a critical reading of a text that, when made public as "research" into the text, was able to be repeated by the audience. One of the aspects of a universal argument is that anyone, no matter what his or her specific contexts or particular personal background, could give assent to it.

In the study of literature, such assent would be given by reading the text in nearly the same way as the author of the criticism; however, there is an unbridgeable distance between the *same* way and an *analogous* way. It is the distance between a justification of a reading and a configuration of it.[4] Readers of the confrontation between Bate and de Man, for example, would have to give assent to Bate's reading of a text where it conflicted with de Man's before they could produce evidence that Bate had refuted his rival. On the surface this seems quite plausible, but it is only plausible to a critic who believes that texts have stable meanings—the premise on which their justification of the interpretations at issue depends. Furthermore, what evidence could Bate bring forth that was *not* a description of the text in question? Yet what else could descriptions of a text be except descriptions of reading acts? In principle, then, reading acts would have to be replicable by any other witnesses to the Abrams and Miller debate in order to obtain the requisite universal assent. To put it mildly, fulfilling this requirement would seem to be fraught with difficulties when one reader assumes the meaning is stable while the other does not.

Despite such difficulties, many critics believe they can refute their rival critics for an important reason—the status of literary study as a discipline hinges on our ability to *establish* evidence for our claims. Unless critics can adjudicate between rival interpretations of the same texts by showing that the evidence for one is valid and that the evidence for the other is invalid, they cannot claim to produce reliable knowledge. I refer to the practice of invalidating as refuting. If you show why the evidence in an existing argument is invalid, you refute that argument. Refuting is a disciplinary practice and is, as such, typically modern.[5]

Critics who argue in order to convince their audiences by justifying their theories can be characterized as modern, and those who relinquish the aspiration to convince their audiences by refuting opposing theories can be characterized as postmodern.[6] Critics who call themselves postmodern but believe in convincing and refuting have, in my view, modern skeletons in the closets of their critical habitats.[7] Why, then, do postmodern critics (like de Man) spend so much time ostensibly refuting rival critics?

Can the Recognition of an Experience Be Refuted?

Critics speak about disproving, invalidating, discrediting, controverting, proving to the contrary, and refuting. Despite such practices, not a single handbook of literary terminology bothers to define refutation (or any of the other terms), much less give an account of the conditions of its possibility. This seems rather odd and provokes me to ask, What are the conditions of the possibility of refuting explanations, justifications, and configurations?

Given an explanation's principal feature—that its axioms or warrants are not debatable—we have to locate explanations within the realm of compact disciplines. These are fields of study whose descriptions or paradigms are widely accepted. In such studies, what Kuhn calls "normal science" reigns. This is the domain of falsification. Here the discovery of anomalies for which the reigning theory or paradigm cannot account could lead to its demise. Correlatively, any particular application of the agreed-on methodology can be refuted by demonstrating that it does not follow the paradigm or that its descriptions of the facts, grounds, or data are inaccurate.[8] As most critics seem to agree, this situation is not characteristic of literary studies.

In the second instance—regarding justificatory arguments intended to convince an audience—as I suggested above, within a given interpretive community the replicability of research results functions as the main test of the argument. Readers give assent to other critics in their interpretive community when reading the texts at issue *in the manner suggested by those critics* proves illuminating. When reading in that manner does not illuminate the text, critics offer counterreadings by way of refutation. Technically, however, readings are refuted only with respect to the logic in which they are presented—for example, by offering counterevidence from the text to dismantle an interpretation. Strictly speaking, in a formal refutation critics point to inconsistencies and logical errors in the reasoning process presupposed by the critical argument. The reading is thus treated as a process of reasoning, presupposing that the reading could not be replicated because the reasoning was faulty.

The refutation of opposing theories on which differing interpretive communities are based is another matter altogether. This particular problem greatly troubled the Chicago School critics, who formulated the theory of criticism known as pluralism. For many pluralists (Wayne Booth comes to mind—especially his *Modern Dogma and the Rhetoric of Assent* and *Critical Understanding: The Powers and Limits of Pluralism*), opposing theories can, in principle, be shown to be complementary, though the task of showing their interrelatedness is often too daunting to complete. Concerning refutation (at least the kind associated with falsification), Booth writes that it "offers what looks like respectable intellectual reasons for treating rivals superficially" (*Critical Understanding* 12). In general, Booth is very suspicious of refutations, characterizing them as "easy and inevitable from an alien perspective" (397). For such a refutation to be viable, the audience must call the argument into question by noting that its factual premises are inconsistent with its theoretical premises. In the case of literary studies, this would be tantamount to taking the argument on its own terms and pointing to ways in which it contradicts itself; however, it is notoriously difficult for rival theorists to treat their opponents' theories empathetically.

The difficulty we have in refuting another theory when it is used in justificatory arguments aimed at convincing is that the warrants of these arguments are themselves theorems from the theory in question. Recall that axioms or theorems themselves need to be justified before such arguments can proceed. Nonetheless, critics intending to refute such arguments usually step outside their premises in order to do so. A critic might argue that Freud's theories disprove Jung's theories, so a Jungian hypothesis in the argument of a given literary critic is also dubious. But what metatheory can decide this for literary study? Cognitive psychology? When this happens, critics usually advance the premises they employ in their own practices to supplant the ones proffered, sometimes using the theory to which they have given their allegiance as a metatheory that discounts the rival theory. Refutation in any strict sense is questionable in such contexts.[9] Disagreements of this sort can be endless.

This brings us to the refutation of configurations, arguments intended to persuade audiences by getting them to reexperience the "data." These present us with more difficult cases because they are so complex, often incorporating reasoning, narrating, and exhorting. Let me put aside for the moment the emotional, imaginative, and hortatory elements of such arguments and focus on their use of reasoning. Recall that Perelman's distinction between arguments intended to convince and those intended to persuade hinges on the difference between universal appeals and specific appeals. If we pursue this distinction, then a literary argument—say, Freimarck's quoted in an earlier chapter—could take either form. The argument as it stands in Freimarck's articulation of it is intended to convince. It nowhere relies on a specific audience but seems to address readers in general. Its implied audience is a well-informed reader familiar with the conventions of literary genres going as far back into our literary history as the twelfth century. Thus, for all practical purposes, the implied reader is a professional critic like Freimarck himself. Rhetorically, however, the appeal is to *any* critic. In this sense, it implies a universal audience. Though, in principle, it addresses a specific audience of persons who have read "Araby," it decontextualizes that audience and thus universalizes it.

Consider making Freimarck's argument to a class of undergraduates at Miami University in Oxford, Ohio (which, as the following anecdote implies, I have done). To do so, I have to tell the Perceval story before I can make the argument work. This is not a minor matter. In effect, I have to give my students an approximate experience of reading *Perceval* before I can proceed. What happens when one of my students (let's call him Todd) misses class the day I recount the Perceval narrative? I ask, "Did the boy in 'Araby' learn anything from his disappointment?" Todd answers, "No." Can I tell him he is wrong or incorrect in reading "Araby" in the way he does, not having reexperienced the text by comparing it with the Perceval story in which, according to Freimarck and others, the disheartened hero learns from his failure? Can I, in any sense, refute Todd's reading of Joyce's story if it does not arrive at the idea that the boy understands more about himself after going to the bazaar? Not according to Todd, who had an excellent defense of his interpretation.

Todd had asked Susan to go to a rock concert, but she couldn't go, so he went alone because he had already purchased the tickets. Once there, he felt depressed. In explaining his view that the boy did not learn anything at the end of "Araby," he volunteered that he didn't learn anything about himself when he went to the concert, pointing out that he was quite understandably depressed since he didn't have a date. He argued cogently that it was a very commonplace occurrence that, when failing to get a date, he became depressed; and he was quick to add that this was an experience with which he was quite familiar. According to Todd, the boy in "Araby" was simply naive and unrealistic. Can I refute Todd's experience? That he did not replicate Freimarck's reading is certainly a consequence of not having had the requisite historical background in medieval romances. But even if he had read *Perceval,* he could still legitimately disagree with Freimarck's reading of "Araby." He can't easily be refuted, even at the literal level, nor can he refute Freimarck in any logical way.

That refutation is an unlikely avenue to consensus in justificatory arguments, let alone configurative ones, seems apparent when we think of debating texts with our students. On the other hand, consensus is not all that desirable either. Our debates with other critics are similar to our debates with students. Our schooling trains us to write arguments intended to convince, and these arguments are thought to stand alone. Our audience is critics in general, no matter what their particular background or predisposition; that is, when writing we address *the* universal critic or *the* informed reader. Do we not, therefore, consistently universalize our audiences within and outside our classrooms? When we write about students, we seem to speak of *the* student; when about critics, of *the* critic; and when about readers, of *the* public. This is not a dialogical trait. So, we might ask, should we continue to develop stand-alone arguments aimed at a generalized audience of specialists? This brings us back to our starting point—the relevance of work in English departments to the general public, which Lodge's *Nice Work* so aptly dramatizes. This time, let's dramatize what usually happens in classrooms when students are addressed in the abstract terms we employ when addressing colleagues.

Most teachers of literature have undergone the following torture: Before a class, they patiently work out a reading of a literary work. In class, they work even harder to get their students to arrive at a reading that approximates the one they prepared. They are not trying to be tyrannical. Their students can hardly make sense of the text assigned in the first place, but on this particular day they cannot quite see the point and produce debilitatingly irrelevant readings that reflect vain attempts to pursue their teacher's instructions. Finally, as the class is winding down, Matt, a student who has looked particularly morose throughout the class, pipes up for the first time to say, "Aren't interpretations a matter of opinion?" This is not an isolated experience. It is endemic to the teaching of literature.

The implication of this scenario is that matters of opinion are usually matters of belief as well. An opinion is an idea or judgment held to be valid by an individual. Belief is the act of assenting intellectually to a statement proposed as valid or the state of mind of one who so assents. The word "belief" adds an element of trust and a social dimension to the experience of thinking that an idea is valid. In my example, Matt chooses the word "opinion" to emphasize that validity is an individual matter in situations where evidence is hard to come by. However, once opinions are placed in a social context where negotiation is required to obtain widespread assent, we find ourselves in a somewhat different realm—the dialogical, where what one believes is at stake. In this realm, Matt's remark suggests that although teachers are individuals with no more authority than their students, teachers nonetheless insist that their students believe the opinions. When we translate Matt's question to bring out its social implications— "Why do we have to debate this matter?"—interpretation ceases to be an individual issue. As long as Matt can regard his teacher's belief as mere opinion, he can disregard it. At the moment it becomes a question of what the majority of the class believes, Matt then can no longer regard it as mere opinion. This is the function of debate. It brings out into the open the social implications of beliefs—the issue underlying the question of refutation.

Debate, which formally sanctions refutation, has been part of the fabric of our society for centuries. However, it seems to have lost much of its potency because, in our media-oriented culture, opinions obtain assent by dramatization rather than as the consequence of refutation. As the media alters our decision-making processes, the question arises whether the university remains a site in our culture where debate is still worth privileging, and, correlatively, whether the debates that take place in universities have to do with other specialists within the university or with the general public. This is presupposed in the question the student asks. When Matt asks, "Isn't it just a matter of opinion?" he probably means, "Isn't it just something that only concerns teachers, who, as specialists, are preoccupied with this matter; and therefore, isn't it something that need not concern me?" His question probably reflects the widespread view that English teachers argue about matters of no concern to the general public. While brooding over this example, we have to keep in mind that students are our most direct link to the general public. Ordinarily we do not have as much contact with business or factory personnel as Robyn does in *Nice Work.*

In his novel, Lodge configures the exchange of views between academics and the general public. Vic is not an academic. He is quite intelligent, well informed about his business, and receptive to new views. Robyn is an academic who succeeds in translating her concerns for Vic. Charles is the sort of academic who remains within the university and continues to employ its specialized language, never really engaging persons like Vic. It is tempting to read Lodge's novel as an indictment of academic specialists, experts in arcane matters irrelevant to the general public. It seems to confirm our disaffected student's claim: there is no reason for the general public to engage in a debate with an academic. Such a reading would not do justice to the complexity of the characterization. Robyn does not abandon her academic view in her exchanges with Vic; instead, having switched places and therefore contexts, she switches her mode of argumentation from justification to configuration.

With Graff, I believe that discussions of literature need to be debated; better yet, they need to be negotiated so that we turn our thinking away from competitive justifications, whose hallmark is refutation, and make our aim the shared cultural configurations of experiences. As I propose in chapter 14, collaborative, socially negotiated work is an appropriate modus operandi for literary critics. This seems preferable to a view that commits us to the fiction of the stand-alone, single-authored argument essay as well as the solitary exam—the subject of chapter 8. Before we turn to examining practices, we need to consider one other aspect of refuting—the replicability of readings.

Unreplicable Readings

Imagine three hundred critics in Dublin at a future Joyce symposium each reading a paper on the *Dubliners* tale "Araby." Not *5 Readers Reading,* as in the title of Norman Holland's book, but *300 Readers Reading*! Early the first morning, Barbara Herrnstein Smith gives her reading, then Jacques Derrida gives his, then E. D. Hirsch Jr., then Norman Holland, then Gayatri Chakravorty Spivak, then Jeffrey, Fredric, Julia, Jon . . . A Lacanian reading by Jane Gallop is followed by a counterreading by Luce Irigaray. Harold Bloom's reading has Mary Louise Pratt's as its sequel. Wolfgang Iser follows Stanley Fish. Richard Ohmann follows David Bleich. And so on.[10]

Many readers sit in the privacy of their homes silently consuming countless texts. That readers reading the same text silently enjoy widely disparate readings is of no critical consequence. We expect the reading acts of different critics to differ. Yet the moment one of the readers, leaving the privacy of his or her study, publishes a claim about a reading, the situation shifts. Private differences become public disputes. How can the multiplicity of disputable readings in literary studies be explained as a coherent body of knowledge produced by a discipline?

Every student of literature at one time or another encounters inconsistencies among readings of the same text. Within the corpus of "Araby" criticism, for example, it is easy to point out inconsistencies in the claims readers make.[11] Freimarck observes that "Araby" "immediately raises echoes of the Grail Quest story-pattern" (366). Other critics who make similar but inconsistent observations include Jerome Mandel in "Medieval Romance and the Structure of 'Araby'"; John Lyons in "James Joyce and Chaucer's Prioress"; and Warren Beck in *Joyce's Dubliners: Substance, Vision, and Art*.[12] Let's take as our test case on the possibility of refutation (in the compact sense) accounts of the plot of "Araby" that at the surface seem quite similar but are more than a little difficult to justify as "descriptions" of the text of "Araby."

> ["Araby" is] the story of a young boy journeying to Araby in hope of winning the favor of an idealized girl. . . . [He] ignores the reality of his bleak, winter surroundings and allows the word "Araby" to suggest the exciting summer world of Romance . . . in a world hostile to romance, Mangan's sister is the object of the boy's "confused adoration." By the time his lady speaks, his naive crush has led to the heroic bearing of her image like a chalice through market streets, and worship in a chapel-like room where the boy presses his hands together and murmurs "O love! O love!" Hearing she longs to go to Araby, but cannot, he promises to return with a gift if he should make the trip. . . . Finally the boy begins his journey, leaving the house to the strains of "The Arab's Farewell to His Steed." The deserted train, . . . passing through the waste land of "ruinous houses" and crossing . . . a river on its way to Araby . . . Inside, the young boy examines vases and flowered tea-sets . . . ap-

proaching the two men and the woman, he is deterred by their attitude and the trivia of their conversation. . . . Here the boy realizes his journey is over and feels humiliated. His failure brings an increase in knowledge, which continuing the story's ironic counterpoint to Romance, does not bring hope or felicity. (Freimarck 366–68)

It is my belief that "Araby" is constructed with rigorous precision upon a paradigm of medieval romance, that the unnamed boy reflects in detail and in general the action and behavior of smitten courtly lovers, and that the story as a whole shows Joyce working with the well-defined structure of a traditional genre, the medieval romance. (Mandel 234)

Joyce's "Araby" is virtually the prototype of the modern short story about a youth's initiation. It concerns a romantic little boy who secretly worships the sister of a playmate. He wishes to please her by bringing her a souvenir from Araby, a bazaar. His uncle has promised him money for this treat, but on the night he is to go his uncle gets home late. When the boy finally arrives at the bazaar the stands are closing and his romantic imaginings dissolve before the tawdry props and people of the closing carnival. (Lyons 127)

"Araby" is also a genuine short story, moving through determining events to self-realization in a Joycean epiphany. . . . Every morning the boy kept watch from his window until Mangan's sister appeared, and then with a leaping heart he ran to follow her in the street until their ways diverged, hers toward her convent school. Of an evening, when she came out on the doorstep to call her brother to tea, the boys at play would linger in the shadows to see whether she would remain or go in; then while she waited they would approach "resignedly," but while Mangan still teased his sister before obeying, the boy of this story stood by the railings looking at her, seeing "her figure defined by the light from the half-opened door" and waiting upon a summons of another kind. He must wait too for his uncle's late return and for the money to fetch the girl a present from the bazaar, Araby; then the special train, almost empty, waited intolerably and he arrived late. Still he drove toward his goal, paying a shilling to avoid further delay in looking for a sixpenny entrance. Once inside, he found the place half-darkened and the stalls mostly closed. Though there was nothing for him to buy, he lingered still, baffled, stultified, prolonging only pretense of interest. What awaits him as the lights are being put out is a facing "with anguish and anger" of his obsessive mood and its frustration, of himself as a creature "driven and derided by vanity" (Beck 109)

Freimarck and Mandel read "Araby" as a romance, but the latter as a straightforward romance and the former as an ironic one. By contrast, Lyons and Beck read "Araby" as a realistic short story about initiation or self-realization, but the former understands the ending in terms of the boy's "romantic imaginings dissolv[ing] before the tawdry props and people" and the latter in terms of the boy's "obsessive mood and its frustration." The plot description of each critic dovetails (not surprisingly) with the interpretative warrants he uses—an analogue to a Grail-quest romance or a realistic short story. In one case the story is described as a romance in order to compare it with other romances; in another it is an initiation story with strong realistic overtones. In each case, what the critic sets out to claim dictates the slant he gives to his plot description. The resulting inconsistencies are not overwhelming, but they not only raise doubts about the accuracy of these descriptions (of the sort I recounted about Freimarck in an earlier chapter), they also raise questions about the criterion critics have for *describing* plots (see appendix). Plots answer the most fundamental question a reader could ask: What happened? In other words, if agreement among critics cannot be reached at this level, evidential criteria for refutation of interpretive claims are impossible.[13] Two issues emerge: (1) Should critics aspire to consistency in their reading of a text? and (2) If so, how can inconsistent claims be assessed?[14]

If two inconsistent claims are made about the reading of a specific text, consistency is ordinarily achieved by refuting one of the claims. Usually the reading that accounts for the most details of the story supplants the less comprehensive one. From the point of view of systematically applied descriptive procedures, "Araby" should be either a romance or a realistic short story, but not both. Nevertheless, most readers accept the notion Freimarck articulates—it is astonishing how Joyce can write a story that is both realistic and yet powerfully evokes Grail-quest romances. These sorts of compromises seem normal. (This is the situation I describe in the next chapter—the vaguer the warrants, the more extensive the acceptable interpretive claims.) Interpretive compromises seem unproblematic unless they are characteristic of a study that aspires to be a discipline in the strict sense. Strict disciplines operate on a principle of falsification or refutation. This reminder provokes us to re-ask our question: On what grounds can the compromised interpretive claims we are studying be refuted?

All readers privately constitute the texts they read. The textual features critical readers offer as evidence in their discourses are dependent on the performance of complex, subtle, and largely unconscious sets of reading acts conducted in private. Every argument is a public conceptualization of a relatively simple aspect of the extraordinarily complex, private activity of processing an entire text. Hence textual features do not have the status of facts that can be explained as the *necessary* results of reading acts. Under these conditions, the refutation of a given critic's claim is difficult if not impossible.[15] As metacritical analyses of various corpora of criticism show, critical claims are not refuted; rather, over a period of time, they are abandoned or neglected. At present there does not seem to be a reliable way of testing literary analyses.

Unfortunately, we are forced to identify professional students of literature on the basis of a battery of tests, both M. A. and Ph.D. examinations and tests given in undergraduate literature courses. Graduate training in the study of literature typically acquaints the relatively naive reader of literature with models of literary texts and ways of reasoning about them. For example, a graduate student might be asked to master theoretical texts such as Percy Lubbock's *Craft of Fiction,* Brooks and Warren's *Understanding Fiction,* Wayne Booth's *Rhetoric of Fiction,* Seymour Chatman's *Story and Discourse,* Ross Chambers's *Story and Situation,* and Peter Brooks's *Reading for the Plot* in the first weeks of a course on prose fiction, and then to develop a critical discourse in which he or she resolves a problem in a text by means of an argument making use of some theoretical hypotheses about narrative structure, point of view, narration, and so forth. How can the instructor reliably test the conclusions at which students arrive when they perform this series of complex tasks?

The situation is even more perplexing than I indicate by my example. Few courses in fiction acquaint students systematically with the range of available narratological warrants for their research. Most admit a bewilderingly eclectic array of warrants, almost all of which go unexamined. (Even in my example, the narratological warrants implied by the texts mentioned are incompatible.) Given this chaotic conceptual situation, how can instructors use any reliable criteria whatsoever? And further, how can instructors assess (test) the effectiveness of such training, coming to such judgments as: (1) Lubbock's model is ineffective; (2) Brooks and Warren's model needs to be revised; (3) Booth's model should be replaced by Chatman's, or both are unacceptable in a poststructuralist period, hence narratology should be replaced with deconstruction; (4) this student merited a higher/lower grade than assigned; (5) that student should/should not be allowed to continue in our program; (6) training of this sort is incompatible with our program; and so on. In short, what are the grounds for refuting any of the claims arising from this situation? (Note: matters of publication and research involving judgments about publishability, promotion/tenure, etc., are no more amenable to resolution.)

However unreliably, tests of literary competence have been conducted in university systems and related public forums since the late nineteenth century. To impose standards of scientific testing on the profession of literary studies hardly seems advisable, yet how can the institution of criticism operate outside of *test criteria?* What can count as a test of a literary reading? It is difficult to avoid the criterion of *the replicability of analyses of texts* as the most general testing standard.

If a reader of a critical essay is persuaded by it, then in some sense that reader is able to read the text at issue in the same way as its author. Similarly, when professors test their students, they invite them to replicate their own readings. When journal editors accept readings for publication, they do so in the confidence that the subscribers will find the readings viable ones, replicable enough to be worth entertaining as justifiable interpretations. In such judgments the published reading/reasoning process of the critic is replicated in private. If we are to test what has heretofore been a private matter, it seems advisable to make explicit the criterion of replicability. But how can this be accomplished?

For critical discourse to be assessed there should be some reliable grounds for refutation. However, as we have already seen, critical discourse is not a simple report of a reading, since evidence for it is based on private, unrecorded reading acts wherein the text is constituted. As the MURGE project showed (see appendix), even technical descriptions of the plot cannot be easily replicated. If plots (summaries of what happened in the text) cannot be replicated, interpretations of texts cannot be tested. If the body of textual data relevant to interpretations cannot be tested, grounds for refutation in critical discourse seem dubious.

Whether modern or postmodern, the institution of literary criticism has never quite solved the fundamental problem that separates it from strict or compact disciplines: it cannot replicate its research. The mark of reliable knowledge[16] is that its production can be duplicated, but critics cannot establish rules for replicating readings. As a consequence, literary criticism is perennially in danger of losing its credibility as a university study.

Examining Exams

Exams have a troubled history in the American university. Their inadequacies, which provoked at least one recorded riot in the nineteenth century, still incite protests. Recently, for example, the merits of a more finely calibrated grading system (adding + and − to letter grades) were hotly debated in the editorial pages of the college newspaper at a university where I was teaching—an issue very similar to the one that incited students at Harvard more than a century ago: "Harvard's way of distributing points and fractions of points . . . not only failed to distinguish between conduct and scholarship, . . . [it] also failed to convince students of its honesty. Instructors could not agree on the scale of points, one critic wrote: 'Some frankly admitted that it was impossible to get within five or ten per cent of absolute exactness; others were so delicately constituted that they could distinguish between fractions of one per cent'" (Veysey 271–72). Like their nineteenth-century precursor who invented a "marking machine," many of my colleagues determine grades on computers, though, unlike one nineteenth-century teacher on record, no one I know offers "marks *less than zero*" (272).

Veysey's observation that "the Harvard plan" for grading "was devised in the 1820s primarily to discipline the conduct of unruly students rather than test their mental ability or keep insecure students in a perpetual state of intellectual preparation" (272) accords with Foucault's remarks in *Discipline and Punish* about the function of exams:

> The examination combines the techniques of an observing hierarchy and those of a normalizing judgment. It is a normalizing gaze, a surveillance that makes it possible to qualify, to classify and to punish. It estab-

93

lishes over individuals a visibility through which one differentiates them and judges them. That is why, in all the mechanisms of discipline, the examination is highly ritualized. In it are combined the ceremony of power and the form of the experiment, the deployment of force and the establishment of truth. At the heart of the procedures of discipline, it manifests the subjection of those who are perceived as objects and the objectification of those who are subjected. (184–85)

Though more than a century later exams are purportedly designed to ensure the uniformity of disciplinary practices, like their predecessors, they often ensure conformity to cultural practices as well. The examination system of the modern university to which we are heirs, Veysey notes, "aimed to graduate a single model of a civilized gentleman—not a variety of eccentric individuals" "by means of a uniform curriculum and a uniform social routine" (271–72). This agenda is correlative to the hidden agendas of nineteenth-century humanities programs that attempted to acculturate an ever-enlarging immigrant population (Vallance 1–9). Recently these rationales have been reclaimed by William Bennett and his successor, Lynne Cheney, as well as by the advocates of "cultural literacy" as espoused by E. D. Hirsch, in the hope of acculturating an ever-enlarging "illiterate" minority of our present population. The normalizing force of exams usually exceeds their disciplinary boundaries. This is particularly true in the humanities. Consequently, exams on literature deserve some scrutiny.

We might begin by considering that exams given in traditional humanities programs can be considered attempts to make students adherents of a canonical culture. In this regard, their successes are most often temporary. Nevertheless, routine exam procedures encourage students to mimic (if not accept) their teacher's beliefs (at least for the duration of the exam), and though their positive effects are not usually long lasting, sometimes their negative effects are. As Foucault's analysis of discipline helps us to see, the negative effects of exams are related to the way they punish and thus subjugate students. They are often experienced as painful exercises in which apprentices, subject to the threat of punishment, must predict what their masters would say or do under the same conditions.

In literature exams, questions about texts are formulated in ways that imply interpretive conclusions. As I implied in the previous chapter, a teacher might believe that "Araby" is a prototype of *A Portrait of the Artist as a Young Man.* He or she thus asks, "Is this story an initiation story?" The question anticipates that students who have been attentive will answer "Yes" and offer a reading to support this claim. From this perspective, the logic of literature exams is a simple extension of inferential logic. A reader offers an interpretive claim based on accepted premises about literary texts and offers textual evidence in its support. When teachers give exams to student readers, they formulate their interpretations as claims to be supported by evidence from texts, anticipating that studious readers will be able to read the texts in a like manner by employing their teachers' favored assumptions about literature.

In the logic of such exams, the terms of the question often contain premises students must recognize in order to assemble the appropriate evidence for their responses. The question "Is 'Araby' an initiation story?" attributes to that text a conventional combination of narrative features associated with the analysis of genres. Most students, however, form their assumptions about genres from the uncritical use of TV guides. "Initiation story" is not a category they use. Thus, unless students attend to the teacher's identification of the generic features of initiation stories in classroom exercises, they will not be able to find them or remember them on an exam. Often enough, students try to remember textual features identified by their teachers without practicing the style of reading that selects them for a reader's attention; but it is nearly impossible to memorize extended arrays of textual details outside the interpretive strategies that generate them. Thus the best preparation for a literature exam is to mimic the reading strategies of the teacher.

Sometimes teachers do not give their students sufficient information about their interpretive strategies. In these cases students rightly ask, "But what do you want me to do?" The crux of the matter is terminological. Technical vocabularies usually supply students with more information about reading strategies than do their nontechnical equivalents. When a teacher asks an apparently commonsensical question such as "What happens in 'Araby'?" it is likely to be a translation into ordinary language of a more complex concept. Though the word "happens" is ordinary English, it is usually understood by critics as part of a framework that includes the concepts "plot," "story," "event," and so on. A teacher who uses it in a question might be implicitly referring to a well-articulated theory of narrative anywhere from Aristotle to Chatman.

Teachers habitually use framing terms in questions because such terms fit into the frameworks of beliefs about literary texts that governed their training. These frameworks usually differ from the ones students employ in their reading. Thus a more particular way of reading than the question seems to imply is frequently presumed by teachers who ask, "What happens in this story?" Unless students read in the manner prescribed by their teachers' questions, their responses will be unsatisfactory. In effect, students who did not comprehend the ways their teachers wished them to read will not understand the *instruction* presupposed by the questions asked. Students will not be able to answer these questions because they did not know what to look for while they were reading the text in preparation for the exam. Such students do not know what warrants the claims that answer their teachers' questions. This experience is one of frustration and anxiety.

The frequency of such painful effects is evidence for Foucault's claim that exams subjugate. Should students be blamed for avoiding such punishment?

Anyone who has spent a few years in classrooms can testify to the ways in which students learn to mimic their teachers' ways of doing things—for instance, their ways of reading texts. Literary training proceeds largely by way of imitation. Such imitative practices are not culturally innocent. Teachers, by and large, subject students to the cultures teachers affirm. This is no less true when teachers, however aptly or ineptly, affirm their students' cultures. However, as I have already intimated, such training (at least in the humanities) seems less and less efficacious. In what follows I express reservations about the appropriateness of giving exams on the interpretation of literary texts. Though exams are the principal mechanism of disciplinary training in most academic studies, we should not assume they are appropriate to the study of cultures, in which interpretation is at least a coping skill, if not a survival skill.

Questioning the Questioners

Sometimes it is difficult for teachers to appreciate the full force of the exams they create for their students. Already in possession of considerable expertise, they do not always comprehend the extent and difficulty of the tasks they require of their students. Assuming, then, that as a likely reader of this chapter you are a teacher, let me ask you to take the following test under the specified conditions by way of a thought experiment.

Imagine that each year you are called back to your degree-granting institution and asked to take an exam that will establish whether you have kept up with the progress of your profession.[1] For a moment, consider yourself a Chaucerian returning to University College. A sleepless night is followed by a hollow Saturday morning in which only your footsteps resound in the corridor. You find the appropriate classroom and choose a desk at random. You are handed a sheet of paper. It has purple type. It reads:

> Choose three of the following questions
> (Spend approximately two hours on each question)
>
> 1. Should the traditional conception of medieval allegory (D. W. Robertson et al.) be revised in the light of recent conceptions of the figural nature of all language (Paul de Man et al.)? As a preface to your answer, defend (however briefly) the possibility of historical understanding. If time allows, indicate how your view of historical understanding relates to recent New Historical developments.
>
> 2. Would an "action" model of a narrative (Tsvetan Todorov's, Teun Van Dijk's, or Gerald Prince's) more accurately disclose the narrative

structure in "The Knight's Tale" than the "satellite/kernel" model (Seymour Chatman's via Roland Barthes's)? You may offer another view of narrative—for instance, Leo Bersani's or Peter Brooks's psychoanalytic ones. If you hold a postmodern view of the reductive linear character of narrative that goes beyond Bersani's or Brooks's, you may write an essay on why narrative structure cannot be "disclosed." This tactic, however, is not recommended.

3. The line "And prively he caughte hire by the quenynte" (l. 3276) in "The Miller's Tale" has been discussed as an item of Chaucerian "realism." Since "realism" usually implies referentiality, can this traditional literary-historical concept be reconciled with prevailing views of the nonreferential nature of literature? In your answer, either support or refute or emend the deconstructive position (of Jacques Derrida et al.) or offer a counterposition (e.g., John Searle's interpretation of speech-act theory, Gerald Graff's pre–1985 view of literature as knowledge, or New Historicist and neo-Marxist attempts to historicize deconstructive strategies of interpretation.)

4. In a semiotic analysis of "The Wife of Bath's Tale," it is not possible to interpret the word "wyf" (l. 957) in the tale of "Myda" as signifying "Midas's wife" in Ovid's tale, for there is no "wyf" in Ovid's tale. Consequently, is it possible that the occurrence of the word "wyf" can be explained as a sign that Chaucer's unconscious substituted it for the sign "barbour," which could have referred to the sign "famulus" (the slave-barber) actually occurring in Ovid's tale? In other words, rather than construing the word "wyf" as a purely potential lexical unit, could we not consider it as signifying, at a minimum, "here is an-image-of-a-wife"? From a semiotic point of view, can it be argued that Chaucer's unconscious simply left the imprint of the image-of-a-woman-as-wifely on Chaucer's consciousness—a relationship that would seem to parallel the physical connection between the natural phenomenon and the sign in Peirce's notion of "index" as he applies it to a photograph? In such an event, Chaucer's unconscious would be the code; and, since we have no access to his unconscious, we then would have to regard the word as "codeless" and, therefore, parallel to Metz's "a kind of Here is" or Barthes's description of the photographic icon as a "kind of natural being-there of the object." (In this sense, it would carry with itself its own actualization, as a kind of "here is," or "voici"—the very word Andre Martinet considers to be a pure index of actualization.) Or, on the other hand, should the word be understood as an indirect and ironic reference to the fact that in Ovid's tale the narrative function of the barber, who is male, is "gossiping"? In your answer be certain to avoid confusions between Peirce's, Eco's, de Lauretis's, and Metz's semiotics and Barthes's pre-*S/Z* semiology.

5. Does Chaucer's "self-portrait" in *The Canterbury Tales* reflect a rejection of reality to the extent that as a "mirror-image" (cf. Jacques Lacan's "le stade du miroir") it allows Chaucer, as artist-child, to

govern his relations with other imagined (projected) people and to turn them into participants in games of master and slave, actor and spectator? You may answer this question by arguing a case against psychoanalytic criticism in general or against the specific use of Lacan's notoriously inaccessible terminology in psychoanalytic readings. This tactic, however, is not recommended.

Six hours later you reluctantly turn in your answers to the three questions you selected. Three weeks later you are called into your chairman's office. Sadly he tells you, "I regret to inform you that I have just received notice from University College that you have failed the exam. Unfortunately, it is the official policy of this university not to renew the contracts of members of our staff who do not pass their annuals."

This exam is preposterous. In some respects it reads like a parody of contemporary literary studies. Yet it raises the question of whether teachers can examine other teachers about their "knowledge" of the interpretation of literature. However, the exam I just offered clearly skews the study of literature toward theoretical concerns. It could be justified on the ground that students of literature must be aware of the most recent challenges to the assumptions that govern their "disciplined" interpretations. It presumes that any teacher of literature should be informed about any currently viable premise of interpretations. In effect, it assumes that teachers should be familiar with every conceivable method of interpretation and all the debates that accompany their practices. This is palpably unrealistic. Let me reframe the exam in the vocabularies of methods of literary interpretation:

Monday: Do a historical analysis of *Beowulf.* Develop either a Marxist, neo-Marxist, or some species of New Historical argument.

Tuesday: Do a formal analysis of Chaucer's "The Parliament of Fowls." Develop either a Russian, French, British, or American formal argument. (Assume that I. A. Richards belongs to a formal rather than a reader-oriented school of thought and construes "rhetorical analysis" as a formal matter.) If you are so disposed, do a feminist analysis instead of a formal one, but be certain to identify which brand you are using. In particular, be careful not to contaminate American feminisms with the work of French feminists. If you do choose to base your analysis on the work of Cixous, Kristeva, Irigaray, et al., be certain to take into account how their work is related to their male precursors'.

Wednesday: Do a semiotic analysis of Shakespeare's *King Lear.* Develop either a Jakobsonian, Peircean, Mukarovskian, Barthean, Lotmanian, or Econian argument. (Bakhtin may be construed as a semiotician for the purpose of answering this question.)

Thursday: Do a psychoanalytic analysis of Pope's *Essay on Man.* Develop either a Freudian, Lacanian, Kohutian, or Laingian argument. Avoid Jungian arguments!

Friday: Do a reader-oriented criticism of Coleridge's "Kubla Khan."
Develop either a Fishian, Jaussian, Culleresque, Iserian,
Schweichardarian, or Radwayian argument. No Bleichian or
Hollandesque arguments allowed!

Saturday: Do a postmodern analysis of *Gravity's Rainbow.* You may base
your reading on any one of the following: Derrida, de Man, Foucault,
Deleuze and Guattari, Lacan, or Lyotard. Avoid Althusser, Jameson,
Habermas, and other highly politicized theorists.

In this version of the exam I added the equally implausible assumption
that every teacher should not only be familiar with every interpretive
method but also with most canonical literature. The abilities, energies, and
resources presupposed by this exam belong to no scholar of whom I have
heard. Not René Wellek, not Eric Auerbach, not Gustave Lanson. So we
can safely say that both of the first two exams are unrealistic. It is unrealistic to assume that every teacher is thoroughly informed about not only
every canonical work but also about every interpretive method. What,
then, would be the basis of an examination of teachers of literature?

We assume that professors of literature are specialists in some field and
practitioners of some method of interpretation. It would appear, then, to
be more realistic to develop an exam on this assumption. However, if any
professor can choose any recognized field and any recognized method, as
my newest proposal assumes, how can we test professors whose practices
are eclectic? And who are the experts who could grade such exams? Even
leaving that perplexing issue aside, though the first and second exams may
seem unrealistic, they do not have the serious flaw that the more realistic
exam I just proposed has. Consider that if the questioner is vague about
the terms of the question, the answerer will have difficulty predicting the
correct response. Thus, though the first and second questions seem skewed
toward any and every theory and any and every text, they are less vague
than any allegedly more realistic exam is likely to be. Allowing for this
circumstance, let us assume that every teacher commands an interpretive
method and is capable of interpreting accessible texts in terms of their own
practices, whatever they might be. Let's try an exam that does not imply a
method, one that is theory-free. Of course, to write this exam we have to
assume some field of competence. Let's try nineteenth-century British. (I
will leave aside here the difficulty you no doubt have noted—the test entails some "list" of works in the specified "field" on which such examinations can be based, the very sort of canonical list that was developed by
earlier educators to impose cultural standards upon a divergent population.)

Answer all four questions on the following poem

The Sick Rose
O Rose thou art sick.

> The invisible worm,
> That flies in the night
> In the howling storm:
>
> Has found out thy bed
> Of crimson joy:
> And his dark secret love
> Does thy life destroy.
>
> 1. What is the *form* of Blake's poem?
> 2. What is its *structure?*
> 3. How does the *pattern* of the poem differ from its *form* and *structure?*
> 4. What is the *shape* of the experience Blake presents to us in this
>   poem?

I offer this particular exam as an instance of the difficulty of asking questions about the meaning of literary works in nontechnical language. This exam implies no criteria by which the answers can be judged to be satisfactory. Any and every answer that is not nonsensical has to be judged a fair answer. When technical terms enter the questions, so do the theories in which they are embedded.

The most theory-free exam that can be given was actually commonplace before the twentieth century:

> Recite the first twenty-five lines of "The General Prologue" to *The
> Canterbury Tales.*

Our nineteenth-century predecessors believed that every educated gentleman should have the classics committed to memory. Many critics still believe we should be able to recite the opening lines of *The Canterbury Tales,* as well as passages from Milton, Shakespeare, and other canonical writers.

Thus far we have not found an exam suitable for teachers of literature. However, many would argue that I have left out the most obvious kind of exam—one that tests our "knowledge" of literature, our scholarship. You may wish to offer counterexamples, but if an exam on literature is to be based on "facts" about texts, I think it would have to take the following form:

> Answer all the following questions
>
> Who was the Parnell to whom Joyce alludes in "Araby"?
> Which names of which characters in Joyce's *Portrait* are real?
> What is the date of Joyce's *Ulysses?*
> On what Dublin street does . . .

The more testable facts about literature can be, the less interpretive they must be. Unfortunately, this proposition can be restated: the less interpretive statements about literature are, the more trivial a pursuit they become.

At the other end of the spectrum, the more questions address interpretive strategies, the more subjective they become:

> Rank the following questions in the order of their subjectivity
>
> In a Station of the Metro
> The apparition of these faces in the crowd;
> Petals on a wet, black bough.
>
> 1. What does this poem mean?
> 2. What does Pound mean by "The apparition of these faces in the crowd; / Petals on a wet, black bough"?
> 3. What does the utterance "The apparition of these faces in the crowd; / Petals on a wet, black bough" mean?
> 4. What does the reader understand by the sentence "The apparition of these faces in the crowd; / Petals on a wet, black bough"?
> 5. What do I mean by this poem?
> 6. What do you mean by this poem?

The most factual answer students could offer in this exam is in response to the very last question, the one that explicitly asks for their subjective interpretation, the only meaning to which they are actual witnesses. Perhaps a lexicographer could claim more objectivity about the ordinary usage of Pound's words, but this is not a very satisfactory account of the meaning of the poem. Moreover, answers to questions 2, 3, and 4 are all appropriate answers to question 1.

I may have overlooked some types of exams or exam questions, but surely none of the ones I have so far offered could constitute a fair exam by teachers of other teachers. Granted that I have slanted the rhetoric of my putative exams toward parody; nevertheless, I have offered instances of the five most common types of exams used in the study of literature (the recitation exam is the exception). My first exam tests teachers' awareness of current controversies about the interpretation of literature; the second tests awareness of methods of interpretation; the third asks for a demonstration of a cogent practice; the fourth reminds us of common examining practices in the nineteenth century; the fifth tests for facts about literature; and the sixth points to the difficulty of basing an exam on the act of interpretation by showing how familiar questions about the "meaning" of texts are inescapably ambiguous. To me, all six of these types of tests on literature are suspect.

If the most common types of questions found in literature exams are suspect when addressed to teachers by other teachers, then what exams would be appropriate for students of literature? It is hard to imagine asking students questions that are different *in kind* from the ones I proposed for the examination of teachers. The questions I suggested above frequently occur in examinations of students. Though the content would be different and germane to particular courses and fields, there would be no substantive difference in the type or form of the questions were they addressed to students. This raises the perplexing question of the relevance of such exams to anyone. If exams on literature are so perplexingly difficult to conduct, why do English departments insist on them? What do teachers of literature hope to accomplish by examining their students on their readings?

Literary Arguments Depend on Analogical Warrants

Any defense of exams in literary study is necessarily based on some account of the activities that are presupposed by the exams. I am reluctant, however, to answer the question I posed at the end of the previous section with a commonplace like "Exams on literature test readers on their critical skills" without specifying what those skills are. Thus, as in chapter 5, I start with critical activities generally understood to make up most critical practices. Rather than begin with a novel theoretical account of exams, I offer the same list of the activities of literary critics as I did earlier. Nearly all critics

1. *read* some text
2. *discuss formally and in public* the texts they read
3. *make sense* of texts regarded by other readers as difficult to understand
4. *make claims* about how other readers should make sense of texts
5. *make comparisons* among texts, especially those similar to the ones they are reading
6. *generalize* about texts, periods, and so on
7. *give evidence for* their readings
8. *try to justify* their readings
9. *seek agreement* with other critics about how texts should or should not be read

As before, I take the notion of argumentation to be a shorthand summary term for the list.

If the description of criticism I offer is as sensible as I claim, *it could justify giving exams.* If critics draw inferences from texts on the basis of warranting assumptions about those texts, then this pattern of reasoning can be repeated, however mimetically. Hence exams can be justified to the extent that they ask students to duplicate the reading practices of their teachers as a way of demonstrating that they have acquired specific interpretive strategies. Please note that this argument hinges, unfortunately, on the possibility that readings, in some measurable ("gradable") way, can be replicated (a view I called into question in the previous chapter). If they can be replicated, then readings also can be refuted if they diverge from the norm. This is one necessary condition of the possibility of an exam on reading as a practice that produces knowledge. (Of course, it can be more easily justified as a test of whether students can adequately mimic their teachers' reading habits.)

Literary study, if you accept the standard description I offer above (letting the question of mimicry go for the time being), aims at the understanding of literary texts, and the purpose of exams is to determine whether a student does or does not comprehend particular texts. By "understanding" I mean making sense of texts by finding patterns in their complex discursive features. Admittedly, not just any understanding will do. The variegated senses of complicated texts are not available to common sense; they emerge from specialized reading communities that share various interpretive strategies. The usual purpose of an exam in literature is to decide whether individuals belong to a given community of expert readers and then to rank their competence hierarchically—undergraduate, graduate, professorial. Exams professionalize readers by making them members of a professional group of readers. Through the passage of exams, amateurs enter "occupations with special power and prestige. Society grants these rewards [power and prestige] because professions have special competence in esoteric bodies of knowledge" developed from "techniques which the professionals apply in their work" (Larson x). In sum, exams make you a more expert reader than you were before studying for them. Exams ensure that by practicing the activities delineated above, amateur readers will develop "competence."

In speaking of reading as a "special competence in esoteric bodies of knowledge," a problem surfaces. Shall we stipulate that the meanings of texts are stable in order to call an understanding of a literary text "knowledge"? Reliable understandings presuppose relatively stable meanings—at least ones that do not shift unpredictably from one interpreter to another, from one period to another. If meanings shift in unstable or undecidable ways, basing an exam on such an unreliable outcome presents something of a difficulty in justifying exams as training in reading competence. The stability or decidability of meaning provides an examiner with the decisiveness called for while grading. Conversely, for postmodern critics who assume the indeterminateness of meaning, exams can only discipline students by arbitrary constraint through the exercise of authority (through the power to punish). Compliance does not, however, entail competence.

Let us assume that meaning can, relatively speaking, be determined, and therefore that literary arguments can be adjudicated on the basis of the logic they presuppose. Let us propose, then, that interpretive claims can be justly made, warranted, and supported by evidence from the text. But even assuming the relative stability of meanings, another problem arises: Is meaning derived from texts as a logical inference from observable facts or by analogy to experience? Are exams tests of facts or tests of taste? The same teacher who might be happy with an array of distinctive answers to the question "What is the meaning of Joyce's 'Araby'?" might be quite disconcerted by a wide range of answers to the question "What is the narrator's point of view in 'Araby'?" Whereas the first question depends on loose analogies among the text and various intertexts or contexts, the second is an inference that can be drawn from specific linguistic markers in Joyce's text.

Let me return to the nightmarish fiction I called "the annuals." In that exam, many of the questions borrow conceptions of texts from other disciplines and use them *by analogy* to literary texts. Since 1977, when I wrote "The Use of the Word 'Text' in Critical Discourse," in which the first version of this exam appeared, we have seen an extraordinary importation of literary theory from Europe. What I said then can be said even more forcefully now. When the conceptions of texts presupposed by readings are borrowed from other disciplines, they are used in literary arguments only analogously. For instance, a text does not have an unconscious. Psychoanalytic critics read texts *as if they were dreams.* Thus, any reunderstanding of the structure of the unconscious (such as Lacan's) is also applied analogously. Lacanian critics read texts *as if literary texts were structured like a language in the way that the unconscious is.* In this conception of the literary text, the primary analogy between texts and *langue* (like a systematic structure—architectonic) is understood through a secondary analogy (like the unconscious—dreamlike) that doubles back on the first (which unconscious is like a systematic structure—*langue*-like), thus creating a "reflexive" tertiary analogy. This explanation of how a text works is like a computer specialist explaining that e-mail is like real mail if you understand letters to be like bits coming from post offices like nodes at whose gateways there are "mailers." Such analogies can be instructive, but they are not logical inferences.

The more one looks at the warranting conceptions of texts that govern readings, even the formal ones New Critics used, the more one uncovers analogies. To say that a text is ironic suggests a conversation between a speaker and a listener in which their tones of voice are clues to their meanings. The reader has to place the text in the context of lived experience. Understanding texts requires an analogy to the reader's experience. Virtually any attempt to discern a pattern in the chaos of intertextuality that flares up in acts of reading demands some analogy to a thing that has a recognizable order. If we speak about the structure of texts and inquire into the pattern a given reader discerns, that structure will be imaged from the reader's experience as architectonic or organic or cosmic or chaotic or . . . Readers make sense of texts by comparing them with other texts in an infinite variety of vague resemblances made graphic through an analogy with some tangible experience. Critical warrants are metaphoric. They are tropes on our own experiences. This is what gives them such power.

Reading experiences depend more on intuitions than on logical inferences.[2] Generally, a reader comprehends a literary text by comparing it with other articulations of experience (often those from remembered conversations), all the while detecting fuzzy resemblances. These articulations or intertexts mediate experiences for the reader. Readings are *not* inferences from the *con*-texts to which the text is compared. Meanings are transferred synthetically (holistically) to the text from its *co*[n]*texts*. For instance, when a reader encounters the sentences "I imagined that I bore my chalice safely through a throng of foes" and "Her name sprang to my lips at moments in strange prayers and praises which I myself did not understand," a series of intertexts, not only from medieval romances, but also remarks about "chalices," "foes," and "gauntlet" (appearing in a related sentence but linked to "through throng of foes," etc.) that *resemble* Joyce's signification in "fuzzy" ways, come to mind. These associations take form by a process of embedding, wherein one articulation frames or structures the others. The embedding usually hinges on the memory of a specific set of sensations associated with personal experiences that readers recall because of their emotional resonances. In short, the text is translated into the meaning of lived experiences and the emotions or feelings they evoke. This translation is not an inference from a set of facts but an insight into intertextual resemblances.

When the meaning of the text is reduced to specifiable literary or historical contexts rather than evocative personal ones, the experience of reading literature is sterilized into cultural themes and motifs. There is no doubt that exposure to literature and its conventions increases the density of meanings that can structure a reading experience. There is also no doubt that the exposure to a specific string of intertexts can produce conforming readings of a specific text. But the situation is quite volatile.

Why Exams Are Experienced as Torturous

A situation in which a novice reader must reproduce the reading of a master reader is certainly constrictive. To make similar sense of the text, the novice must make every effort to remember the intertextual contexts the master characteristically uses. This constrains the apprentice's intuitions. Conventional wisdom says that such exams, however constrictive, nonetheless acquaint novices with traditions of intertextual relations and inculcate interpretive strategies that establish apprentice readers as members of professional reading communities—as experts called "scholars." There are, however, several difficulties with such training.

From the point of view of the trainee, exams that grant or deny readers a particular academic status are indeed torturous (in the sense of anxiety-producing), but this is not the form of torture on which I wish to focus here. The tortures I have in mind, as Foucault notes in the passage I quoted earlier, appear to be those modern equivalents of primitive rites of passage that make exams memorable events in one's life. From my point of view, these tortures derive from the appurtenances of objectivity accompanying exams. Though often employed to describe the quality of critical activity, the term "objective" seems less a descriptor of exams on literature than does "subjective." The conventional wisdom that frowns on identification questions, true-or-false questions, matching columns, and other forms of objective tests seems quite appropriate in cultural study. However, literary exams still follow procedures and often employ formats that presuppose objectivity.

Objectivity is established when any observer can describe an event in terms that match those of other observers. The social trait that accompanies an objective report of an experience is that "all speakers assent to such [reports] under the same stimulations" (Quine & Ullian 16). In the case of an examining committee, say, for the M. A. degree, a student's reading of a text must gain the assent of all the examiners who have read that text, whether or not they have taught the examinee. The notion that a reader can be examined by another reader with whose personal reading practices he or she has no acquaintance presupposes that readings are objective matters. But here we run into something of a problem. If belonging to a community of readers requires exposure to their intertextual repertoires, can we assume that all the members of an M. A. committee are members of the same interpretive community? Obviously not. This is why the annuals I described earlier are a nightmare. In that exam at least a dozen radically different schools of reading are represented. If we add the unmentioned schools of criticism (as I do in the second version of the exam), we arrive at a remarkable number of interpretive communities. Considering how little uniformity exists in such broadly gauged communities, the scenario quickly becomes Kafkaesque. (Are Fish, Iser, Bleich, Holland, Schweikart, Radway, Jauss, Culler, and Riffaterre in the same interpretive community?) Students facing an exam that claims to be objective are likely to be tortured by the complexity of their task. (What would be a precise answer to the question "How would the meaning(s) of Julio Cortázar's 'Axotol' be derived by *a* reader-oriented theorist?" And is not this question both less complex and more "objective" than the question "What are the meanings of Julio Cortázar's 'Axotol'"?)

Schools of reading are not in as comfortable relations to each other as some advocates of pluralism might be inclined to suggest. Critics characteristically contend with each other. Yet the underlying disagreements about literary texts that separate readers do not usually surface when those readers are appointed to exam committees. In fact, the enormity of the differences among examiners is most often covered over by their willingness to coauthor denominalized questions. Teachers, in the interests of clarity, speak about critical schools as denominations of criticism. The work of several thinkers is linked together by resemblances among them that, in effect, generalize the group by leveling the differences among the theorists involved to arrive at the lowest common denominator of belief. When this occurs, many of the key concepts lose their specificity and are "denominalized"—reduced to a common denominator. The term "deconstruction," for example, has been denominalized to the extent that M. H. Abrams can call Stanley Fish a "deconstructive" critic (*Is There a Text* 268). Such denominalizations of critical terms characterize the formulation of exam questions. This results in the third example of the annuals I offered earlier, the exam inviting a demonstration of a critical practice, which removes the arcane and highly specialized terms from the exam questions and uses the vaguest of terms instead (form, pattern, shape, etc.).

This situation is even more torturous than the first. Now there is virtually no hope of identifying the interpretive community whose perspective is required to answer the question. The range of possibilities is not narrow enough for reliable hunches. For example, imagine that your friend suggests that she will buy the next round of beers if you can guess the number she is thinking of. You promptly blurt out "Five." When she informs you that you were mistaken because she was thinking of 345 and that you are wrong by some 340 numbers, you would be likely to regard her game as unfair. The range of possibilities is too large. A narrower one is necessary, say 1–10, or better 1–5, or, to be really fair, 1–2 (giving you a 50–50 chance). However, *if you wanted her to win,* you would not object. We have to consider that English professors do not object to an extremely wide range of possible answers on exams and encourage this likelihood by the use of denominations in their questions. In literature exams, the range of possible answers usually exceeds the limit of probable ones. This ratio sounds ideal for students—the vaguer the question, the wider the possible range of answers—but this situation can have adverse effects. It leaves students without any defense. Posing questions in vague terms that offer no clues about how readings should be conducted in order to obtain consensus from the exam committee does not prevent any examiner from interpreting the vague question to imply a specific mode of reading. This renders any alternative answer incorrect. For all practical purposes, the more denominalized the exam, the more it is a guessing game. Students who have scoped out their instructors can prosper in such circumstances, but students who decide to define the terms for themselves (or worse, who decide to use the idioms of a "hot" theory) run an awful risk of offending the members of the committee who are either opposed to the theory or likely to perceive any theory but theirs to be naive.

Whereas exams that invite you to demonstrate your reading practices are familiar to contemporary literary students, most students are less familiar with the tortures associated with quoting passages by rote or memorizing countless facts, activities required by my fourth and fifth exams, respectively. Though these exams are now easy to dismiss as reductive, it is worth recalling how widely they were used not only in the nineteenth century but earlier in this century. These exams have a singular virtue when it comes to grading them—they are based on the "facts" of the text. It would probably surprise critics who are younger than fifty that graded recitals and quizzes on the names of characters in stories and the details of poems were the most common form of examination of literature (especially in classical literatures) in their older teachers' youthful studies. The *critic* did not that long ago replace the *philologist*—quite a different breed of taskmaster who has come down to us as the legendary pedant—a pedagogue who has given way to a much less dogmatic (if not relativistic) teacher.

This brings me to the sixth example (the meaning of meaning exam), an attempt to take into account the individual differences in reading styles that examiners typically embody. Unless explicitly asked for their own interpretation, students must assume in such exams that they are being asked implicitly to duplicate the readings of their instructors. In most respects, this is what happens to undergraduate literature majors as they pursue their education. As they travel from one course to another, they learn to mimic the reading styles of their teachers. When tested, they reflect those styles and strategies in their own readings. The torture starts only when what works in one class does not work in another (which puts Graff's comments on the unconnectivity of classrooms in a troubling perspective). Since students are rarely appraised of the different assumptions on which the various classes they take rely, they must construct the whole picture from the parts to which they are randomly exposed. This task is torturous because it is so confusing. Moreover, the confusion multiplies as the differences among teachers are obscured when they denominalize the views of other teachers. For the most part, teachers present views of texts so general as to make the differences among competing schools of criticism appear nonexistent. Most textbooks demand a denominational style, one that flattens out the differences among readings and thus among readers. Marxism seems little different from New Historicism, which is hardly distinguishable from historicism or literary history (in general), a perspective easily conflated with textual scholarship and, thus, with close readings that rely on tropes shared by New Critics and deconstructors, who use Foucault when they are not quoting Lacan's version of Freud in their personal metaphors for reading, and so on. It's a hodgepodge.

Nonetheless, to the extent that a teacher can acquaint particular students with his or her ways of reading, those students have a better chance of passing the exam. But what is accomplished by such an exam? Specialized exams, dependent as they are on a spectacular array of highly personal intertexts from the enormous catalogs of literature now mostly out of print, take professional reading out of public spheres or communities. Highly specialized interpretive communities have limited social uses. Trekkies write for persons interested in the canon of *Star Trek* episodes. Their constituency is rather small. Experts in other literary phenomena have seen their constituencies diminish. As I noted in my comments on Graff's *Beyond the Culture Wars,* this is a problem related to our policy of patterned isolation.

Future Dilemmas

It must be obvious by now that I have little, if any, faith in the efficacy of exams on literature. I do believe they can inculcate in students habits of reading that loosely resemble those of their teachers. However, since I am not an advocate of an American cultural canon of literature, I do not find this result necessarily beneficial. We face some interesting but frustrating dilemmas as we approach the twenty-first century. Let me mention two. The first I will call the dilemma of solidarity or difference. The second I will call the dilemma of significance or insignificance.

On the one hand, if we taught everyone to read the same texts in the same ways, we would provide one condition of the possibility of cultural solidarity. This, of course, has long been identified as an important rationale for the study of literature—it educates the citizens of this country to share a common literary heritage. This rationale was quite powerful in the nineteenth century and led to the establishment of long lists of texts that every American should read and to the establishment of nationwide tests on these materials (Vallance 1–9; Veysey, chapter 4; Graff, *Culture Wars,* chapter 2). Historically speaking, literature departments are failing in this mission. Not only have their members become such specialized readers of the literary canon that it is now almost inaccessible to the public that allegedly entrusted them with the mission in the first place, but the public does not regard the canon of its educators *as its own.* Once the perquisite of the literati, as many commentators have pointed out, the mission of acculturation has been taken over by the media (especially TV).

On the other hand, if we taught everyone to read different texts in different ways, we would encourage cultural diversity. In many respects this is a more common rationale in the literature departments I know about than the rationale of cultural solidarity. Ironically, we are failing in this newer mission as well. Specialization in literary criticism does not create diversity in ways that reflect the diversity of our culture but, instead, in ways that reflect the diversity of professors. Most training in literary criticism is text-oriented. The problems of reading texts are defined as problems professors have with texts rather than as problems nonprofessional persons have reading those texts. Critics who attend to the problems ordinary readers have with texts (e.g., composition teachers) are rarely advocates of the latest schools of criticism and generally find the sophisticated modes of reading engendered by deconstruction, Lacanian psychoanalysis, Jamesonian neo-Marxism, or even traditionally belletristic schools unhelpful in dealing with the problems students bring to them about reading texts—an attitude for which they are pilloried by some of their colleagues. Unhappily from my point of view, to students who have been indoctrinated to believe they need information to contextualize their readings, Hirsch's *Cultural Literacy,* which simplifies intertextuality to a few brash and selective commonplaces, appears to fit the bill. Lack of prior reading is the main problem in teaching reading. Students don't read much. As Iser might put it, they have little in their literary repertoires. But Hirsch-like tactics hardly encourage diversity in the sense of cultural differences. Quite the opposite—they discourage it.

The second dilemma, significance or insignificance, is even worse. We like to believe that what we do has significance. Thus, for students to pass difficult exams on literature has significance. It means that they have accomplished something of importance. However significant such accomplishments may be to the individuals involved, however much students feel enriched by their ability to emulate their teacher's readings, this feat does not have the social significance we like to attribute to it (Graff, *Culture Wars,* chapter 5). As Evan Watkins remarks in *Work Time: English Departments and the Circulation of Cultural Value,* "it matters less *how* you were taught Romantic poetry say—what socialization or countersocialization of expectations took place—than what grade you got at the end of the process" (6). From this point of view, however significant we believe our work to be as a "socialization or countersocialization," it lacks social significance. Exams, then, have less significance as instruments of acculturation than they do as the generators of grades. As Watkins notes, classes can be understood as a "particular complex of relations among students and the instructor engaged in the study of *Paradise Lost.*" This activity is thought to be valuable. However, "it's not value in quite the same sense as one might speak of the value of Milton's altering the conventions of English blank verse" (16). As Watkins suggests, "unless you imagine that the whole process of drawing up a syllabus, assigning readings and papers, making comments on the results students generate, 'translating' those comments into a number grade, and filing a grade report at the end of the term is just a meaningless ritual, then the social relations that exist in the classroom represent an organization of work whose result is 'value' in some sense" (17).

That value can be concretely identified as a grade, for "you don't report to the registrar that *Paradise Lost* is a revolutionary fusion of contradictory ethical claims, or even that John has a remarkable grasp of English history for a sophomore. You report that 60239 got a 3.8 in Engl 322, which in turn, in a couple of years, is then circulated to the personnel office at Boeing as 60239's prospective employer. There's a chance the workers in the personnel office at Boeing will hear something from 60239 about the fusion of ethical claims in *Paradise Lost,* but not a very good one. They will, however, hear about the 3.8 in Engl 322, which they can read and exchange against any number of similar 'value terms'" (17–18).

From Watkins's perspective, from the point of view of the value that is *circulated* socially as a result of readings of literature, the salient social significance of an exam in literature is that it results in a grade. We may wish to make greater claims, and we may base them on individual testimonies, but the social significance of our work (acculturation) has been diminishing since the late nineteenth century. I do not take as bleak a view as Watkins does, but I believe his analysis is telling. If we are to speak about the social significance of what we do, the values put in circulation by what we do are as good a test as any.

This brings me to the other horn of this second dilemma. What could be significant enough about what we do that it would be circulated as a value? This is a question that, to a startling degree, has been successfully answered by E. D. Hirsch and his followers—we could provide lists of great books, offer digests of them, and index it all in an encyclopedia of important cultural concepts. This strategy could make literature as accessible as pop culture. By the extension of such motives, the Hirschean approach could be modified to commodify the culture in the ways the media have developed for mass entertainment. Then, perhaps, our work will be on the best-seller lists, as Hirsch's has been. Then, finally, our work will be in general circulation like copies of the latest rock albums. Then our exams might take the form of trivial pursuits.

One of the underlying issues Graff pursues in *Beyond the Culture Wars*— whether critics are generalists or specialists—I would formulate in the following question: Do exams in literature train students to be model citizens by shaping their attitudes, or do they train students to be model critics by shaping their methods of inquiry? Though it underlies what I have been saying, I have not yet answered this question. Instead, I have put it into another context wherein it appears as a dilemma. As you might have noticed, the dilemmas of solidarity-divergence and significance-insignificance are simply different perspectives on our ambivalence toward discipline. On the one hand we have inherited a mission to create a national heritage from which a national character might emerge as we shape the attitudes of the citizens we teach by giving them canonical readings. On the other hand we have inherited a long-standing ambition to be as exacting as our neighbor disciplines, the sciences, in our research methods, and to accumulate significant knowledge. As we near the twenty-first century, these two nineteenth-century rationales for our profession have produced a particular dilemma. The more we move toward cultural uniformity by training readers to read alike, the more we move away from the specialization of reading. Yet the more we move toward specialization, the more we move away from diversity. Exams normalize; difference is unexaminable.

The more one examines exams, the less they seem to accomplish what they were designed to do—make critics—and the more their secondary effects—making docile citizens—keep us in business (at least for the time being). If, however, exams do not examine—that is, cannot reliably distinguish between an adequate reading and an inadequate one, are there any grounds for refutation in literary study? If not, what do exams accomplish? This brings me to the topic of the next chapter.

Constructing Intellectuality

CHAPTER 9

n 1936 Cleanth Brooks, together with Robert Penn Warren, published *An Approach to Literature,* the precursor of *Understanding Poetry* (1938), *Understanding Fiction* (1943) and *Understanding Drama* (1945). These texts flourished in the early fifties when both Brooks and Warren were teaching at Yale as colleagues of René Wellek and William Wimsatt. In the interval, Brooks published a classic of critical practice, *The Well Wrought Urn* (1947), which was followed two years later by René Wellek and Austin Warren's *Theory of Literature,* a theoretical justification of the formalism Brooks's practice exemplifies.

Within two decades (1936 to 1957), Cleanth Brooks became one of the best-known practitioners of New Criticism in America. Elmer Borklund remarks that *"The Well Wrought Urn* exerted a good deal of influence during the 1940s and fifties partly because Brooks writes persuasively and partly because the views developed there, simplified and copiously illustrated, form the basis of *Understanding Poetry,* the anthology-cum-commentary which taught generations of American college students . . . what to look for and care about in poems" (92). Furthermore, Brooks's practice was authorized by a well-established group of critics (R. Warren, A. Warren, Wimsatt, and Wellek) who had ties to other well-known figures like John Crowe Ransom and Allen Tate. Their beliefs were effectively disseminated in a series of textbooks, and New Critical questions set the parameters of literary study for at least two generations of literary critics. Yet the assumptions that justified New Critical practices, although made explicit in *Theory of Literature* (and elsewhere), were seldom mentioned in the textbooks that illustrated them. Since the students who used these textbooks did not usually read these theoretical texts, an authoritative group of "implied authors" invisibly governed literary study for nearly thirty years.[1]

This chapter examines the construction of intellectuality in literary criticism by looking at how the Vanderbilt/Yale school of New Criticism trained two generations of literary critics through a set of pedagogically effective textbooks. It links literary study with professional, disciplinary, and institutional interests by showing how New Criticism achieved the status of "normal study" or orthodoxy.[2] By examining documents that do not usually concern historians of literary criticism, namely, textbooks, noting in particular their "margins," we can see how exercises and glossaries inculcated New Critical orthodoxy. In sum, questioning leads to schooling and schooling leads to schools.

Questions

Questions play a crucial role in literary studies. They empower readers. When a reader questions a text, he or she experiences a particular disposition toward it that is expected to lead to some control over it. By comparison with the naive reader, for whom a text is an opaque screen, a critical reader has X-ray vision and can see through it. Unlike readers powerless before the text, a critical reader discloses hidden symbols and illuminates shadowy patterns. To learn these skills, however, one must apprentice oneself to master readers. Their terms tell readers what to look for.

Questions govern the conduct of critical discourse. As speech acts, they invite specific responses. They make others think about a specific topic in a particular manner. Questions proceed from particular warranting assumptions and call for evidence that confirms them. They require the respondent to employ similar warranting assumptions. Answers seem appropriate only when they have the rhetorical and logical structure prescribed by the question. Appropriate responses, in effect, entail norms for critical conduct. By analogy with "normal science," we can speak of "normal study."[3]

Brooks and Warren's "Introduction to Fiction" chapter of *An Approach to Literature* illustrates the way the terms of questions tell readers what to look for in a text. After a series of extended definitions of terms such as "plot," "unity," "logic," "interpretation," "belief," "point of view," "exposition," "conflict," and "climax," an exercise ends the chapter:

1. What is the theme of the story or novel?
2. How can the characters be defined?
3. How are the characters related to the theme?
4. How are the characters related to each other?
5. How does the conflict express the theme?

In order to answer these questions fully, readers have to ask themselves additional questions:

6. At what point does the reader first become aware of the theme?
7. How is the conflict complicated or intensified?
8. Where does the climax occur?
9. Is there a central character?
10. If there is no central character, how is the continuity of interest held?
11. Who tells the story?
12. What is the point of view?
13. How is the point of view indicated in the story?
14. Is it ever shifted in the course of the story?
15. Is it ever inconsistent?
16. How is the exposition handled?
17. What proportions of scene, narrative, and comment are used?
18. Are there transitions of place and time?
19. How are they handled?
20. What is the atmosphere?
21. What means does the writer employ to communicate this atmosphere? (28)

Each question Brooks and Warren ask instructs students to perform a particular task in a special manner. Some questions presuppose operations readers normally perform while reading in private, but many are classroom-specific instructions. For students unfamiliar with Brooks's textbook, the question "What proportions of scene, narrative, and comment are used?" is difficult to answer. Only students using this textbook diligently would know what the terms of the question required.

Questions presuppose reading acts.[4] Each question above instructs a student to generate a distinct kind of reading. When that student becomes a teacher and asks the same questions of his or her students, the questioning begins to have a history. For instance, it is no accident that Hugh Kenner, Brooks's dissertation student at Yale, writes, "All that is in front of the naive student is the poem. . . . A half-hour spent on the doctrines of romanticism insures that meanwhile a dozen odes will die in their entirety. Any strategy for entering directly into the text, and encouraging the strange capacity of its words for engaging one another and absorbing attention, is clearly preferable to a pedagogic habit that lingers amid peripheral data, because in no other way can the life of the poem be saved, the life that alone confers interest on other orders of lore" ("The Pedagogue as Critic" 45).

In Kenner's mode of New Critical reading, words "engage" each other. In this passage he disseminates what he learned from Brooks (probably via I. A. Richards's notion of the interinanimation of poetic language, via Coleridge, which recalls Roman Jakobson's theory of poetic language). The particular "life of the poem" that Kenner's students save is the language of a text; they are not required to enliven poems through their sociopolitical contexts. This is how Kenner was schooled—Brooks and Warren's list lacks historical questions. Critical schooling produces critical schools.

Schooling

Every master teaches his or her apprentice the secrets of the trade. The uninitiated are dumbfounded in the face of tasks skilled performers effortlessly accomplish. The amateur drops, slices, burns, stumbles, accidentally deletes, and otherwise fumbles the task. The pro knows how to pause, hold, sight, move, and otherwise gauge his or her effort. All one's energies are schooled to the task.

Schooling in reading hinges on teaching students warranting terms such as "plot," "unity," "irony," or "Grail quest," which are both frameworks for reading texts and premises for arguing about them.[5] When warrants appear as terms in questions, they instruct students how to read texts as literature. Every question, every instruction, presupposes a framework of instruction, a way of reading the text. How many students would look for "the climax" if they were not instructed to do so? Would they look for ironies and paradoxes? Though they might make sense of the text, would they "look for" its "theme" if not asked to do so?

Warranting terms—or, as they are more idiomatically known, critical frameworks—are intrinsic to the process of reading, since they locate anomalies or "gaps" in texts. Apprentice critics are asked in exams to "fill in" these gaps in a standard manner. As pedagogical devices, questions are the principal instrument of literary training. They normalize critical acts and hence certify the professional reader as a critic who has been tested against a standardized way of reading texts and can be regarded as non-deviant.[6]

Exam questions have the power to qualify a novice reader as an apprentice or certify an apprentice reader as a master. Power ordinarily is defined as "A's ability to get others to act or think in ways which otherwise they would not act or think, specifically *in the ways which maximize A's interests*" (Parenti 5). Because, in order to answer specific questions, apprentice readers must perform these rather than those reading acts, they act and think as the questioner wishes. As Gerald Graff notes in "The Life of the Mind Stuff," such motives do not necessarily maximize students' interests (*Culture Wars* 86–104).[7] Consider, for example, answering the Brooks and Warren question "If there is no central character, how is the continuity of interest held?" To answer this question, students must read the story within the framework of the teacher's conception of textual unity, a practice that schools readers in New Criticism. The question about Conrad's "The Lagoon," "What advantage is there in having Arsat tell the story at the moment of Diamelen's death?" (69), is not one students instinctively ask. Students' conceptions of shifting points of view, if they have any, would not provide the correct answer. Can they answer the question on the basis of common sense? Could we successfully answer the question in Wolfgang Iser's terms? Who decides the parameters of the appropriate answer?

Whose power is it? The teacher exercises power, but only in a delegated form.[8] When teachers borrow textbook questions, they school their pupils in a school whose authority they have borrowed. The insidious aspect of this power is that examiners exercise it in the name of the critical school and rarely have to assume personal responsibility for the conduct the question enforces. For instance, examiners almost never spend the time required to answer their own questions and have little sense of what the questions actually entail. Moreover, the aim of the inquiry is often mystified.

As we saw in the previous chapter, the less clear the warranting concept is in the mind of the questioner, the less explicit its formulation, the less legible the conditions of answering it, the less visible the teacher's power, the more powerless the student. Teachers who claim to believe that reading should be theory-free protect their basis of power by hiding behind "ordinary" terms while examining students. By not making the conditions of a given performance explicit, by keeping the conditions of their power invisible, they give themselves unwarranted authority. This is the characteristic way of exercising power within the institution and is a species of what Bourdieu calls "misrecognition"—mystification.[9] In short, asking questions disciplines students in a profession.

Training in literary study develops the disciplined work habits to which we usually refer as competence, but it also develops professional attitudes. In the scene of the classroom, teachers are not only competent guides for uninformed followers but also confident masters of naive apprentices. Teachers not only have to make students read literature; they have to make them confident readers who value the experience. Evaluators not only ask "Is this performance a good instance of its kind and thus rewardable?" but also (borrowing the notion of "felicity conditions" from speech-act theory) "Is this performance 'sincere'"? From one side we see the professional face of the critic; from the other we see the double or alter ego—his or her disciplined face. The critic is both a professor and a disciple.[10]

When we look at training in literary study as the manipulation of work habits, we are easily led to Foucault's treatment of discipline. For Foucault, the "means of correct training" include "a mechanism that coerces by means of observation," identifiable "offenses," and "punishments" that are "corrective."[11] However, whether we wish to argue that the characteristic mode of training in reading literature is positive or not, discipline is a condition of literary study. Criticism cannot develop without judgments about what sorts of work are valuable (and hence rewardable). Since this is so, it is important to ask, Who authorizes the criteria for rewarding work?

Critical Schools

Prior to the New Critical revolution, criticism was based on external evidence, usually historical. When formalism revamped the institution of criticism, it altered the paradigm of literary argumentation to emphasize internal evidence. This change would have been impossible without *schooling*. The formal analysis of texts (close reading) superseded several varieties of historicism as the orthodox pedagogy in literature classrooms. Such schooling was authorized by a critical school.

But what is a critical school? Is it a school of thought? A school of practice? A school of critics? A theoretical school? The answer is yes in all cases. Practice leads to schooling to schools to movements, each with a history. Brooks's career can be charted by the networks (schools) in which he was taught and taught others. Our understanding of his role in the history of literary studies cannot be separated from our understanding of New Criticism as an orthodox school of thought promulgated at many universities.[12] How did New Criticism supplant its predecessor? One explanation is that the rationales for New Criticism paralleled the rationales for the modern American university in the decades between the two world wars.

In *The Emergence of the American University,* Laurence Veysey establishes that, during the eighteenth and nineteenth centuries, American universities justified themselves in the following ways:

1. The *service* rationale: universities should address themselves to changes in the needs of the general populace and to the condition of their well-being. The modern university should offer the public a practical means of enhancing its social status, while creating an educated citizenry (57–120).
2. The *humanistic* rationale: universities should acquaint their students with their culture (180–251).
3. The *research* rationale: universities should be centers for the accumulation of new knowledge (121–79).

According to Veysey, these three rationales merged at the turn of the century to form the modern university (342–80). They authorized particular roles for faculties.

As both Gerald Graff and Burton Bledstein point out, prior to the 1880s the university professor was a generalist who taught a wide range of subjects in a ministerial manner (Graff, *Professing Literature* 81; Bledstein 171). This role fit the humanistic rationale of the time. Once it merged with the German model of research, the ministerial aspect of the teacher's role disappeared. Profession merged with discipline. The development of professionalism was governed by distinctly disciplinary ideals of learning. Amateurs gave way to experts.

These ideals have been rather consistently identified in the modern university.[13] I mention here the five axioms or doxa of disciplinary study most relevant to the development of literary criticism:

1. *Knowledge can be accumulated.* In the university knowledge can be understood as symbolic capital, a resource provided by the university through its faculty for its students (Parsons & Platt 3, 5).[14]
2. *Knowledge is valuable because it is objective, logical, systematic, and verifiable* (24, 70–71 [definition], 71–72, 73).
3. *Rationality is the ground of validation.* The modern American university maintains standards of rationality (18–19).[15]
4. *Learning is acquiring.* Undergraduates typically learn through the device of "pedagogic" questions, the answers to which are developed higher up in the structure through research and passed down as information acquired by repeating the inquiry already conducted. The assumption is that such an apprenticeship prepares students for life, teaching them to behave in a disciplined manner with respect to sharply defined fields. For students to learn, study has to be generalized in a manageable way, the complexities of actual situations being difficult to comprehend (3, 15, 19, 107–8). In other words, the preconditions of learning include the formalization of research and the universalization of knowledge.
5. *Learning can be evaluated* by examiners who design the questioning process to test students' acquisition of knowledge (108).[16]

An Approach to Literature, which exemplifies New Critical praxis, fits in well with the doxa that define the modern American university as a system of learning. It might be useful at this point to enumerate the ways in which *An Approach* is "authorized" by the rationales and axioms I have delineated.

1. New Criticism obviously teaches students modern rhetoric and close reading, thus clearly fulfilling its obligation to serve them (see Brooks's textbooks). But we should not take its service to the general populace in too narrow a context. One of the principal ways universities serve their students is by shaping unformed subjects into recognizable individuals. The modern university offers members of the general populace a means of achieving their potential as individuals—persons who can be differentiated from their peers by ranked accomplishments.[17] New Critical inquiry allows students to enhance their personal well-being and social status because New Critical readings individualize readers by singling out those students who can be said to have knowledge: "Any person with a healthy love of life wants to develop, through experience, his own possibilities. The study of literature is one of the things that can lead to the discovery of new dimensions of the self" (*An Approach to Literature* 1).

2. New Critical inquiry is grounded in a tradition of humanism qualifying students as members of the culture: "Such a thing as culture exists. . . .

Literature appeals to us . . . insofar as [it] opens a new world for us, and a new view of the old world we have lived in, it also indicates new kinds of response to the world" (1).

3. New Critical inquiry invites disciplinary research in that it places boundaries between literary questioning and other forms of questioning (2) and trains its students in rigorous inquiry.[18] The value of literature is inaccessible except through the "study" of literature—"People do read books and magazines, novels and stories for amusement, of course . . . [but] an understanding of the meaning of literature can come only from a study of literature itself" (2).

Brooks and Warren point out that literature studies the same "realities" other disciplines study but through an autonomous form of understanding. Thus they justify literary study as a discipline in its own right. In "What Literature Is" they contrast an autopsy report, a legal indictment, a newspaper account, and a pop fiction account with a poem about a murder, identifying the last type of writing as the proper object of literary research (1–8).

We can also survey the ways in which *An Approach* incorporates the doxa fundamental to the mode of modern learning:

1. New Critical inquiry allows for the accumulation of knowledge about literature, understood as "advances" in reading a work.[19]
2. New Critical inquiry values insights that are objective, logical, systematic, and verifiable:

   We have concluded that the action of fiction is different from the random piece of action given us by life in that it (1) is unified and complete, (2) has a certain logic of organization, and (3) embodies an interpretation. Indeed, each of these things implies the others, for there cannot be unity in fiction without a logic of organization that does not embody, to a degree at least, some interpretation. Furthermore, we have seen that the discussion of such a thing as the plot or action of a piece of fiction immediately involves the writer's conception of his characters and theme. These things, action, character, and theme, are aspects of a unity which we call the novel or story. The story of the novel gives an effect, an experience; and that experience is what we finally value in fiction. (15)

3. New Critical inquiry validates its claims by way of logical argumentation. Brooks and Warren's "Discussions" make claims, offering passages from works as support for them. They define their warranting terms in "Glossaries."[20]
4. New Critical readings can be treated as acquisitions. Students can recognize readings as "learning" about literature: "Fiction extends [the reader's] experience of life, and at the same time feeds his fundamental curiosity about life and its meaning. Our curiosity about life can take a number of forms. But though they are always involved with

each other in the fictional work, we can separate them out for inspection" (9–10).
5. New Critical inquiry can be tested or examined—textbooks that contain exercises designed to apply its principles presuppose this.[21]

These assumptions about education appear intertextually as themata in Brooks and Warren's praxis. If we examine their "Glossaries," we can identify the axioms of modern education mentioned above as presuppositions. Here, form is the center around which the material of an imaginative work is organized:

> *Form* The arrangement of various elements in a work of literature; the organization of various materials (ideas, images, characters, setting, and the like) to give a single effect. It may be said that a story is successful—that it has achieved form—when all of the elements are functionally related to each other, when each part contributes to the intended effect.[22] Form is not to be thought of merely as a sort of container for the story; it is, rather, the total principle of organization and affects every aspect of the composition. It is the mode in which the story exists.

> *Theme* The special view of life or special feeling about life or special sets of values which constitute the point or basic idea of a piece of literature.

> *Unity* The sense of oneness—of having a total and final meaning.[23]

The axioms we delineated above reappear as themata in these definitions. When literary works are understood to be systematic, coherent structures, it is not surprising to find that they have unity—"total and final meaning," which, of course, makes them "knowledge." Literary works are understood in terms of "themes," views of "life" that contain "values." In Brooks's delineation of his approach, we can discern the profile of the modern critic.

A successful critical approach, it should be noted, attends to the problems readers find during their readings. It generalizes practice without turning it into method reading, a misunderstanding of praxis, which simply reads all texts in the same way. Readers are schooled by such praxes and become members of a group of practitioners. The definitions I have quoted simplify available conceptions of "form" or "unity"—for instance, Wellek and Warren's discussions in their *Theory of Literature*.[24] Nonetheless, if we contrast these terms with Barthes's conception of a text as plural, we can see that they belong to the critical denomination to which we usually refer as New Criticism. When their rationales match those of the institutions that house them, critical practices becomes "normal study." Intellectuality, like sexuality, is socially constructed. In the next chapter I look at this process from the point of view of the subjects involved.

Academic Subjects

CHAPTER 10

Like other persons, critics occupy "subject-positions."[1] They are ranked—assistant, associate, and full. These titles entitle them to a "position" in the institution of criticism and a status relative to other positions. Through the ways critics talk and think about themselves and are talked and thought about, they are subjected to positions relative to others in the hierarchical structure of power relations that makes up the university. Subjects are identified by the positions they occupy.

In Althusser's famous view, we acquire our subject positions by being called to them: "I shall then suggest that ideology . . . 'recruits' subjects . . . or 'transforms' . . . individuals into subjects . . . by *interpellation* or hailing, and which can be imagined along the lines of the most commonplace everyday police (or other) hailing: 'Hey, you there!'" (174). A person so interpellated or hailed recognizes "that the hail was 'really' addressed to him, and that it was *really him* who was hailed (and not someone else)" (174).

A person, by being called a "literary critic" or a "professor of English," is called, or hailed, by the institution in which the terms "critic" and "professor" function. That person recognizes that he or she is, indeed, a professional critic and thus believes in the reality of his or her calling and all it entails within the institution of the university. In Althusser's view, "The existence of ideology and the hailing or interpellation of individuals as subjects are one and the same thing" because ideology, in his view, produces subjects (175). Subjects are positioned by the discursive formations to which they are subjugated.[2] Persons are subject to discourses that position them in particular mappings of a world. Universities map the world by departmentalizing it. Each department studies some aspect of our world; each has as its subject matter a particular field.

It is not accidental that when literary study was first justified as an autonomous field of study to be approached philologically, it became a department devoted to a specific subject matter. Departments, a key in the institutionalization of the professions, are bound historically to the concept of a field. There are several reasons for this development, each of which can be related to the parallel development of specialized disciplines (Veysey 142, 321).[3] The "old-time professor, a jack-of-all disciplines" (Graff's "generalist") was replaced by the "specialist" (Graff's "scholar"). "The dominant characteristic of the new American universities" in the latter decades of the nineteenth century "was their ability to shelter specialized departments of knowledge" (142). The rationale for the administrative strategy of departmentalization is a specialized subject matter or field, and this, as I have already noted, gave rise to what Graff calls the field-coverage principle in literary study. It was Daniel Coit Gilman, the first president of Johns Hopkins, who, as an administrator, took an innovative role in departmentalization. In 1875 he wrote: "I incline more & more to the belief that what is wanted in Baltimore is not a scientific school, nor a classical college, nor both combined; but a faculty of medicine, and a faculty of philosophy: . . . that each head of a great department, with his associates in that department,—say of mathematics, or of Language or of Chemistry or of History, etc. shall be as far as possible free from the interference of other heads of departments" (Veysey 160). Gilman's letter presupposes "autonomous fields of inquiry" known only by the professional specialist in that area. The period that followed his innovative administration of Johns Hopkins witnessed the spread of departments across the American university system. The creation of new departments was deemed justifiable because departments housed autonomous disciplines demarcated from others by their differing fields of inquiry. Veysey notes that in the latter half of the nineteenth century "there was a tendency among the more enterprising students to enter new fields regarded until then as mere sub-specialties of an established discipline, and to develop the specialty into a new discipline. Such a tendency was undeniably visible in the American university during the 1890's; it could be seen at work, for instance, among psychologists and sociologists, the latter having often begun their careers as economists" (321).

Though no longer apparent, the rationale for a university department is disciplinary—a department is the home of an autonomous field of study. Professors of literature were quartered together because they studied a common field. By entering that departmental field, an apprentice could be schooled as a specialist. By subjecting oneself to a specific subject matter, one became a special sort of academic subject.

Academic Subjects and Their Discursive Fields

The notion of a field of study is metaphoric. It suggests a site at which truths can be harvested. It belongs to a tradition of metaphors we have inherited from the nineteenth century:

> The metaphors used to describe scientific knowledge significantly reveal its assumed permanence. Knowledge was an island whose territory was continually being advanced into the ocean of the unknown; knowledge was a great temple, built of monographic bricks (not easily corroded by time or weather). Or, . . . a bit more flexibly, knowledge was a great river. To be sure it sometimes changed its course and left villages high and dry. But the metaphor presumed a basically stable source. A river obeyed the law of gravity and it never turned into a mirage. Such images of knowledge sanctified the researcher as one of the lasting contributors to civilization. The quest on every side was for definitive studies—studies that would never have to be done again. (Veysey 141)

This attitude is common among those who profess literary study. Definitive scholarship is still an active ideal for some students of literature. A belief in the sort of refutability in which Ira Remsen placed his faith is not nowadays everywhere regarded as a myth. What glues this attitude together, binds it in coherence, and sustains the faithful is the conviction that sets of facts exist as a site of knowledge, as a field, as a factual ground requiring special disciplinary techniques suitably applied to yield a harvest of knowledge. From a disciplinary point of view, fields contain objects that can be induced to yield truths by special procedures.

A field is a site that can be visited. The field of literary study, literature, exists at sites we call libraries. Critics traditionally cultivate the facticity of works gathered there as literature. They conveniently divide the labor by assigning themselves rows of books as their special plot in this vast field of study. Earlier workers in the field had accomplished the massive task of clearing up periods, genres, and authors. Still, for traditional scholars there remains an infinity of facts to be researched.[4] In this landscape, texts are objects about which discoveries can be made, adding to the accumulation of knowledge about a field.

When the critics I have termed "modern" speak of criticism, they still assume the field of literature is tilled by the disciplinary techniques of reading.[5] They speak resolutely about knowledge of their fields. They produce research in a specific literary field, published as knowledge of that subject matter. Their interpretive claims are grounded or refuted by the factual stability of such fields in justificatory arguments. Literary works are arti-*facts,* objects thought to be independent of their readers. This traditional construction of them as a subject matter comprised of arti*facts* is misleading. Though artifacts might seem to have laws and constraints on which humanistic fields are defined, these are, on the contrary, *produced by* methods of objectification. Modern literary critics speak as if they deal with something real, something that tells them the way the world is. They justify their work as a way of storing knowledge about literature, a way of preserving a long tradition of humane values.

Like normal science, literary study normalizes those subjected to it. As "normalization operates through the creation of abnormalities which it then must treat and reform" (Dreyfus & Rabinow 195–96), so objectification operates through the creation of subjectivity, which it then must identify as error and correct. Disciplinary mechanisms maintain a discursive field of objects by creating a particular form of subjectivity. When subjects feel a need to incorporate that subjectivity *as their own,* they become "objective." Only subjects can objectify. By submitting to training as a professional reader, a person is disciplined to form a text as if it were an object. Thus the strategy of a disciplinary regime is to correlate the subject's cognitive activity with the discursive formation of the culturally valorized objects called canonical texts. Examinations are one such strategy. Exams, the litmus tests of aberrant subjectivity, fail to do what examiners claim they can do in the case of criticism. Nonetheless, schooled in acknowledging that his or her intuitive claims are false, the critic confesses that he or she has been wrong. If contrite, the critic is obliged to discipline his or her subjectivity. This brings me back, full circle, to my point of departure. Schooling is another term for the formation of subjects. Modern schooling creates subject positions.

The Formation of Objects Called a Subject

The field of literature, as I mentioned above, is tilled by means of the disciplinary techniques of literary study. When modern critics speak of literary study, they ordinarily allude not only to a subject matter but also to a well-formed set of critical practices. The former is usually called German literature, or English literature, and so on; the latter is an approach to it, sometimes associated with a school. As a result of the practices of a school, knowledge about literature is thought to be accumulated and is published as research in the field. In the nineteenth-century academy, for example, the most typical technique for studying literature was philology, on whose production of knowledge "normal" literary study still depends.[6] Like libraries, schools can be visited. A school like New Criticism, for instance, can be studied through an "archaeological" exploration of Vanderbilt, Louisiana State, Kenyon, and Yale, in whose archives we are likely to find vestiges of the earliest forms of New Critical schooling.

Central to the modern view is the factual stability of literary works, on the basis of which interpretive claims can be grounded or refuted.[7] Works of literary merit are objects, arti*facts,* thought to be independent of their readers. Until recently, the modern notion of a field of study seemed rational; however, from the perspective of Foucault's work, we can ask ourselves, What if objects are the result of objectivity, just as sex is the result of sexuality? Though it might seem to have its own laws and constraints whereupon scientific and humanistic fields are defined, an object is something that, on the contrary, is *produced* by the apparatus of objectivity. Once we consider that the field called "literature" is an "enunciative field" (Racevskis 70–73), the traditional view of it as a field of knowledge collapses as quickly as a house of cards, one built by a supreme illusion. If, for instance, we view literary study as a discipline that controls the production of discourse, "fixing its limits" (Foucault, *Archaeology of Knowledge* 224), then literature is a library, a way of cataloging discourse by grouping together discursive forms that schools perceive as a common object because they have produced it by a constellation of disciplinary and nondiscursive social practices (Dreyfus & Rabinow 59–67). Literary objects, in Foucault's terms, would be relations "established between institutions, economic and social processes, behavioral patterns, systems of norms, techniques, types of classification, modes of characterization" (*Archaeology of Knowledge* 45) that make references possible. A space unfolds—a library—which, again in Foucault's terms, might be called a "field of statements." Just as various "economic, political, familial, institutional, architectural, pedagogical, and discursive relations coalesce into the modern university only because of something which has been called 'the idea of the university'" (Dreyfus & Rabinow 66), so similar relations coalesce only because of something called "literature."

However, what we take to be literature, how we approach it, and what we do with it in classrooms is a part of a discursive formation that includes economic and social practices that do not allow for its autonomy. Edward Said's *Orientalism,* in showing how the field of orientalism is intimately linked to nonliterary discursive practices, is a brilliant illustration of this phenomenon. In "The Rhetoric of Survival: The Germanist in America from 1900–1925," Henry Schmidt shows how the study of German literature was suddenly and arbitrarily reshaped in order that Germanists could remain institutionally viable while America was at war with Germany. David Shumway shows in *Creating American Civilization* how the emergence of the field was bound to available discursive formations.[8]

Literature as a field is not only impermanent but also unstable—the literary works that constitute it are themselves constituted by readers. A set of words is objectified once it is identified as a literary work, but it does not become a subject for study until it is made into an interrelated set of literary signs. Here we must distinguish between *the literary work,* the social activity that defines a set of words as literature by locating it in a discursive formation, and *the literary text,* the private activity that transforms it into literary signs (Dreyfus & Rabinow 62). Whereas the work is an object formed by discursive social practices that are public, the text is a subject formed by the performance of reading acts. Literary study is thus the practice that informs a given performance of reading.

The literary text, as distinguished from the literary work, is, borrowing Kenneth Burke's term for the moment, a "symbolic action" whose constitutive act is the identification between a reader and an array of words formed as an extension of a subject-*activity* (*Philosophy of Literary Form* 8–16). In this view, readers project their subjection onto works, making them texts. Moreover, the projection (knowing) is strategic, motivated by a particular outcome desired by a given reader. The text is an extension of the reading subject and is the subject matter (in the sense of the subject materialized) of that reading. The reader as subject is characterized by discursive forms that make that reader who he or she is. His or her performances as a reader become articulate as verbal formations that make a work significant, that is, render it a text, a subject materialized in the reading. Literature, as a subject matter, a field of study, has as its precondition the objectification of subjection.

This modern view of literature has been sustained for at least a century. How so? In the next section I will argue that the key is literary training, a disciplinary technique. The discipline of literary study involves the correlative notions of a subject matter and a mode of addressing it. Fields, as intellectual constructs, are maintained by schooling. The precondition for schooling apprentices in objectivity is their resolve to discipline their subjectivities. This is the theme of the next section.

The Formation of Subjects Called Objective

In order to sustain a discursive field of objects, disciplinary mechanisms, having created a particular form of subjectivity, become operative when subjects feel a need to subjugate that subjectivity *as their own.* Thus, the strategy of a disciplinary regime is to objectify the subject-*activity* as a correlative to the discursive formation of objects. As Dreyfus and Rabinow point out, Foucault's analysis of the Panopticon "as the paradigmatic example of a disciplinary technology" shows how power operates "by inducing in the inmate a state of objectivity, a permanent visibility" (188–89). The examination is "the technical heart of these new procedures" (173).

The professionalization of literary studies is bound up with the technique of giving exams that allegedly test the student's knowledge of a given subfield. But even from the outset, exams failed to do this. In his history of the American university, Veysey writes,

> After midcentury, social pressures began pushing hard against the immature state of academic culture. Increasingly after 1840, for instance, both parents and students expected competitive written examinations. Now grades and honors placed the emphasis in American education on personal achievement, the individual desire to succeed, and the race between students. But an effective plan of examinations, grades, merit rolls, and scholarships awarded by the college required a professionally competent faculty in which the members individually shared the values of competition, ambition, achievement, and success. (271–72)

The introduction of examinations into the university curriculum was not greeted with applause. Students went on a rampage against them at Harvard in 1790 and "claimed that they had not entered college with this understanding, and when their petition was denied one student threw a stone into the examination room" (272). But, as the nineteenth century progressed, students eventually became convinced that exams and grades were fair and necessary. (We might speculate that this came about when students learned to believe in "objectivity.")

Exams about literature standardize it through the objectification of the subject-*act*ivity of reading. Questions on exams about literature call for answers that make appropriate specific critical performances. By doing so, they normalize literary study by asking students to treat certain works as sets of facts, as evidence for their readings, a procedure that has as its precondition the notion of a field as a set of objects.[9] Such exams fail to do what examiners claim they can do, suggesting that their survival points to success in terms of some other, hidden agenda—exams are forms of confession.

As we noted previously, the more one examines exams, the less they seem likely to accomplish what they have been allegedly designed to do: test a student's knowledge of the subfields of literature.[10] Why then have they survived? Following the insights of Foucault, we might consider that they succeed in accomplishing a hidden agenda, namely, they do not determine that their subjected subject recognizes an object, but they determine that the subject does not object to the practice of objectification (normal study). They render subjects objective, that is, docile. The expectation that students will demonstrate knowledge of a subfield such as eighteenth-century British literature by readings of canonized works can be realized only on the condition that there are acceptable and unacceptable readings. The traditional assumption of examining committees is that readings are testable knowledge. When students successfully provide the established readings and commentaries, they are given credentials authorizing them as specialists in a given subfield and allowed to identify themselves as such in their curricula vitae. Hiring, tenuring, and promoting all depend on the process of submitting credentials, a form of submission to the conventional wisdom of the discipline. Exam committees are precursors of departmental hiring and tenuring committees. Examiners are precursors of editors and publishers, who seek the advice of experts in various subfields. In this relentless process of examination and reexamination of field-dependent credentials, the crucial disciplinary strategy is to make the subject subjected to his or her subjectivity.

Exams are confessions. As Foucault makes clear in his *History of Sexuality,* "the medical examination, the psychiatric investigation, the pedagogical report, and family controls may have the overall and apparent objective of saying no to all wayward or unproductive sexualities" (45). "For Foucault, the nineteenth-century medical examination, like other forms of circumscribed confession, exposed to figures of authority the individual's deepest sexual fantasies and hidden practices. Moreover, the individual was persuaded that through such a confession, it was possible to know himself" (Dreyfus & Rabinow 173–74). Internalized as an attitude, objectivity produces a stable field of study, in effect, by punishing persons, by teaching them to believe that subjectivity is erroneous. It is effective as a disciplinary technology only to the extent that subjects are subjected to their subjectivity, to the extent they feel they have *truly* come to know who they are and are penitent. A regime of objectivity can be effective in a virtual field such as literature only when subjects feel subjugated by their own subjectivity. As Dreyfus and Rabinow remark,

> The key to the technology of the self is the belief that one can, with the help of experts, tell the truth about oneself. It is a central tenet not only in psychiatric sciences and medicine, but also in the law, in education, in love. The conviction that truth can be discovered through the self-examination of consciousness and the confession of one's thoughts and acts now appears so natural, so compelling, indeed so self-evident, that it seems unreasonable to posit that such self-examination is a central component in a strategy of power. This unseemliness rests on our attachment to the repressive hypothesis; if the truth is inherently opposed to power, then its uncovering would surely lead us on the path to liberation. (175)

Persons who fail exams are not hired, are fired, receive rejection letters on the basis of an examination of their credentials in a given field, and have difficulty in maintaining self-esteem. In such "failures," one allegedly discovers the "truth" about oneself in the admission of one's mistakes and fears a lack of expertise in a field. Having confessed the lack, the candidate forms a desire to conform to the standard view of the field. When subjects believe the image in the mirror of their confessions, they become objective. Through the combined disciplinary techniques of the objectification of a subject and the subject's subjection to the objective, the discipline of literary study intensifies its hold on us.

Because in this chapter I have taken a postmodern perspective on the question of disciplinarity, identifying discipline with modern criticism, it seems necessary to end it on a cautionary note. Much of what I have said can be taken in either of two ways: on the one hand, it can be read as a critique of modern literary criticism; on the other, it can be read as an ironic commentary on postmodern criticism. As I noted in chapter 1, many postmodern critics have modern skeletons in their closets. Exams, you might remember from my earlier remarks, are the biggest skeleton in the postmodern closet. To become critics, postmoderns must confess the sins of their subjectivity by submitting to exams no less than do modern critics. Further, critics (like myself) who think of themselves as postmodern have to flinch every time they give an exam. For similar reasons, they should also flinch when they try to falsify the views of other critics in the competition for the scarce rewards the academy offers; this is the topic of my next chapter.

Truth Wars

CHAPTER 11

Perhaps one of the most infelicitous New Critical utterances was a statement made by John Crowe Ransom in "Criticism Inc.": "It is from the professors of literature, in this country the professors of English for the most part, that I should hope eventually for the *erection* of intelligent standards of criticism" (328; italics mine). He goes on to remark about our need to be more "scientific, or precise and systematic" (328). It is easy to forget not only that the professors to whom he refers were predominantly men but also that they wanted to "erect" systematic procedures to make literary studies a better fit in universities designed to house disciplines. They were responding to what Laurence Veysey has called "the emergence of the American university."

By the late nineteenth century, as we have seen in the preceding chapters, an intellectualized conception of discipline led institutions of higher learning to reorganize along disciplinary lines, and this, in turn, led to a significant structural change that produced what is often called the modern American university. The pattern I have traced is now worn well enough that it can be followed quickly: The rise of the professions led to the development of disciplines of study, which led to the creation of departments to house them. For the most part, the organization of a newly formed study as a discipline was modeled on the successful institutionalization of scientific research. Literary studies followed this pattern. Before the turn of the century, philology gave literary study the disciplined appearance of a science of literature. Then literary history did the same. New Criticism gives us a more recent legacy of attempts to reformulate literary studies as a discipline. The overt intention of New Critical theory, in classics like "The Intentional *Fallacy*" (italics mine) or *Theory of Literature,* was to make literary criticism objective, reliable, verifiable, and so on.

But it is that *men* endeavored to make criticism a discipline along scientific lines that most interests me in this chapter. I presuppose a tie between the institutional construction of intellectuality (which I discussed in the preceding two chapters) and the social construction of sexuality, in this case masculinity. Structured hierarchically on the basis of a reward system, universities tend to produce intensely competitive critics. Their prototype is the persona Marc Fasteau calls "the male machine,"

> a special kind of being, different from women, children, and men who don't measure up. He is functional, designed mainly for work. He is programmed to tackle jobs, override obstacles, attack problems, overcome difficulties, and always seize the offensive. He will take on any task that can be presented to him in a competitive framework, and his most important positive reinforcement is victory. . . . This ideology makes competition the guiding principle of moral and intellectual, as well as economic, life. It tells us that the general welfare is served by the self-interested clash of ambitions and ideas. (1)

Like his business counterpart, the male-machine critic is programmed to win the reward, counter rivals, and take on tasks in which he can be challenged and emerge victorious. The discipline of the critic emanates from a competitive rather than a cooperative ethos.

Though women have argued for the value of literary study as a discipline, the canonical theoretical statements are made by men. The unselfconscious maleness of their insistence on a science of criticism is notable. As Gayle Greene and Coppelia Kahn remind us, "a male perspective, assumed to be 'universal,' has dominated fields of knowledge" (1–2). Literary criticism is no exception. Consider, for example, I. A. Richards, John Crowe Ransom, and René Wellek.

Richards wished to put literary criticism on the solid footing of a discipline. As Elmer Borklund points out, Richards began his career "by virtually dismissing the entire critical tradition" prior to him (440). Richards writes: "A few conjectures, a supply of admonitions, many acute isolated observations, some brilliant guesses, much oratory and applied poetry, inexhaustible confusion, a sufficiency of dogma, no small stock of prejudices, whimsies and crochets, a profusion of mysticism, a little genuine speculation, sundry stray inspirations, pregnant hints and *apercus;* of such as these, it may be said without exaggeration, is extant critical theory composed" (*Principles of Literary Criticism* 6).

Simultaneously, in America, John Crowe Ransom took a similar view but couched it in business terms, unwittingly reflecting the extent to which universities had become corporations:

> Professors of literature are learned but not critical men. . . . Neverthe-
> less, it is from the professors of literature, in this country the professors
> of English for the most part, that I should hope eventually for the erec-
> tion of intelligent standards of criticism. It is their business. Criticism
> must become more scientific, or precise and systematic, and this means
> that it must be developed by the collective and sustained effort of
> learned persons—which means that its proper seat is in the universi-
> ties. . . . Rather than occasional criticism by amateurs, I should think
> the whole enterprise might be seriously taken in hand by professionals.
> Perhaps I use a distasteful figure, but I have the idea that what we need
> is Criticism, Inc., or Criticism, Ltd. ("Criticism Inc." 328–29)

Wellek believed we were still recovering from "a disaster." For him, literary criticism, which had been "taken over by politically oriented journalism" during the nineteenth century, became "degraded to something
purely practical, serving temporal ends." "The critic," he laments in "Literary Theory, Criticism, and History," "becomes a middleman, a secretary,
even a servant, of the public" (3). A decade after the publication of *Theory
of Literature,* he complained that literary scholars were too much on the
defensive: "Our whole society is based on the assumption that we know
what is just, and our science on the assumption that we know what is true.
Our teaching of literature is actually also based on aesthetic imperatives,
even if we feel less definitely bound by them and seem much more hesitant
to bring these assumptions out into the open. The disaster of the 'humanities' as far as they are concerned with the arts and literature is due to their
timidity in making the very same claims which are made in regard to law
and truth" (17). Unfortunately, something of a masculinist bias emerges in
his examples when he goes on to say, "Actually we do make these claims
when we teach *Hamlet* or *Paradise Lost* rather than Grace Metalious. . . .
But we do so shamefully, apologetically, hesitatingly. There is, contrary to
frequent assertions, a very wide agreement on the great classics: the main
canon of literature. There is an insuperable gulf between really great art
and very bad art: between say 'Lycidas' and a poem on the leading page of
the *New York Times,* between Tolstoy's *Master and Man* and a story in *True
Confessions*" (17–18).

In a somewhat different vein, Wellek defends the possibility not only of
correct interpretations but also of correct evaluations. Though the complexity of art might make interpretation difficult, he stresses that

> this does not mean that all interpretations are equally right, that there
> is no possibility of differentiating between them. There are utterly fan-
> tastic interpretations, partial, distorted interpretations. We may argue
> about Bradley's or Dover Wilson's or even Ernest Jones' interpretation
> of *Hamlet:* but we know that Hamlet was no woman in disguise. The
> concept of adequacy of interpretation leads clearly to the concept of the

> correctness of judgment. Evaluation grows out of understanding; cor-
> rect evaluation out of correct understanding. There is a hierarchy of
> viewpoints implied in the very concept of adequacy of interpretation.
> Just as there is correct interpretation, at least as an ideal, so there is cor-
> rect judgment, good judgment. (18)

For Wellek, the only factor that could keep literary criticism from being a
"secretary" to the public was falsification. That we could correctly understand that "Hamlet was no woman in disguise" would allow us to make
the "good judgment" that *True Confessions* was degrading. In Wellek's view,
the study of literature was *Literaturwissenschaft,* "systematic knowledge."

In retrospect, it is remarkable still that the main opponents to New
Criticism in the sixties did not question the view that literary criticism,
even though it could not muster exacting objectivity, should be modeled
on the sciences. They regarded New Criticism as not scientific enough.
Northrop Frye, in his "Polemical Introduction" to *Anatomy of Criticism,*
outflanks the New Critics by arguing the case for a science of literature
rather than for a scientific method of interpretation. E. D. Hirsch's *Validity
in Interpretation* critiques the theory of "the intentional fallacy" by arguing
that we can validly determine intention. In the sixties, when anti–New
Critical ferment began, system and method were, nonetheless, privileged
terms. The most wide-scale attempt to make criticism into a science belonged to a movement that would have supplanted New Criticism by making its scientific tendencies explicit, namely, structuralism. It is now an
often-told tale how structuralism engendered poststructuralism.

To poststructuralist or postmodern critics, whose intellectual formation
is deeply indebted to feminism,[1] modern theories of criticism are phallo/
logocentric. In his *The Pleasure of the Text,* for instance, Roland Barthes ironically invites us to

> imagine someone (a kind of Monsieur Teste in reverse) who abolishes
> within himself all barriers, all classes, all exclusions, not by syncretism
> but by simple discard of that old specter: *logical contradiction;* who mixes
> every language, even those said to be incompatible; who silently accepts
> every charge of illogicality, of incongruity; who remains passive in the
> face of Socratic irony (leading the interlocutor to the supreme disgrace:
> *self-contradiction*) and legal terrorism (how much penal evidence is based
> on a psychology of consistency!). Such a man would be the mockery of
> our society: court, school, asylum, polite conversations would cast him
> out: who endures contradiction without shame? Now this anti-hero ex-
> ists. (3)

For the most part, modern criticism is based on the notion that readings
can be objective, impersonal, and detached, that there is a discipline of
literary criticism. Though traditional critics differ widely in their assump-

tions about interpretation, they appear similar in their logocentrism when contrasted with postmodern critics. Working within this system, modern critics contend that their readings are demonstrable because textual or contextual evidence can show that rival readings are not logically supported. Since readings that are accepted as true at an earlier moment in time can at a later date be shown to be false, the engine of this system is falsification. New readings supplant old readings. This is a familiar pattern to anyone studying literature. Most critics strive to come up with new readings and, in order to do so, have to clear their paths by falsifying the previously accepted ones. To our postmodern sensibilities, the theory of falsification, exemplified in the tendency among traditional critics to identify the fallacies of their rivals, is recognizably modern. And, as I noted earlier, the term "modern" refers to the historical period characterized by the infusion of discipline (in Foucault's sense) into the structure of Western society. In modern literary criticism, to be disciplined is to argue with sufficient rigor to refute critical counterclaims.

Critics, including postmoderns, are usually judged by the success of their arguments. Their merits are therefore often indirectly measured by the degree to which they have falsified their rivals' claims and the degree to which their own arguments are deemed falsifiable. In literary studies, falsification takes the general form of the judgment "Professor X is mistaken/incorrect/wrong when he says . . ." (As I noted in chapter 2, postmodern critics utter such statements, thus rattling the bones of the modern skeletons in their closets.) The falsification of critical judgments makes evaluations, promotions, and other academic awards possible. Moreover, these uses of the notion of falsification depend on a belief that governs the modern institution of criticism, namely, that a claim about a text can be proven false. Thus a belief in a critical orientation can be seen as tantamount to faith in "the truth of the text" (de Man's remark about the irreducible authority of the text comes to mind).

The term "falsificity," which I use ironically, identifies the particular conflation of errors on which the modern institution of criticism is based. Falsificity is the principle that it is logically wrong (and therefore culpable and punishable) to mistake the incorrect for the correct. Falsification parallels Gerald Graff's field-coverage principle as an institutional device that produces patterned isolation, since it drives critics apart and makes it difficult to connect their views. According to this principle, to submit as criticism an illogical or "unjustified" discourse (however otherwise reasonable) is wrong and hence must be punished—marked by an F, cast out of editorial houses, denied an award, or deemed a heretical practice. In other words, what characterizes modern literary criticism is a principle of falsificity.

The institutional construction of intellectuality (discussed in chapter 9) involves a correlative construction of sexuality. The instance I offer here as an example is competition, a target of feminist critique for decades and "a feminist taboo"[2] in the "sexual/textual politics"[3] of the academy. This masculine trait of the disciplined critic, his competitiveness, demands re-investigation. In the present academy, competitiveness and argumenta-tiveness are inextricable. One climbs the ladder of career success in literary study by competing with rival critics for similar awards. This mode of ca-reerism is masculine.

The Construction of Intellectual Sexuality

Literary criticism is a career. Like other careers invented in the nineteenth century, it changed the lives of *men* because it articulated *their* aspirations as ambitions. Burton Bledstein describes the shift in the sense of the pur-posefulness of a man's life during the nineteenth century as a shift away from a belief in a "calling" to a choice of a "career," a shift easily discerned in changing ways ministers, lawyers, doctors, and educators spoke about their professions. A "calling" was not the choice of a person, but a career most certainly was. Bledstein's remark that a career was a choice for "young men" leaves unspoken that it was not a choice for women.

The shift Bledstein describes was hierarchically and competitively con-figured not merely as a change in status and roles provoked by analogies to ladders and races, but also as a change in the social construction of mascu-linity provoked by images of gentlemen:

> The inner intensity of the new life oriented toward a career stood in con-trast to that of the older learned professional life of the eighteenth and early nineteenth centuries. In the earlier period such external attributes of gentlemanly behavior as benevolence, duty, virtue, and manners cir-cumscribed the professional experience. Competence, knowledge, and preparation were less important in evaluating the skills of the profes-sional than were dedication to the community, sincerity, trust, perma-nence, honorable reputation, and righteous behavior. The qualifying cre-dentials of the learned professionals were honesty, decency, and civility. (173)

The career professional, by contrast, thought in terms of advancement. The nineteenth-century gentleman gave way to the twentieth-century busi-nessman, who prospered in "a competitive society in which unrestrained individual self-determination undermined traditional life styles" (174).

Bledstein remarks that in the development of nineteenth-century pro-fessionalism, ambitious men were instrumental in "structuring our disci-pline according to a distinct vision—the vertical one of career" (ix). From this point of view, the development of literary study matches Bledstein's delineation of the relationship between the growth of the university and the rise of professionalism. To become a literary scholar is to be professionalized, to take part in a social process involving the interjection of an "intellectual competitiveness." The masculine qualities of exemplary male professors were imitated and became the traits of an idealized career profile. Exemplary male professors became role models for success within the structure of the academy, a phenomenon that shaped the field of literary study as we now know it.[4] We are the heirs of roles explicitly designed for the new gentleman, the businessman.

The history of literary study, as I have argued elsewhere,[5] can be understood as the collective biography of exemplary *male* academic figures. The crisscrossing movement of their careers influenced the newly developing field of literary study. Its historical development is, in most respects, an account of these critical movements, which are usually associated with key *men* who inspired schools of thought. Figures like Child, Brooks, and Lanson are historically significant because they became exemplary figures. These men were exemplary because, in doing what they believed ought to be done, they became examples for others. Modern literary study developed as a profession to the extent that the manner in which a particular *man* studied literature was widely imitated, to the extent that *a man's way* of doing criticism or scholarship became a trait in the composite profile of the ideal professor of literature. Invariably, *men* were the models underlying the ideal profile of the scholar-critic at specific junctures in the development of literary studies. Over time, this idealized career profile became a composite of masculine traits derived from the superimposition of the portrayals of exemplary male scholars. Women working in the academy, in order to succeed in their careers, had to acquire these traits. As Hélène Cixous reminds us, a discourse "signed with a woman's name doesn't necessarily make a piece of writing feminine. It could quite well be masculine writing" (52).

Nowadays, to be a professional critic authorized by the institution of criticism still requires submission to an idealized career profile whose masculinity derives from male models. Since this profile is nowhere made explicit as such and in toto, I have called it the *Magister Implicatus* in *Token Professionals and Master Critics* to personify and thus concretize the sum total of performances now demanded for accreditation as a professional critic.[6] As we currently know him, the *Magister Implicatus* is a personification of an ideal male career. At present he stands for the professionalization of the male scholar from the very first exam through various forms of discipline to the final authorization of his work. In his traditional guise, he is the personification of the patriarchal institution, the site for training, disciplining, and schooling men. It is his male interests that are served when critics are bonded to the patriarchal institution.

Because careers allow for professional advances along a ladder of institutional success (degrees, salaries, ranks, etc.), the *Magister* through his exemplariness inspires critics to compete with one another for awards. It is on this one trait of the *Magister Implicatus,* his competitiveness, that I will focus attention.

Falsificity: A Mindless, Man-Driven Theory Machine

In the present academy, competitiveness and falsificity are inextricably bound together. Critics are judged by the successes of their arguments, whose merits are measured by the falsification of rival claims. "And merit is, of course, determined by competition. How else?" (Longino 253).[7] The success of a critic is therefore inextricably linked with the extent to which he competes with rival critics.

Competition is usually defined as a striving for a certain object, position, prize, and so on, usually in accordance with fixed rules. Rule-governed striving is the generating principle of career success. Each juncture of the career path presents to the careerist a goal for which he must compete—a grade, a degree, a job, a promotion, a grant, and so on. In every case, the competitor is judged on the merit of his critical arguments. Hence, if we consider that arguments displace earlier arguments through falsification, the successful competitor is the successful falsifier. Falsification and competitiveness are isomorphic in this system.

As Helen Longino points out in her essay "The Ideology of Competition," "competition always involves a contest among individuals seeking the same thing when not all can obtain it" (250). Some competitions, she argues, are based on the availability of a single prize, as in a race where there is only one first prize. As a consequence, the salient factor is differences in abilities of the contestants. Such competitions are staged to establish who is the best in a particular performance. There are many examples in literary criticism—competing for a job, a grant, an award. In other competitions the scarcity of the object sought (the reward) creates a "survival of the fittest" context and the game has to be played until winners are determined. In literary criticism, competing for publications, jobs, promotions, and salaries has the structure of a win/lose (vs. prize) competition. In this type of competition the salient factor is not necessarily ability but perseverance, fortitude, endurance, doggedness, and so on.

When we look at literary criticism as an institution through the lens of competition, that is, when we study the ways in which critical argumentation has been institutionalized as a competition, a peculiar distortion of critical inquiry comes to light. In order to decide between winners and losers in the various career games we all play, administrators, in choosing to focus on the success of critical arguments, force critics to reify their understanding. Knowledge, as Pierre Bourdieu argues, becomes "symbolic capital" (*Outline* 171–83). What we know has to be quantifiable, measurable, and therefore cumulative. We might say that intuitions have to be converted into information in order to be accumulated. In this system, the goal of criticism is to accumulate objective knowledge, hence the critic who has accumulated the most knowledge gets the most rewards. Central to this system is falsification.

Let's take Graff's example of the OMP (old male professor) and the YFP (young female professor). The OMP believes that X is the meaning of poem "Dover Beach." He argues his case on the grounds of the beliefs A, B, and C, which he takes to be factual. The YFP believes that y is the meaning of "Dover Beach." She argues her case on the grounds of a, d, and q. What are the OMP's options? Well, obviously, he could agree. He could say, "I was mistaken in believing B and C." If he does so, he admits his reading is false and he is no longer eligible for an institutional reward. False arguments are not rewarded. So in order to maintain his reading, the OMP has to say either that d and q are irrelevant or that not-d and not-q are the facts. In other words, to survive the competition among readers, he must maintain his beliefs; otherwise he admits to error and loses status or merit.

In *The Psychology of Intelligence,* Jean Piaget terms "assimilation" the form of intellection I have just described, namely, the tendency to assimilate all new experiences into the cognitive frameworks one already possesses. He contrasts this mode of intellection with "accommodation," wherein inquirers allow new experiences to break down the frameworks they are accustomed to using. It can be safely said that the institution of criticism encourages assimilation. It does not help your career to go around explaining how you are in error.

Considering that the institution of criticism encourages assimilation and therefore falsification as the cognitive strategies best suited to the accumulation of knowledge (information), we might, recalling Cixous's use of "the proper," term this cognitive style "appropriation."[8] Appropriation is the acquisition of knowledge understood as an entity (identities, samenesses; i.e., information). It is the assimilation of concepts into a governing framework. Appropriation is an arrogation, a confiscation, a seizure of concepts. Ideas can be owned and sold at will. They are proper-ties. A contrasting mode of intellection, like intuition, a term I prefer to the term "insight,"[9] often involves the in-appropriate, the disconcerting, and so on. Intuitions are unspecifiable.[10] Intuitions are multiple, diverse, ad hoc, and diffuse. Whereas logical problems have single solutions, intuited problems have plural solutions and often appear illogical. Intuited problems are therefore in-appropriate because painful, humiliating, disconcerting. Moreover, intuitions are not appropriable, making them even more in-appropriate because nothing gets accumulated.

Ostensibly, for most postmoderns the veracity of criticism is not a matter of logic (that skeleton stays in the closet). Thought is not single, unified, centered, present. Though I cannot rehearse postmodern critiques of logocentrism here, I believe I am not alone in thinking that texts do not provide a factual ground to interpretive claims, that writers and readers are discursive subjects who cannot be codified, that distinctions between correct and incorrect are purely conventional, that truth is a signifier like all others. In short, in postmodern theorizing, the very possibility of falsification is thoroughly undermined as an intellectual endeavor (which does not prevent pomo critics from practicing refutation).

If falsification does not lead to objective knowledge, then why do we continue to accept it? Obviously, it serves some other purpose (and accounts for the existence of pomo closets). In the case of traditional criticism, the purpose is to regulate competition. Competition always requires rules. Falsification is the governing rule. Thus modern criticism is no more than a competition governed by an arbitrary rule interpreted by those institutionally empowered to do so. Falsificity is a mechanism of a disciplinary apparatus to regulate competition. In an academic context, regulation of competition refers to the rules that govern the attribution of merit to critical performances. Every competition has to have fixed rules to ensure that someone will win. Falsification is a regulating mechanism in the sense that it is like tagging the person who is "it." Falsifying reminds one of the fiction boys use in childhood war games—when an enemy is shot, the victor shouts "You're dead!" and moves on to surprise the next opponent. Falsification is a similar device used by successful competitors to establish their progress (over the corpses of rival critics) along the way to winning. In critical games, though rationalized as a reward for possessing "the best idea" among one's opponents, the competition is for a grade, a degree, a job, a publication, a promotion, a grant, an appointment. The awarding of these prizes in no way guarantees the value of the inquiry. Another irony in this system is that whereas rules—like falsification—are designed to regulate, to keep under control the aggression involved, they have the effect of increasing it. Falsification, though construed as a regulator, functions only as a measurement of the logicality and frequency of successful counterclaims; hence it has the effect of multiplying falsifications.

This system intensifies competition and leads to what I call intellectual machismo, the tendency toward an exaggerated expression of competition for the acquisition and appropriation of ideas. It is an exercise of power. In this sense it is an instance of domination. The instigator, the person who picks the fight, confirms his sense that he is better than his rival, often by creating a situation in which the rival, taken by surprise, is overwhelmed. In this scenario knowledge is power. Oddly, since it is an intellectually trivial pursuit, this war game has the character of a parlor game. The machismic critic scores by knowing the most recent article, the exact date, the most stinging review, the precise reference, the received opinion, and so on. A side effect of these games is that it becomes impossible for the critic whose intellectual style is machismic to admit error. It is regarded as a fault, an embarrassment. This is a ridiculous posture. Ironically, the machismic intellectual, by telling what is obviously a kind of lie, places himself in a ludicrous position if he wishes finally to reach some understanding. Nevertheless, the machismic intellectual's discourse is permeated by utterances like "Professor X is wrong." Because, in the institution of criticism, falsification is bound up with the notion of "wrong-doing," intellectual machismo has a Rambo effect. The heroic critic is obligated morally to rescue thinkers from the prisons of illogic, to stand up to illogic when no one else cares. He is armed to the teeth with falsifications. Nothing but his self-esteem is left in his wake. He is the supreme falsifier, appropriator, assimilator.

Assimilation, the hallmark of appropriation, mechanizes falsification. When undertaken aggressively, it becomes a machine that falsifies everything in its path. The machine is a simple idea-mower, a handy procrustean mechanism. The machismic intellectual already has a set of beliefs to encompass his world. When he encounters someone else's belief, one of two events occurs. Either the announced belief squares with his own and can be assimilated as a confirmation of what he already believes, in which case verification occurs as a kind of negative falsification (I'm right, so he's wrong); or, as is more often the case, the announced belief does not square with his and is assimilated into his belief system as an error. In the latter instance, the Ramboist (this is, after all, a school of thought that needs a name) finds counterevidence in his stock of beliefs, or identifies a lapse in logic, or invokes an authority (someone who believes what he believes). In short, since he cannot accommodate a belief that is inconsistent with his belief system, it enters his framework as a false belief. In his Ramboistic war games, critical arguments are not distinguishable from quarrels. Quarreling is "a dispute or disagreement, especially one marked by anger and deep resentment" and "implies heated verbal strife" that "often suggests continued hostility as a result" (*Webster's New World Dictionary*). This describes the Ramboistic criticism (faultfinding) in which machismic critics engage.

Though arguments are said to be logical, dispassionate, detached, impersonal, objective, and so on, and in this sense can be regarded culturally as masculine, looked at closely, especially in the light of a critique of falsification, the arguments offered by critics, as the MURGE project showed, are surprisingly difficult to distinguish from quarrels. Oddly, the more one examines arguments, the more one finds quarrels. Similarly, the more one looks at intuition and the confession of error, the more it looks like a strong, incisive, powerful mode of knowing.

Falsification is little more than a competitive tactic governed by arbitrary rules interpreted by those institutionally empowered to do so. Falsificity is, speaking metaphorically, a regulator, a mechanism of a disciplinary apparatus to control competition, a machine. The very mechanism that would ensure replicability and thus establish literary study as a "true" discipline merely regulates the careerist impulse in literary study.

Competition in humanistic study presents a double bind, especially for women: compete with your colleagues cooperatively. At a more fundamental level, this bind works more viciously: falsify knowledge in order to understand—an epistemological equivalent of "Make war for peace."

If, as I have argued, such rationales for professing a discipline of modern literary study are questionable, how is it that they have such a long and enduring tradition? How is it that disciplinary practices seem the natural way of doing things? How is it that pomo critics inconsistently continue these practices? In part, the answer to these questions is bound up with our willingness to accept the aims of the modern university that employs us. At a time of immense cultural shifts—economic, social, and technological—it may be time to rethink our aims.

Through a Postmodern Lens

CHAPTER 12

When I look through a postmodern lens at what we do as critics, the thought that we have a common goal, that we are aiming at a single target, seems troubling. On the one hand, if we had an aim, it would restrict what many critics could or might do; it would set up a target everyone had to hit. On the other hand, if we have no aim, then we cannot justify our work within the university system. From a postmodern point of view, it seems accurate if not shrewd to explain that, "like the peasant in the old story, we first shoot the holes in the fence and then paint the bull's-eyes around them."[1] We don't usually like to admit this, but now might be the time to do so.

For instance, Stephen Greenblatt, the alleged founder of New Historicism, remarks, "My own work has always been done with a sense of just having to go about and do it, without establishing first exactly what my theoretical position is." He goes on to say, "A few years ago I was asked by *Genre* to edit a selection of Renaissance essays, and I said ok. I collected a bunch of essays and then, out of a kind of desperation to get the introduction done, I wrote that the essays represented something I called a "new historicism" (Veeser 1). After admitting that he had indeed painted a target around what he had hit upon, he then makes this startling confession: "I'd never been very good at making up advertising phrases of this kind; for reasons that I would be quite interested in exploring at some point, the name stuck much more than other names I'd very carefully tried to invent over the years. In fact I have heard—in the last year or so—quite a lot of talk about the 'new historicism' (which for some reason in Australia is called Neo-historicism); there are articles about it, attacks on it, references to it in dissertations: the whole thing makes me quite giddy with amazement" (1). Of

143

course, many great discoveries have been made by accident, but this looks less like discovery and more like invention. Until someone asked him how what he was doing was different from what other critics were doing, he didn't seem to be aware that he was aiming at any special result.

For the most part, when we think of our aims we think of them comparatively, contrasting the purpose of literary study with similar pursuits in endless individual efforts to clarify our aims. Often we disguise the fact that we are talking about our aims by speaking instead of our methods. Comparing the study of literary texts with the study of dreams, for instance, it could be remarked that the study of literature does not attempt to cure authors in the way that psychoanalysis attempts to cure dreamers. And this is a useful remark, for it keeps the wished-for outcome of our critical conduct within the domain of the possible. But such remarks come post facto, and they suppose that the purpose of literary study is marked by its differences from other academic pursuits. This satisfies our sense of being autonomous. Each to his or her own, we seem to imply. However, comparisons always bring the perspective of the other with them, sometimes because it is the other who is empowered.

One comparison in particular has been imposed on us by our institutional history. Since the late nineteenth century, we have compared literary study to scientific study in order to formulate our rationale. As a result we are inclined to remarks like "The aim of literary study is to accumulate knowledge about literary works." In such alleged observations we unwittingly compare the purpose of an intellectual pursuit like chemistry to our own. It is no more possible to imagine literary study as a form of chemistry than it is to imagine chemistry as a form of literary study; yet we speak of the production of "literary knowledge" although in the comparisons of our efforts to those of scientists it commits us to the production of "facts," a disciplinary goal. In disciplinary discourse, the term "knowledge" is enmeshed semantically with concepts like facts, truths, principles, erudition, study, clarity, certainty, information, and bodies of truths, that is, with a type of understanding that can be accumulated, stored, and retrieved. Even our everyday use of the word "knowledge" carries with it similar semantic resonance:

1. acquaintance with facts, truths, or principles: general erudition
2. familiarity or conversance, as by study or experience
3. the fact or state of knowing: mental apprehension
4. awareness, as of a fact or circumstance
5. something that is or may be known: information
6. the body of truths or facts accumulated in the course of time
7. the sum of what is known

The senses of the word given in the standard dictionaries—"conversance by experience" and "awareness of facts or circumstances or situations"—

lean toward the empirical. In the comparative way we think of our endeavors, the production of knowledge is not ordinarily associated with poetry or fiction (or, I might add, with intuition). In academic circles, the word "knowledge" is usually reserved for the results of argumentative practices that rely on logic. Thus, when we think of ourselves as acquiring knowledge, our pursuit is likely to be governed by disciplinary practices.

If we call our aim "knowledge," we may be limiting the scope of our understandings. By calling something by an inappropriate name, one can come to imagine it to be what it does not have to be. If traditional critics call readings "knowledge" and imagine something that can be accumulated or advanced or stored for later retrieval like "information," then the trace of a picture of what they do when they do bibliographies, image studies, and the like misleads them. In traditional terms, knowing has a product—knowledge—as its outcome. But the outcome of critical conduct could be imagined in a number of alternative ways.

The potential that familiar frameworks have for inhibiting our understanding is illustrated in psychology classes by asking students to solve what appears to be a simple puzzle. Given a series of dots arranged in the form of a square, they are asked to connect all of the dots with only three straight lines. Many students fail to solve the puzzle because its solution involves going outside the square box the dots form. It is quite amazing to realize how confining the framework of the square is in solving this puzzle. As Wittgenstein observed in the *Philosophical Investigations,* many of our difficulties are tied to a lack of imagination.

If literary study is freed from its disciplinary context, what we call *knowing* can be *wanting to understand.* When we consider the study of literature not as a product but as a performance, not as a disinterested accumulation of facts but as the fulfillment of a desire for meaning, not as an objective scrutiny of objects but as a subject reflecting on his or her subjection, then the language of desire seems more appropriate than the language of discipline.

Reading is a symbolic action. Actions are driven by states of desire. Desires are constitutive of cultural subjects. Reading is wish-fulfilling. Instead of imaging the outcome of reading as something collected and stored, it could be imagined as dreaming, even though the outcome of dreaming is discernible only through the desires of the dreamer. Critics might envision belief, which suggests *wanting to understand,* rather than having knowledge, in the sense of information, as the outcome of literary study.[2] In a technocracy knowledge is customarily valued and belief disparaged. Only in the absence of knowledge does one have to believe, so they say. Not surprisingly, therefore, when an institution tries to inform its cultural subjects about literature it disciplines them to think that, unless *wanting* to understand is replaced by *knowing* that they have fully understood, they have not done their jobs.

Paradoxically, in this view, because knowledge is disinterested, it must lack interest. But reading, like dreaming, is wish-fulfilling. Especially in first encounters, reading literature makes one believe in desires in which one did not earlier believe. When I was quite young, I read sports novel after sports novel and wished I could become a major leaguer. One day my school librarian, who noticed I was making my second round through most of the baseball novels in the library, suggested I read a different kind of book—*Kristan Lavaransdatter*, by Sigrid Undset. I was amazed to feel quite different desires forming in the virtual world that huge trilogy created for me. And again, when I first read *The Brothers Karamazov*, the figure of Aloysha stirred in me desires I had never had before.

Possibility engenders hope. When persons stop reading, they limit the range of their hopes because nothing is desirable if it is not believed to be possible. Literary study leads one to self-understanding because it helps one learn what is desirable.[3] Unless you construe literature as knowledge of the "real" world, the worlds it describes are fictions. At best they are virtual. Thus our understanding of these worlds is an understanding of what is possible. Once we learn something is possible, we can desire it. Censoring literature, for example, operates on the premise that if we can imagine doing things we never before dreamed of doing, we may actually do them. The formation of desire is a significant aspect of the formation of cultural subjects. Engendering desire is as culturally momentous as engendering other forms of indispensable life-sustaining energy.

My criticism of the modern understanding of the aim of literary study—to *determine* or *establish* the meaning of texts—is that it rationalizes the accumulation of information (see chapter 4). I see no reason why we should place ourselves in the awkward position of claiming to give our students *self*-understanding by reducing the understanding of oneself to information. Why shouldn't we teach them about their subjectivity, that is, their subjugation, their subjectedness, their interpellation in discursive formations as cultural subjects, in order to engender in them desires for alternatives?[4]

Critical Imagination

Foucault remarks that "if you wish to replace an official institution by another institution that fulfills the same function—better and differently—then you are already reabsorbed by the dominant structure" (*Language* 232). As long as literature remains a field of study that yields knowledge, critics will be subject to disciplinary constraints. But can we envision a postdisciplinary field? This is a difficult task. Hoping that it will provoke a discussion that might lead to rethinking the notion of a discipline of literary study, I outline a postdisciplinary practice in this chapter and then in subsequent ones fill the outline in a bit.

With Kenneth Burke, I believe that texts are performed on works as symbolic actions. To read literary texts is to develop plans for one's personal conduct based on revising one's beliefs. Reading, in this view, is strategic, tactical, preparatory. It does not constitute knowledge available in literature about the real, but imaginative solutions to personal or social problems that depend on imagined possibilities. In this view, critical reading makes explicit an interest in literature as potential strategies for dealing with our selves.[5]

In the 1990s, Burke's provocative view of literature, which he once defined as "the dancing of an attitude," seems a fitting aim for literary studies as it broadens its horizons into cultural studies. Furthermore, this view restores prominence to the imagination, a type of intelligence that has the cultural power to restore prominence to our work. As I argue in *Token Professionals and Master Critics,* disciplinary regimes discredit the imagination. Under the aegis of slogans such as "emotional," "subjective," and "irrational," the imaginative is reduced to the aberrant. However, the imaginative is the locus of resistance to the conceptualization of experience.

As long as we continue to treat the imaginative as a negative force, we imprison ourselves in a disciplinary construction of the actual. The imaginative, on the other hand, is a precondition of making the impossible possible. It is the source of the impossible whose possibility we are prohibited from addressing. If we treat the imaginative in the way Foucault treats power, as pervasive and productive, positive and negative, then to read literature can be to resist the ways things are. In this sense, to read literature is to theorize alternatives to our lives.

We are accustomed to thinking of literary study as a field. There exists a particular subject matter, a field, with respect to which "a specific exemplar of successful work" (Dreyfus & Rabinow 60) is carried out, forming what we call a discipline. But if we alter our notion of literature as the field of literary study, moving away from the modern view that it is a site of objects and toward the view that it is a set of performances loosely regulated by social practices that are continuously violated, the notion that literary study is a discipline has to be modified. If literature is something already always there prior to the critic's reading, then it would be a field in which "a specific exemplar of successful work" can produce knowledge. But if we take the view that literature is a set of performances, then an exemplary mode of reading only *imagines* that field, creating instances of a preferred set of beliefs (see Annette Kolodny's "Dancing through the Minefield"). Ordinarily the imaginative is considered problematic in that it produces erroneous beliefs. From a postdisciplinary point of view, it only produces instances of belief. The imaginative has the potential for making the impossible possible if the impossible is not systematically suppressed in the culture.

Critical practices thus become ways of working against the prevailing order. Critical reading would be understood as "equipment for living" in Kenneth Burke's phrase—a form of self-reflexivity and a precondition of change. Literature (or culture) would not be a site at which paradigmatic research work discovers knowledge about the world.

There is an important political difference between these two views, between what I have been calling the modern notion of literature as a field of study and the postmodern notion I am now presenting of literature as the imagination of alternative cultural environments. Understood as a field of study, literature is a domain of knowledge about actual human conduct. As traditionalists tell us, literature teaches us *about* ourselves, meaning about our human nature. Understood as a cultural possibility, literature is an arena for a dialectic. The modern view has the effect of telling us that we see ourselves in the mirror of literature, believing we are like Antigone, Oedipus, Hamlet, Emma, or Brother William. By contrast, for postmodern critics Hamlet does not afford us knowledge about ourselves; he inhabits a possible world we created in the virtual spaces of our minds that may configure our own world. Consider, for instance, Dante's *Inferno* as literature. This work does not give us knowledge about a netherworld we may one day be forced to visit; it offers an analogy to the world we experience.

If we move from canonical to popular literature, it is easier to see literary worlds as alternatives to ours. Science fiction, for instance, presents us with scenarios we now deem impossible. Our culture in part reproduces itself by getting us to believe that alternatives to it are impossible. Thus, literature, as an alternative world, provides a critique of our culture when it images as possible what our cultural belief system deems impossible. For instance, in a time not so long ago and one still heralded in literary study, it was "known" that women were the daughters of Eve and God was a man-spirit, and therefore it was also "known" that it was impossible for women to be more rational than their husbands. The net product of the modern disciplinary view is a set of ideas. The net product of a counterdisciplinary view is a set of strategies, or "options" (Racevskis 75).

Disciplinary apparatuses govern our behavior by governing our use of symbolic actions, our tools for theorizing our conduct. If modes of reading are construed as normative, they inculcate habits of reading that reproduce acceptable sets of ideas about human nature. The reproduction of values has always been one of the functions of literary study because readers constitute texts. Thus, when particular reading procedures are regarded as acceptable, the net weight of the disciplinary technologies of normalization ensure normal readings. If these normative readings are understood to be knowledge of the natural state of man, truths about human nature, universal laws of moral conduct, and so on, then we have an apparatus of cultural reproduction.

Resistance to such normalization is tolerated in the academy. As Henry Giroux observes throughout *Theory and Resistance in Education,* there is ample evidence of such resistance. However, as I have already mentioned, if resistance takes the form of a "better" way of doing what we are doing, it has little effect on the process of reproduction. Changing the canon to include more works by women and blacks is not likely to disturb the liberal humanistic tradition that sees the role of literary study as essentially apolitical—the impracticability of its truths being the ground of their value. Given the unlikelihood of consensus on the meaning of works by women, blacks, and others, not much change would occur in society.

If literature is construed as an imaginative world it is possible for us to inhabit, then criticism becomes a critique of human conduct and predominant cultural values because they are perceived in the light of alternatives to them. If you are buying a house, the second one you visit is a critique of the first, the third of the second as well as the first, and so on. The critique may have a positive valence—the first is more suitable to your lifestyle than the second, an understanding you appreciate when you examine it in the light of an alternative to it. In *The Art of Discrimination,* Ralph Cohen makes a case that literary study is comparative throughout its operations. This observation has many implications, one of which is that criticism is the adjudication of alternatives. If so, literary criticism is, then, the adjudication of the cultures we inhabit, since by engaging in it we judge how imagined alternatives compare to them.

The underlying aim of this cultural criticism is to develop the conditions of the possibility of *changing* the cultures we inhabit.[6] If pursued, one's field is not an object for paradigmatic research but rather discourses that need to be reimagined on account of their deleterious social effects.[7] Feminist criticism is exemplary in this respect. In this context, the idea of new readings takes on a completely different character.

Critical reading can be a form of theorizing, a form of practicing theory, a political act, as Foucault suggests when he remarks that "the intellectual's role is no longer to place himself 'somewhat ahead and to the side' in order to express the stifled truth of the collectivity; rather, it is to struggle against the forms of power that transform him into its object and instrument in the sphere of 'knowledge,' 'truth,' 'consciousness,' and 'discourse.' In this sense, theory does not express, translate, or serve to apply practice: it is practice" (*Power/Knowledge* 207–8). Though it often is not, having been prohibited by our commitment to discipline, reading literature can be an outcome of a willingness to intervene powerfully in the discourses that produce social ills.

A Postmodern Project: Studying the Cultural Formation of Subjects

What does it mean to be the sort of postdisciplinary intellectual Foucault describes? Intellectuals articulate public concerns, but if they are members of a school of specialists their avowed relationship to the public is as experts to amateurs. They put themselves in a position of interpreting the concerns of the public *for them,* a relationship of dominance and power. I agree with Jameson and other commentators that professors of literature need to resume their traditional roles as intellectuals (Giroux et al., *Teachers as Intellectuals*). However, as I argued earlier, from a postdisciplinary perspective, literary intellectuals should not be defined as specialists in fields.[8] I also contend that fields should not be understood as the centers of intellectual communities. Not only do we not need more interpretive communities, but the concept of a field or a specialty is unnecessarily restrictive. In literary studies, fields are "discursive formations" constituted by researchers as privileged domains of work. Such domains can be constituted in any way whatsoever, and defining them in a highly technical vocabulary known only to specialists makes them inaccessible to the public. Literature becomes a scripture that only the literati can translate and interpret. Such a caste system is unwelcome in cultural study. It makes intellectuals seem to be the high priests of culture.

Intellectuals address necessary changes in the public spheres that make up our cultures.[9] In "The Need for Cultural Studies," Henry Giroux, David Shumway, Paul Smith, and I argue that intellectuals should develop such projects to make students agents of their cultural formation rather than interpreters of various fields of it. Rather than promoting cults devoted to individual genuses, literary critics could be more broadly concerned with the effects of such acculturation, with the formation of cultural subjects. This requires a different sense of self-understanding than the one invoked as the modern aim of literary study, yet it is not an unfamiliar one. Official objectives rarely describe what goes on in practice. In "Self as Subject in English Studies," William Cain writes that it "is striking how often critics invoke the self as the authoritative ground for their disciplinary mission" (*Crisis in Criticism* 76). He points out that "the unresolved problem of English studies [is] in the problem of subjectivity. On the one hand, the study of literature is felt by many to depend on (and to glory in) the individual work and distinctive merit of each interpreter. But it is precisely this individualistic strain, so others argue, that English must erase if it wishes to nominate itself as a true 'discipline,' as something other than the field where subjectivity romps" (81). Cain notes that the discipline "celebrates the 'selves' of readers and interpreters," adding that "it aims to refine and monitor their critical instruments" (82). Still, the discipline—in order to remain a discipline—"cannot finally tolerate any method that emphasizes selves and thereby seems to invite subjectivity and the slide into chaos" (82).

But, he writes, "there are deeper reasons for the persistent nomination of the self or subject as the embodiment of English studies" (78), and he concludes that subjectivity "should not imply the labor of the solitary individual, but should instead refer to the condition of each 'subject' as social actor and agent" (84). I would add that many literary critics are already preoccupied with the ways cultural subjects are formed. Postmodern critics are already concerned with subjects, not objects called texts. As I argued in chapter 10, the text is an extension of the reading subject and is the subject matter (in the sense of subject materialized) of that reading. If literary scholars redefine the humanities as cultural studies in which they are concerned not with the construction of objects but with the construction of subjects,[10] they might then, as Cain puts it, stop seeing their work as "the labor of the solitary individual" and begin seeing it as "the condition of each 'subject' as social actor and agent" (84).

Ironically, we are paid not for what we consider to be our work (research) but rather for our service. Thus, a turn toward becoming person-oriented is consistent with our service to the university. Our aim needs to be service, but reunderstood. A shift from text-orientation to person-orientation would change the old research priorities in which the impersonal takes precedence over the personal. It would address a profound contradiction in our profession of a discipline of literature—our aspiration to impersonally study the intensely personal. Such an aspiration has a hollow sound in a postmodern era.

Modern versus Postmodern

I am convinced that literary study should not be governed by disciplinary ideals and aims, both because it cannot meet them and because few critics wish to be so governed. Thus I conclude that the professional study of literature should be either abandoned or reconceived. The first inference makes surprisingly good sense. If reading literature cannot be a discipline, why should literary study be part of a university structure? This, of course, raises the question, What are universities for? Presumably they exist to develop intellectuals, but scientists or disciplinarians are not the only types of intellectuals.

Disciplines are valued in large measure for their capacity to make discoveries that affect lives. The sciences have been so successful in this regard that science has become the prototypical discipline. Unfortunately, disciplinarity has become a totalizing ideal of intellectual activity. We need to go beyond counterdisciplinary critiques and envision a postdisciplinary or, more broadly speaking, a postmodern mode of inquiry. By the expression "postmodern" I mark only the exhaustion of a particular way of thinking, without identifying any clear-cut set of new procedures or any paradigm shift.

Nonetheless, it is possible to envision a postmodern research program. Though what it might look like is not yet clear, nevertheless we can see some possibilities emerging in critiques of the institution of criticism: a postmodern inquiry tries not to be totalizing, nor to subscribe to a disciplinary epistemology or to a logic of consistency; instead it is concerned with subjects rather than objects. Actually, we are already living in a postmodern era. My four caveats could be taken as descriptions of current critical attitudes.

First, few critics nowadays seek a totalizing theory. Literary study is better understood as a cluster of research projects with very specific, ad hoc, and sometimes incompatible aims, rather than as the unfolding of the implications of a single paradigm. Despite squabbling among schools of criticism, most critics accept the incompatibility of existing research paradigms and do not seek to reduce them to a single "correct" one. Second, the work of fewer and fewer critics depends on disciplinary forms of argumentation (explanations or even justifications). Most critics pay little attention to the logical rigor of their arguments despite their use of an argumentative rhetoric. Third, few critics rely on a logic of consistency, that is, on systematicity, the hallmark of disciplinarity. Instead, most implicitly employ an analogic of coincidence. Finally, few critics take literature as a subject matter about which facts are discovered; most understand it as a discursive environment in which cultural subjects are formed. Many critics, especially younger ones, are concerned with the ways reading and writing form students as cultural subjects.

At present, the large number of competing models of writing/texts/reading interrelationships are disconcerting because they appear incompatible. When critics are confronted with such inconsistencies, the only alternative to a disciplinary point of view is to consider the model falsified and look for another. However, for all practical purposes, critics have abandoned the ideal of coherence. Though modern historians describe it as a discipline, literary study can be shown to operate in flagrant disregard of the defining characteristic of a discipline—the logic of consistency. It should be noted that in literary inquiry, anomalies and lacunae do not lead to the overthrow of a reigning paradigm. From a postmodern perspective, paradigms are irrelevant. Literary research is ad hoc; results are aimed at very specific social changes. Its significance is often explicitly political. Unlike disciplinary researches, postmodern ones are not understood as constituting facts but as instruments for changing the culture. It is not that we know the truth about, say, literacy, but that we can change habits of writing and reading, or habits of not writing and not reading. As a consequence, microcultures might change. In this respect the political character of literary studies surfaces. At least it is no longer hidden under a disciplinary coat.

A Different View of Research

I have argued that, historically, critics have construed literary study as a form of knowledge. As a consequence, they have made research (compiling knowledge) one of their central aims. It has long been believed that students of literature should be trained for this task. And indeed, in the course of the last century, scholars have accumulated vast amounts of information. But recently the status of this store of knowledge has been called into question.[11] What can count as research in a postmodern period?

I offer a modest research program based on a different imaging of *research*. I suggest that in a postmodern period some of us working as critics might choose another aim based on a different premise—that literary study can be a form of configuring. My choice of the term "configuring" is motivated by the belief that in a period of our intellectual history when the traditional subject of humanistic discourse has been decentered, attention to the interactions among persons brings back into focus the human agents of cultural transformation.[12]

Configuring is a purely heuristic gesture that makes no claim to represent anything. A configuration presents the shape an experience might take in a particular and ad hoc intersection of historical contexts. It is a metaphoric mode of thinking—the critical imagination at work. Configuring stands in contrast to the procedure of assimilation usually associated with the accumulation of knowledge. Our professional history, in more respects than we admit, has mimicked the successful professionalization of the sciences. In practice, however, humanistic understanding has much more to do with imagination than with logic.

The traditional subject of the humanities, human beings, requires understanding of a configurative sort. For instance, we usually believe that we understand others more humanely if we are told their personal h*istories*. Such storytellings, taken collectively (seen as analogues), are the sources of *our* social, political, and cultural histories, which cannot be understood without notions of myth, ritual, drama, and so on—all literary categories. Myths are narrative. Rituals are dramatic. Drama is action; action is behavior; persons behave. We do not necessarily understand human behavior by accumulating information about it; and though we do not ordinarily think of narrative as a mode of understanding, it can be so understood. Kenneth Burke's notion that discourse is a form of symbolic action is a case in point.

In his view, we dramatize or narrativize nearly everything. Letters, essays, treatises—all are forms of symbolic action. To put an action into words is to narrate. A symbolic action is, quite simply, the telling of an action—in Burke's formulation, dramatizing experience. As symbolic actions, readings are virtual and constitute a field of possible actions for critics. As a consequence, literature can be understood as a set of possible acts existing historically as the discourse of its articulate readership. To criticize literature, so understood, is to reflect critically on the relation between literature and culture—the repository of acceptable behavior—and to "tell" in "readings" which possible acts are important to, or inhibited by, a particular society.

Contemporary critics of literature cannot be called ill-advised if they reflect on their field critically as an unfolding sequence of possible worlds, some of which are the history of our culture, others of which may yet be realized. Readings are not neutral matters. If we take a broad view of texts as semioticians sometimes do (to include films, paintings, buildings), culture can be said to be *composed of readings* that make up a world of virtual experiences. Furthermore, other forms of discourse (e.g., arguments) can also be understood as symbolic actions. Once a depersonalized argument is placed back in its context of debate (quarrel or controversy), the actions it presupposes become visible. Considering that arguments take place in particular social contexts and situations that are often quite volatile, we understand that they often begin in desire and conflict. From this perspective, arguments can be perceived as the human dramas they invariably are.

I use the word "configuration" to identify the form of understanding that underlies acts of narration. When we teach students in departments devoted to the study of literature, are we teaching them about literature by informing them about what we (and our scholarly colleagues) believe to be the meaning of a given literary work? Or are we teaching them how to read literature by encouraging them to configure what they read as a strategy for making explicit the bias of texts that constitute the culture? In the first case students have more ideas, and in the second they can take more effective social, political, and cultural action. In the first case students are perceived as recipients of culture, in the second as agents of its transformation.

As members of literature departments who define the field of literary study by the terms we use to speak about it, we must take responsibility for its development. The terms of our critical discourse de*term*ine what we attend to as critics. I propose that we teach students how to develop "readings" *configuratively.* This aim differs from the modern one. I do not propose this as *the* aim of literary study but as *a* worthwhile aim. It generates a postdisciplinary research program motivated by an interest in transforming the culture rather than preserving it.[13]

In her feminist reading of Adrian Lynne's film *Fatal Attraction,* Susan Faludi, for example, juxtaposes the configuration of the femme fatale and everyday configurations of women to show how incongruous Lynne's depiction of Alex Forrest as a career woman is. Faludi's "graphic criticism" also includes two cartoons as "evidence" in her configural argument.[14] One of her cartoons shows two young girls playing "pretend" beneath the caption "Fatal choices." One says, "I'll be the single working woman bitch, and you be the mommy," to which the other replies, "I never get to be the single woman. I'm telling!" In the first cartoon, Faludi gives us Lynne's *model for* culture against a backdrop of how such *models of* adult behavior affect children (Geertz, *Interpretation* 93–94). This cartoon is followed by another, in which two young women discuss their dating experiences. One, identified as a "good girl," remarks, "When a guy dumps me, I buy a big bag of semisweet chocolate, then I get into bed and cry and eat until I hate myself." The "bad girl" of the pair remarks: "So like if a guy dumps me, usually I like to run over and pour acid on his car and kill his pets." In this instance, Faludi places the configuration of good/bad girl in Lynne's film against the cultural backdrop of dating conventions to bring out the incongruity. What gets exposed in this tactic is the spuriousness of the link between Lynne's depiction of Alex Forrest and the actual behavior of career women in our culture. Therefore, *Fatal Attraction*'s value as a representation of our culture is called into question. Faludi's configural argument raises the question, If this is what we could do, should we do it?

I cite Faludi's essay as an instance of a configurative argument because she matches one configuration with another. She does not attempt to refute Lynne but rather demythologizes the cultural configurations in the film by showing them against a background of everyday life. The effect is humorous, satirical, and critical. As a tactic, Faludi's critique—especially the cartoons—is *in kind* very much like the ad in Bush's successful presidential campaign that depicted his opponent's policy toward "law and order" in the image of a prison with a revolving door, a configuration (rather than a justification) that influenced millions of voters. Had Bush presented his views in a lengthy justification, it is not likely that his "interpretation" of Dukakis's position on prison reform would have had much interpretive force. Configurations work by shaping attitudes. Just as you cannot critique a feeling through concepts, you cannot *feel* the hollowness of a particular cultural disposition by a conceptual analysis. In such cases, counter-emotions are more significant than counterclaims. A configural critique has the feeling of betrayal, not falsification. It's seeing the minister of God in bed with his disciple.

The postmodern inquiry implied by Faludi's criticism of *Fatal Attraction* involves many of the activities in which we already engage. Though a postmodern inquiry may seem at first glance to call for the acceptance of a revolutionary paradigm, instead it sometimes only calls for drawing a bull's-eye around what we have already hit upon. However, to be honest about it, we probably need to speak about "target practice" in somewhat different terms. This is the spirit of the next chapter, in which I discuss arguments as narrations.

Alternative Cultures

CHAPTER 13

Virtual events have real effects. Though we desire what we do not have and can only imagine it, nonetheless we really desire it. Furthermore, many virtual states are more satisfying than real ones. Receiving some letters from admirers of his "biography" of Sherlock Holmes during World War II, Vincent Starrett wrote, "I knew that I was back in the world of sanity again." He preferred to dwell in the "thick, yellow fog" of Holmes's London to the "bedeviled, phantasmagoria of Europe" at the time. Starrett's preference is not extraordinary. The virtual worlds of fiction, poetry, drama, opera, symphonies, TV, films, biographies, histories, and news have been with us for a long time. So has the world of advertising.

As we know from advertisements, the production of desire in audiences is often induced by narrative means. Whereas conflicts can be readily rendered in conceptual terms as contradictions or anomalies, desires cannot. The conceptual equivalents of desires seem pale by comparison with the allure of the objects desired *as that allure is felt.* In this regard we might note that disciplinary studies have greater success in rendering fictional conflicts as competing beliefs than they have in rendering desires as compelling concepts. Conceptualizing desire has an effect similar to reading the ingredients on a box of candy (acetylated monoglycerides [emulsifier], partially hydrogenated vegetable oils [cotton seed and/or soybean], anise oil, etc.)—it clashes with the feeling of desire for the candy inside (licorice). Arguments about the desires our cultures produce in us that conceptualize the experiences involved tend to supply us with an idea of the ingredients and turn us away. I believe these observations to be relevant to the study of cultures. Along with its many other features, culture is a virtual state (because of the role imagination plays in its formation) wherein desires are cultivated.

In this chapter I take Graff's cultural studies proposals a step further than he has ventured. Calling a conflict a culture war presupposes a culture burdened by difficult problems. Though solutions to such conflicts have in the past been found in combat (religious wars come to mind), it is appropriate to explore a less adversarial configuration. Graff's interest in the culture wars is linked to his proposal that we teach the conflicts. However, inviting persons to identify with one or the other side of a conflict is not the only way to engage them in the activity of interpretation.[1] Narratologists have proposed that readers, for the most part, become engaged in narratives in three ways—they identify with (1) the protagonist in a conflict, (2) the protagonist's desires, or, most often, (3) the conflicting desires of the protagonist and antagonist. As a complement to teaching the conflicts I propose teaching desires. As I implied in the previous chapter, teaching desires is a shorthand expression for teaching the cultural production of desires, the principal means of forming cultural subjects.

Let us imagine for a moment that literature was to be discussed not by way of conceptions of it but by way of analogies to it, not by way of concepts but by way of configurations of experiences. This latter mode is probably the prevailing mode in public discussions of cultural artifacts. Film audiences identify with the structure of desire as an effect of various characterizations. For example, when *Fatal Attraction* was first released, theater audiences screamed out loud in the climactic scene in which Beth kills Alex (in my experience, some of them shouted "Kill the bitch"). This suggests that the film's audiences were "informed" by a desire that is integral to the narrative.

Thinking through Analogies

Much of what I have said in the first part of this study implies that critics should explore alternatives to the disciplinary protocols that structure their understanding in the form of logical arguments. Disciplinarity induces an excessive conceptualization of our understanding. One way of rescuing the "emotional curves" of literary works from the oblivion disciplinarity has in store for them is to take the surreptitious metaphors that warrant our interpretations as configurations.[2] In the chapter of *Metaphors We Live By* entitled "How Is Our Conceptual System Grounded?" George Lakoff and Mark Johnson claim that "most of our normal conceptual system is metaphorically structured; [that] is, most concepts are partially understood in terms of other concepts. This raises an important question about the grounding of our conceptual system. Are there any concepts at all that are understood directly, without metaphor?" (56).

Lakoff and Johnson make their point by discussing the word "up." Ultimately, they argue, "up" cannot be understood "purely in its own terms but emerges from the collection of constantly performed motor functions having to do with our erect position relative to the gravitational field we live in" (57). They configure this experience with the following story: "Imagine a spherical being living outside any gravitational field, with no knowledge or imagination of any other kind of experience. What could UP possibly mean to such a being? The answer to this question would depend, not only on the physiology of this spherical being, but also on its culture" (57). In this chapter I make a similar case for the warrants we use in literary arguments. In effect, I suggest that we construe what we do, not as a disciplinary argument based on inferential logic, but as a style of thinking better described as configuration.

Configuring is a style of thinking whose domain is rhetoric. Its genre is persuasion. However, it is not a disciplinary (explanatory or justificatory) argument. It persuades through narration. In many rhetorics, argument is a logical arrangement of propositions: evidence from which claims are inferred through warranting assumptions. A configuration is also an arrangement, not of statements or propositions, but of "narrative" expressions or, to use Burke's more familiar phrase, "symbolic actions." Configuring, as a modality of persuasion, is structured in ways that can be compared to arguments. First, it puts its audience in mind of specific experiences as evidence. Second, interpretations function in configurations much as claims do in arguments, though they are not, strictly speaking, inferred. Third, arguments depend for their efficacy on warrants—assumptions or general principles or laws that link the claims to the evidence. This is the theoretical aspect of an argument. The link between the evidence and the claim provided by the warrant is a logical inference. The link between the interpretation and the experiences described in a configuration is an intuition.[3] The analogue in a configuration parallels the warrant in a classical argument.[4]

Recall Freimarck's interpretation of "Araby." For him, the meaning of "Araby" was that "the boy realizes his journey is over and feels humiliated. His failure brings an increase in knowledge." This is not an inference from the facts of the text but a meaning derived from perceiving the text as an analogue to the Grail romances:

> In the grail castle the knight's success depends on his asking the right question concerning the grail which is carried past him. The woman questions the boy: "I looked humbly at the great jars [grails] that stood like eastern guards [the cherub at the East wall of Eden?] at either side of the dark entrance to the stall and murmured: 'No thank you.'" The wrong answer has been given and the boy asks no questions. The lights go out. When the knight does not ask the correct question in the castle it disappears and he wakes up at the edge of a cliff by the ocean, or in a

manure wagon being driven through a town where people insult him because of his failure to heal the land. Here the boy realizes his journey is over and feels humiliated. His failure brings an increase in knowledge, which, continuing the story's ironic counterpoint to Romance, does not bring hope or felicity. (368)

Freimarck, from the perspective of adulthood, looks back on his own adolescent experiences in a way that Joyce provokes. This self-reflexive attitude was not a part of my student Todd's experience (he did not experience an "increase in knowledge"), nor was reading Grail romances. As a consequence, Todd did not arrive at the conclusion that the boy's "failure brings an increase in knowledge." There is nothing in Joyce's text as such that would allow for that inference. It is only the perception of the text as analogous to the Grail romances that allows a reader to attribute to the boy in "Araby" a Christian gloss on the significance of the failure to answer the question when the knight appears in the Grail castle. For Freimarck this seems to confirm his experience of what it means to become an adult, an experience bound up with the frustration of expectations. Freimarck is persuaded by Joyce's narrative. It sheds light on his own experiences.

While in the act of persuading, a configurer like Joyce behaves, in many respects, like Benjamin's storyteller. He wishes to share experiences with his audience. His story is anecdotal and fragmentary but no less a story. His narration tends to overwhelm the syntagmatic sequence of the anecdote with commentary. His configuration lacks the pace of most narratives. The commentary delves into various constellations of meaning that cluster around the experience the anecdote reveals. These constellations interpret the experiences of his audience for them. His configuration is meant to be persuasive. For instance, he might hope to persuade his audience to seek another form of life than the one that comes out badly in his account. His configurations parallel other types of narratives; they are tragic, ironic, comic, or satiric. In each case, his purpose is persuasive. He does not describe reality, only possibility. He configures possible worlds. He offers plans, strategies for coping with a hostile world. He persuades by leading his audience to believe that some possible experiences are worse than others. If some persons in his audience believe this is so, then they may take action and form a different culture than the one they have inherited. But not everyone will. Configurations are matters of contestation.

The Contrast between Analytic and Analogical Arguments

In the academy, disciplinary reasoning authorizes a professional. When a text is rejected for publication, it is usually criticized for not being well argued—evidence is thought to be lacking, coherence missing, and so on.

The criteria invoked are disciplinary in character—logical errors in systematic reasoning. The merits of interpretive claims are evaluated in terms of a hierarchy of logical practices. Our discursive formation is disciplinary. Though our arguments cannot match the standards set by those studies from which the idea of a discipline was developed—the so-called hard sciences—we still employ much of the disciplinary language framed in the nineteenth century by philologists and historians who borrowed it from the institutional rationales of their day.

The thesis that the humanities are distinct from the sciences has a long history. I, for one, believe the two have different aims. Whereas scientific studies aim at the simplification of experiences in order to control them, the humanities aim at understanding the complexities of experience in order to cope with a world one has no hope of controlling. Ronald Crane put it quite well in *The Idea of the Humanities.* In his leading essay, "The Idea of the Humanities," he contrasts the values of the humanities with those of the sciences:

> There is a very real sense . . . in which the direction of the humanistic arts, when they are properly cultivated, is the opposite of the direction properly taken by the sciences of nature and society. The sciences are most successful when they seek to move from the diversity and particularity of their observations toward as high a degree of unity, uniformity, simplicity, and necessity as their materials permit. The humanities, on the other hand, are most alive when they reverse this process, and look for devices of explanation and appreciation that will enable them to preserve as much as possible of the variety, the uniqueness, the unexpectedness, the complexity, the originality, that distinguish what men are capable of doing at their best from what they must do, or tend generally to do, as biological organisms. (11–12)

Crane's articulation, I believe, still represents a majority view in the humanities, namely, that the humanities concern themselves with the diversity and uniqueness of experience.

Literary critics, I contend, find it counterintuitive to "move from the diversity and particularity of their observations toward [a high] degree of unity, uniformity, simplicity, and necessity." As a result, intuitive warrants are quite appropriate to their understanding. Confusion enters the picture when critics structure their observations in the traditional academic form of an argument where their warranting analogues are treated as inferences germane to conceptions of experience. In my view, this intellectualization of experience simplifies experiences by conceiving them as codes, themes, and forms. As I suggested at the outset, the fabric of desire we speak of as motive can be reduced to a concept, but not without stripping it of feeling and emotion. There is an alternative to such disciplining of literary study.

Reading is an activity. Thus one can tell the story of a reading. Such descriptions reveal that readers tell themselves the stories they are reading. When we read "Araby" we virtually tell ourselves a story about a young boy. During the course of that retelling, we wonder about allusions to Irish songs and political figures, notice recurring images, stumble over obscurities. Though most readers can be educated to make the process into a puzzle and turn their storytelling into a series of inferences, their activities are not especially logical. Few would halt their activity in order to analyze. Analyzing is counterintuitive during a reading. Most readers hate to do it. Reading is not analytical; it is analogical. Criticism is analytical because it is expected to be logical. But "logical" is a slippery adjective.

The narrative "logic" (by analogy) appropriate to storytelling is equally appropriate to descriptions of reading acts. It depends on the identification of actions as "turning points" in changes from one state to its "inverse." In place of the traditional logical formulation—if *x,* given *p,* then *q*—it introduces the "logic" of stories—if this desire, then its embodiment in this action results in this state of affairs. This "logic" is not inferential. It is a rhetoric of motives, not a logical argument.

We often have to remind students whose criticisms are plot summaries that it is one thing to enjoy reading a literary work and quite another to analyze it. I wish to dismantle this distinction. Criticism is not contrary to reading. We insist on analysis as something dominated by an inferential logic in order to maintain our status as a discipline. However, reading is an understanding of how configurations of experience do or do not resemble our personal histories. Such understanding is intuitive, not logical. It depends on an apprehension of resemblances, which are metaphorical or analogical. Students who supply us with plot summaries instead of analyses know that retelling the story is a form of understanding the motives it configures.

I am not inclined to defend literary-critical "arguments" on the basis of their *approximation* of the reliability, or veracity, of formal arguments, as does Arthur Danto in *Narration and Knowledge,* or their *conformity* to evidential criteria, as does Walter Fisher in *Human Communication as Narration.* These attempts leave us in the same quandary that Vattimo's notion of "weak reason," which I discussed earlier, leaves humanistic study. I prefer to speak of the work of literary critics *in its own right* and not as some weak variant of a stronger reasoning process. By calling the relation between narration and experience an "intuition," I hope to advocate literary study as *a type of understanding* that has to do with interpersonal relations— interactions motivated by desire.

Narratives are complexes of "motives," which were reduced to "causes" in Aristotelian logic. Kenneth Burke's pentad is based on such alleged "logic":

efficient cause	instrumental cause	material cause	formal cause	final cause
agent	agency	setting	act	purpose

Burke's pentad, however, is not a theory of causality. It is a heuristic. It delineates motivation, which is tied to desires and, therefore, to representations of subjects.[5]

Though we formulate arguments to satisfy disciplinary constraints, the experiences these "arguments" discursively arrange can also be depicted narratively as experiences of reading. The human activities that give rise to statements like claims, warrants, and descriptions can be understood as symbolic actions that are not intelligible outside the states of mind they presuppose. Anthony Kenny gives an account in *Action, Emotion, and Will* of how we express action in the English language. In his view, every action expressed by an active verb presupposes an unwanted state of affairs that, after the action is taken, is altered in the hope of a more desirable state of affairs.[6] Though the states preceding and following an act are not always made explicit, actions imply them. Wherever this scheme of action applies, Kenny argues, there will be room for three main types of interpretation of action: by reference to the unwanted state of affairs that preceded it; by reference to the wanted state of affairs that was, or was expected to be, its upshot; or by some form of interpretation that alludes to both of these together (90–91).

If we consider the layout of an argument in the terms Toulmin does in *The Uses of Argument,* we see that Kenny's scheme of action parallels it. The almost mathematical formula "given x, if y, then z" becomes in Kenny's scheme "observing x, if we value y, then we interpret x in the light of y to mean z."

claim	warrant	evidence
action of believing	action of valuing	action of reading

Sentences in critical discourse that function as evidence are, in one way or another, descriptions of the act of reading. Similarly, interpretive claims describe acts of belief derived from the reader's worldview.

Because all of these virtual acts take place in the mind, they belong to the reader's psychosocial history. Writing about reading in the genre of an argument obscures the ways in which reading is a way of world-making. In reading literature, we construct a fictive world that has its own history. Sherlockians give testimony to this phenomenon when they write biographies of Holmes and Watson and discuss when specific events in those persons' lives took place and where on Baker Street they lived, or imagine that Holmes was a patient of Freud.[7]

Configurations of Alternative Cultural Worlds

Howard Gardner's chapter on "The Personal Intelligences" in *Frames of Mind* suggests not only that personal intelligence is distinguishable from logico-mathematical intelligence but also that it involves the abilities to read intentions and desires and to interpret the symbolic codes by which our culture legitimates itself—rituals, religious codes, mythic and totemic systems. Interpersonal understanding is linked, in his view, to the ability to plan our lives, to adopt role models from our experience of others. It is our ability to "build on our imagery and imaginative powers" that allows us to create such models. The overriding ability Gardner describes is a developing "sense of self," a term for "the balance struck by every individual—in every culture—between the promptings of 'inner feelings' and the pressure of 'other persons'" (242).

Such self-understanding is fundamentally configurative. When we attempt to understand another human being, we do not seek information (how tall, what IQ)—instead we seek stories, anecdotes, personal histories. The underlying configurative nature of our enterprise has much to do with our cultural formation as subjects. As I said above, literary arguments have a configural basis. As Richard Rorty puts it in his attack on our "misguided attempt[s] to be 'scientific,'" "telling stories about how one's favorite and least favorite literary texts hang together is not to be distinguished from— is simply a species of—the 'philosophical' enterprise of telling stories about the nature of the universe" (79). Rorty's remark coincides with Kenneth Burke's dramaturgical notion of human understanding. Fredric Jameson is also persuasive about the significance of narratives in cultural studies. He writes evocatively in *The Political Unconscious* that the "divergent and unequal bodies of work [of the great pioneers of narrative analysis] are here interrogated and evaluated from the perspective of the specific critical and interpretive task of the present volume, namely to restructure the problematics of ideology, of the unconscious and of desire, of representation of history, and of cultural production, around the all informing process of *narrative,* which I take to be (here using the shorthand of philosophical idealism) the central function or *instance* of the human mind" (13).

Despite its advocates, narrative understanding has come under heavy attack. Its critics, including Jameson, worry about both the totalizing potential and the teleological structure of narrative. Lyotard's critique of metanarratives in *The Postmodern Condition* is now almost axiomatic:

> Science has always been in conflict with narratives. Judged by the yard-stick of science, the majority of them prove to be fables. But to the extent that science does not restrict itself to stating useful regularities and seeks the truth, it is obliged to legitimate the rules of its own game. It then produces a discourse of legitimation with respect to its own status, a discourse called philosophy. I will use the term *modern* to designate any science that legitimates itself with reference to a meta-discourse of this kind making an explicit appeal to some grand narrative, such as the dialectics of Spirit, the hermeneutics of meaning, the emancipation of the rational or working subject or the creation of wealth. (xxiii)

Jameson echoes Lyotard's critique in his discussion of expressive causality, "the fullest form" of which is a vast interpretive allegory in which a sequence of historical events or texts and artifacts is rewritten in terms of some deeper, underlying, and more "fundamental" narrative, of a hidden master narrative that is the allegorical key or figural content of the first sequence of empirical materials (28). Lyotard's and Jameson's remarks testify that narrative is fundamental to understanding ourselves as denizens of a world, but this very condition of our understanding makes us prey to "grand narratives" with totalizing visions that end epochally.

At this juncture, an important distinction between a narrative and a configuration comes to light. Narratives are propelled by desires and hence have a profoundly wish-fulfilling character. This is not necessarily the case with configurations. Some involve desires, but others involve conflict, and still others, inquiry. Configurations exist as parts of narratives but do not themselves necessarily embody a narrative telos. Similarly, configurations may function as warrants in analogical arguments that depend on narrated reading acts but, again, are not necessarily narrative (teleological). They are narrative elements.

Configurations, in other words, are not inescapably carriers of narrative teleology. At the same time, they are analogical and powerfully linked to the concrete conditions of our lives. In short, they can communicate possibilities without imposing utopias. This feature is not of small importance. Configurations, as I have been delineating them, are virtual (exist only in the mind as analogues to experiences) and are therefore expressive only of possibility. I distinguish them from histories (narrated descriptions of experience). They exist in virtual space and time.

The virtual is something whose possibility is compelling though it does not actually exist as such. It exists, for example, in a dream, a wish, something imagined. The virtual is an effect of language. If one dreams of a unicorn, no unicorn can be produced for scientific examination. Nonetheless, that a unicorn could be genetically created is possible. At this moment, a unicorn remains a word for an image. This possibility gives us an alternative to the world as we know it.

By configuring our experiences, however virtually, the emerging possibilities influence our behavior. The delineation of possibility poses the question, What if? Configuring the virtual is always a heuristic. It is not an inference; it is an analogue, an analogue for many experiences. Often configurations are parts of a story and form a putative history. When this happens, the story that has been told configures the problems of the persons who hear it, and they respond by seeing it as their story. At this point it becomes history. The "veracity" or "verification" of the story is that in configuring a pain (problem) it allows for its resolution. But the configuration is not a paradigm or model of reality.

A configuration translates an experience for an audience. The translation occurs in a peculiar manner. Instead of exchanging a word or phrase in one language for a parallel one in another language, the configurer delineates his or her experience *as an analogue,* that is, as a transform of the experience. The main effect of this transform is that it goes beyond the configurer's experience, not in the sense of transcending it but because it calls to mind a series of possible transformations of the audience's experiences. It generates a series of analogues that allows a very wide range of analogies to the audience's experiences. As a transforming analogue, the configuration links individuals to each other as an audience. An audience is created via a concurrence of experiences. The analogue allows for an extremely wide range of different experiences and hence of difference. Configurations are transformative—when persons become members of the audience, they reperceive their experiences, and this opens up possible ways of being in the world. In sum, configurations are of alternative cultural worlds.

Reading Cultures

Recently, influenced by Graff's *Beyond the Culture Wars,* I see literary critics conflicted over the need to compete or concur. This dilemma reflects an ambivalence in our aims as critics. It underscores our choice of enabling protocols for our critical practices. Most literary critics, I would guess, aim to acquaint citizens with their culture. But some critics do not regard it as their responsibility to make better cultures for everyone involved. This task is regarded by many as political rather than literary. For the group that wants only the culture that privileges *their* experiences, competition is a requisite protocol. They must make their culture victorious (*Culture Wars* 10). For the group that seeks better *cultures* for everyone involved, *concurrence* is the requisite protocol. It is not a question of establishing their view of culture as the dominant view but rather of addressing the pains and sufferings that acculturation brings for everyone. Unfortunately, disciplinarity breeds competition because it is based on a logic of falsification. As I have argued throughout this study, cultural criticism, if its aim is transformative, should not pursue disciplinary goals.

Reading is indistinguishable from forming a culture. Every act of reading that occurs results in beliefs. Our culture is made from the fabric of our beliefs. When critics compete with each other over interpretations, they diminish cultural differences by stamping them out. Similarly, when critics argue as if they were drawing inferences from facts, they have no alternative except to falsify other claims and thus compete. And finally, when critics present us with concepts, they reduce our cultural experiences to a simple and general uniformity that, once again, belies the complexity of our cultural differences.

In the next chapter I show how configurations allow us to describe alternative worlds that put our own into perspective.

Critical Concurrence

On the spring of 1991 I taught an undergraduate course in cultural criticism in which the students collaborated with me on an essay. In many respects this experience confirmed Gerald Graff's view that debate helps students connect what they learn in different classrooms. As the course developed, students drew heavily from other courses they were taking in order to contribute to the collective essay we were coauthoring. The class also illustrated the need for critical concurrence in collaborative projects. It is the latter point on which I focus in this chapter.

The class began very dramatically in January of 1991. It was an evening class. I recall entering the room for the first time and sensing that something was wrong. As I reached the front of the room, Charles Deiner, a student who had been in my Introduction to Criticism class the previous semester, announced, "We've just bombed Baghdad."

Since half of the class were former students of mine, several, like Chuck, having just taken my Introduction to Criticism class, I had decided in advance to have the students generate the syllabus for the class. After the conversation about the beginning of the Gulf War quieted down, I hesitatingly started the class by indicating that in our first meeting we would design the syllabus, suggesting that we begin that task by going around the room to hear from each person what concerns brought them into the class and what they hoped to learn from it. The first person on my left was Brian Alexander, who indicated that he wanted to learn more about "cultural manipulation." He had been following the news leading up to the bombing of Baghdad and was distressed to think that he had been prepared by the media for what happened earlier that evening.

His suggestion caught on like wildfire. All the other students in the class seemed to take their lead from Brian. However, as they expressed their views of cultural manipulation, it took different forms than the news. One student wanted to study the Mapplethorpe controversy then brewing in the Cincinnati papers. Another wanted to work on the film *Pretty Woman,* which had disturbed her. Another wanted to analyze "trash news," referring to shows like *Hard Copy* and *A Current Affair* (the title of his paper was "NewsPorn"). One student, whose cultural heritage was Eskimo, wanted to do a study of the way his tribe was manipulated. The atmosphere of the first day was charged with ideas.

In the next session I proposed that the class collaborate with me on an essay in which we would develop our negotiated ideas about cultural manipulation. I had never done this with an undergraduate class, but I felt confident about the makeup of this one because I already knew more than half the students. Realizing that the disparities in our discourse would create a problem, I proposed that I draft the essay bit by bit, bringing sections of it to class for editorial discussion, and that they write customary papers on the topics they selected, which I would then use as examples in the collaborative essay. This proposal stunned the class when I announced it, and they looked perplexed. So, having made the proposal, I suggested that I leave the room for fifteen or twenty minutes so they could discuss my proposal among themselves without worrying about how I might react to their problems with it. When I returned to the room they were in a heated discussion and asked me to wait for a few more minutes. Returning a second time, I was greeted by a spokesperson, who said they were generally willing to pursue my plan but had a few questions. One student was not willing to be involved at all. He had been in my Introduction to Criticism class, and I respected his well-defined interests, so he arranged to do a paper on another topic, in addition to joining in on the class discussions and doing the readings we selected. By the end of the session we had worked out various details of the class's organization.

The next several weeks proved to be more than mildly interesting. The first problem we faced was to agree on what we meant by "cultural manipulation." This presented us with two additional problems—coming to terms with the terms "culture" and "manipulation." We had several lively discussions of what culture was and read various definitions of it. Several students contributed essays they had previously read in sociology or literature classes to the reading list for our class. Many of the students in the class were from Western College, an interdisciplinary program that is an independent college within Miami University (which has undertaken some experiments with Graff's proposals). Many of these students had explored conceptions of culture in courses there. I introduced students to Said, Foucault, Althusser, and other thinkers with whom I was familiar.

Though the discussions of culture were lively, the discussions of the term "manipulation" were even livelier. Whereas most students had minimal investments in being members of a culture, they had major investments in agreeing that specific cultural experiences were or were not manipulative. What became clear in our discussions was that until we could identify specific experiences as instances of manipulation and describe them in detail, we were merely ships passing in the night. The identification of these experiences proved very difficult. Whereas for some students any news broadcast constituted cultural manipulation, for others this was far from the case. The most helpful texts in our deliberations were class handouts from a sociology course Brian had taken on propaganda (confirming Graff's view that debates such as ours encourage students to connect what they are doing in one class with other classes they are taking).

The point I wish to make here is that it is futile to agree on a conceptual definition of a problem unless there is some sort of recognition of the problematic experiences involved. It was quite apparent that the abstract discussion of manipulation often disguised real differences of view. The moment concrete instances came up as illustrations of the concepts, the debates were renewed. Once we agreed on specific instances of manipulation (which had to be negotiated), our differences of view had positive effects on our understanding of the issues involved. For example, the easy agreement we had about the concept of culture disappeared when we tried to agree on instances of cultural manipulation. On the other hand, once we agreed to identify particular experiences as ones in which we were being manipulated (one or two students held dissenting opinions but "went along" in order not to be obstructive), the dissenters made the rest of us much more cautious in our articulations, much less inclined to overstate our positions, and so on. In sum, constructive disagreement requires some sort of critical concurrence about the experiences under investigation.[1]

Agreement Makes Productive Disagreement Possible

As a rule, critics differ. Disagreement is a social structure, a play of difference, a principle of creativity. Historically, innovators have disagreed with their predecessors. By profession, artists are as unlike one another as sentences. We assume disagreement is an expression of intellection that distinguishes outstandingly insightful individuals from others. At its most fundamental level, it is a form of differentiation. The social function of disagreement is individuation; it marks one's differences on a preexisting scale. To disagree with others signals one's individuality.[2]

All of these remarks apply to literary-critical disagreements. Many critics, usually male, quickly learned that the designation "brilliant" generally follows upon a polemical disagreement, not upon informed agreement. Many other critics, especially women, who by cultural habit happen to be accommodative, are often construed as sycophants even when they are more articulate about an idea than the interlocutor with whom they are agreeing manages to be. Some cynics suggest that if you want to succeed as a critic you need only attack someone famous. Brilliance is marked by dissent. Disagreement individualizes. There are, however, parameters to public disagreements.

Published criticism is a public performance. Like other performances, it ordinarily presupposes certain protocols, ceremonial forms established as proper and correct in social exchanges. Legally, a protocol is the original note or minute, drawn up by a notary and duly attested, that forms the authority for any subsequent deed or agreement based on it. In either case, protocols are the rules that govern a negotiation. They are, metaphorically, the rules from which all the moves in the game are derived. Protocols represent the expectations we have about the appropriate ways to conduct ourselves in public. Unexpected actions are experienced as a social shock—an aria sung by a member of the audience in the middle of a lecture would be disconcerting. Displays of individuality are not at all times tolerated.

Nor are such displays at all times appropriate. Imagine the Supreme Court governed by a protocol stipulating disagreement. Not that one does not, or should not, expect Supreme Court justices to disagree. On the contrary, one relies on the likelihood of their disagreeing. However, one would not find any comfort in their disagreement if it came under a protocol wherein the justices were "licensed" to compete with each other by calling attention to their disagreements, never obliged to reach any decision. Of course, no court has such a protocol. The protocol of any court is an agreement to agree if at all possible, that is, to collaborate.

I have now identified two sets of protocols for the production of knowledge, one structured by an agreement-to-disagree system of exchange, which I will call "competitive," and the other structured by an agreement-to-agree system of exchange, which I will call "collaborative." The former invites departures from the group; the latter invites concurrences within it. There are courtesies and proprieties associated with each of the two sets of protocols, but they are not of particular concern to us at the moment. I focus on the initial agreement about the form of exchange, however implicit or explicit, that governs the behavior of the group, particularly when the group is audience to a discourse by one of its members. I call to your attention a not often mentioned phenomenon—critical protocols.

Rhetorically, critical disagreements shaped by competitive protocols are forms of truth-telling. You agree with your audience that the truth of the matter needs to be told and, therefore, that untruths that are believed need first to be unmasked. You agree with your audience that your discourse is a set of propositions, truth claims, that must be falsified if they can be.

Rhetorically, critical agreements shaped by collaborative protocols are forms of belief-telling. To agree to agree is necessarily to agree to believe. Disagreement is limitless. Agreement is limited. Collaborative protocols set limits on the extent to which the beliefs in question are to be construed as either appropriate or inappropriate. It is a matter of "believing" or "doubting" because, in academic contexts, disagreeing is usually related to logic and speculating, while agreeing is usually related to praxis and deciding. Agreements are required in contexts wherein there is a need and a willingness to take action. When two or more persons find themselves in a situation in which they have to do something in concert, agreement is a prerequisite. For example, agreeing that "this is a romance" is meaningful when some action needs to be taken—for instance, reading a text. Notice, though, how an interest in coming to an agreement on the genre of a text sets limits on the scope of possible disagreements. Arguing that a given medieval romance is flawed because its characterization is "unrealistic" becomes pointless.

Protocols and Change

Habits are rarely changed by ideas. I am not, of course, suggesting that ideas play no role in changing conduct, but rather that, although ideas conceptualize the problems of conduct, solving those problems requires taking action. Criticism, like all other forms of conduct, does not change by the invocation of a superior idea. What people do by habit will change only when those habits change. Habits change only when people begin to do what they always do in a different way and experience that the difference counts. The only way to change an established praxis is to encourage performances from which a different praxis can emerge.

No change in literary study can take place without changing our habitual practices. First we'd have to change our view of the relations among practice, pedagogy or praxis, and theory. Practice ought to be the precondition of theory, and theory the precondition of praxis; however, in institutional settings practice is often untheorized, and theory is often impracticable. Unfortunately, no matter how unreflective a practice might be or how reductive a theory might be, praxis, the discourse of training, remains even more intractable in its effects than either of them because it usually serves the interests of the institution.

But even if we changed our ideas about practice, theory, and praxis, these changes would take effect only with the institution of different protocols. Recall the change of terms from all students are *required* to attend Sunday church service to all students are *expected* to attend Sunday church service.[3] This change in protocol marked the change of a religious college into a secular university. It was a change in the language of the rule for following rules.

Protocols are the key to changing systems. The most significant axioms of systems are rules for rules, structuring structures, and the like. As the New Critics proved when they placed criticism above scholarship, it is possible to introduce new protocols into university systems, especially protocols for intellectual exchanges.

In the context of Graff's proposals to debate, I propose that a protocol to collaborate replace our present polemical protocol to compete. The latter is the protocol that generates attempts to falsify claims in a disciplinary mode of argumentation. Though omitted in our official view of literary study, collective inquiry historically has been the most effective means of changing critical conduct. The moral of the intersections of the careers of Cleanth Brooks, Robert Penn Warren, William Wimsatt, René Wellek, and Austin Warren is that their intellectual exchanges changed the shape of literary inquiry for three generations of literary students. Unfortunately, such collaborations usually result in the sort of schooling that produces schools whose students follow competitive protocols. Assuming the inevitability of institutions, how can alternatives to the present system be institutionalized in a way that allows for recursive restructuring rather than an impermeable fixing of existing structures? This is a difficult problem to solve because institutions have self-regulating features.

Before critical practices can be expected to change, critical protocols, the rules for following rules, must change. But critics only follow protocols that lead them to the objects of their desires. At present, by making them compete for limited rewards, universities induce conflicting desires and fragmented self-images in literary scholars. However, it is to the advantage of critics, intellectually and politically, to collaborate rather than compete (see chapter 15).

If the protocols of collaboration (by which I mean concurrence based on an acknowledgment of differences) replaced the protocols of competition, other changes would follow. For instance, error would become a heuristic device. Protocols that tolerate difference emphasize agreement and de-emphasize falsification and competition. If we demand that scholarship be definitive, we relegate research-in-progress to a state of ignorance, emphasize disagreement, and valorize falsification. Competition divides and segregates, divorces and segments. It induces paranoia.

This is a moment in our history when we need to act collectively before the electronic revolution we are undergoing invisibly reinstitutionalizes us and reshapes our professional conduct.

Concurrence Is Not Consensus

Literary criticism is intellectual work. What if it were based on protocols of compassion, commitment, collaboration, concurrence, and community? I list these as alternatives to the modern protocols of criticism I have critiqued in previous chapters. Compassion is an alternative to control, commitment to disinterest, collaboration to competition, concurrence to appropriation, and community to individuality.[4]

Let me begin with the need for intellectual compassion. Compassion, as "sorrow for the sufferings or troubles of another" (*Webster's New World Dictionary*), is necessary for a commitment, which is necessary for the collaboration that brings about the concurrence that builds a community.[5] I contrast it with intellectual machismo. Intellectual compassion allows one intellectual to enter imaginatively into the problematic of another. Problems occasion pain and suffering. Pain demands resolution. Collaboration, a desirable alternative to competition, depends on the ability of intellectuals to feel the pain or suffering of others as if it were their own. Competitors thrive on the pain they cause others. The intellectual antagonism competition spawns interferes with the resolution of problems communally. In a competitive environment, concurrence is out of the question. Competitors abstract problems from the painful experiences they articulate and solve them as if they were puzzles to be solved faster and more fashionably (as well as with more élan) than anyone else can solve them.

Problems are not equivalent to puzzles. A literary problem is not only perplexing; it is also frustrating and painful.[6] It occasions suffering. Because a problem is also perplexing and difficult, it calls for the articulation of many questions. Each question is different. Questioning requires the breaking down of preconceived frameworks because of the difficulty of formulating the problem in a way that does not simply appropriate it. Collaborative inquiry is not an instance of differing perspectives ultimately coming together in a unified framework. Intellectual concurrence (rather than appropriation) is sought. This requires an agreement to agree without denying differences.[7]

Concurrence, an agreement to join intellectual forces to get something done, is a plausible alternative to appropriation *only if* the differences among the researchers are allowed free play. In this form of collaboration, researchers are invited into the group not because they represent the same point of view but because they represent different and even incompatible points of view. Since getting-at-"my"-truth no longer governs the inquiry, quarrels are abandoned while concurrence is sought because any idea that helps solve the problem is valued. Removing contradictions or inconsistencies from one's discourse is less important than resolving the cultural conflicts we call racism, elitism, and sexism. Concurrence of this sort is particularly desirable in literary research.[8]

Literary criticism calls for intellectual collaboration. The form of critical collaboration I have been advocating converges on the apprehension of a problem. Out of compassion, critics band together seeking to alleviate the problem. This happens in literary criticism when a group of differing intellectuals, bound together by the acknowledgment of a textual/cultural problem, concur about a possible reading of it. By concurring they do not seek conformity; they seek the coincidences among their differences. In this collaboration, concurrences about the problem and the solution are transpersonal. Intellectual compassion and care are what hold the group together, not a common ideal or telos. In this form of collaboration, intellectual subject positions are not configured competitively. Differences are crucial. Reading is not an appropriation by an individual; it is the political concurrence of a group.

Collaboration is inescapable in the practice of literary study, despite the patriarchal institution's insistence on individualistic readings. Why do we so rarely acknowledge it? In "Competition, Compassion, and Community: Models for a Feminist Ethos," Maria Lugones and Elizabeth Spelman write that "the desire to excel, the desire to avoid obscurity, and the desire for distinction become definitive of a competitive attitude in a context of opposition and they come, in their turn, to be shaped by this context. For at the heart of the desire to excel in the context of opposition, is the desire to excel not merely in some non-comparative sense, but to excel over others, to better them. . . . The overriding preoccupation is with standing out against the performances of others" (236). As they remind us, competition is "essentially self-centered" (237)—it makes "one's own success and well-being . . . impossible without someone else's failure and/or misery" (241). Still, they argue, there is an alternative to the politics of competition—communal excelling.[9]

Collaboration takes place within an aggregate of communities—the polis. An intellectual community stands out as a concurrence of intellectuals.[10] This does not prevent different intellectual communities from engendering sometimes competing collaborations: "There are contexts in which the desire to avoid obscurity and the desire for excellence are not only compatible with but necessary ingredients of projects that are properly communal. In those cases these desires are incompatible with an individualistic conception of excellence and of the participants in the project" (238).

Though the word "community" includes the word "unity," communities are not unities. Obviously, a notion of community can be deconstructed by pointing out that it implies an essential, central unity, the "presence" of some entity. My concern here is not so much with the aberrations of a metaphysics of presence but with the naive assumption that communities are, in fact, unities. I do not mean to suggest by privileging the word "community" that every person in a community communes, that is, moves through the understanding of common goals and ideals toward identity or sameness. Though the word unfortunately suggests some kind of entity that is unified, it is possible to think of a community as a theater in which intellectual play is dramatized. In this play, the dramatis personae, each with distinct characteristics uniquely performed, act together toward a resolution of a problem. This is a play of differences that concurrently respond to a problem differentially perceived.[11] In this play, critics enjoy differing subject positions and their characters change; that is, they exchange subject positions. The bond of an intellectual community is intellectual compassion, the imaginative entry into another's problem.

In the terms now under discussion, critical inquiry is the compassionate accommodation of difference.[12] Such inquires are, by this definition, collaborative. But to be housed in universities, collaborative inquirers (research groups) must, in some sense, *share* problems with communities. And, ultimately, communities of intellectuals can only legitimize themselves in the institution of criticism to the extent that they inquire into problems characterizing the various public spheres that make up our cultural formation.[13] These are not individualizing possibilities, and considering them brings us circuitously back to a consideration of theory.

Although falsification cannot and should not be recuperated by postmodern critics, in the context of communal inquiry it seems foolish if not impossible to try to do without the heuristic value of error. Problems surely are related to errors. To inquire requires error. It is the breaking apart of preconceptions. Inquiries are written (or, in a grammatological sense, inscribed) as questions. Just as texts are intertexts that encompass myriad cultural formations, so inquiries are texts. Knowing this is theorizing.

Theorizing is not necessarily making theories. Theory-making is patriarchal. Theory is often used as a weapon. Theory is an effective instrument of falsification. And so on and so forth. But systematic theories that feed into competitive schemes are only the husk of theorizing. It is in the understanding of a problem through differing intuitions of it that theorizing occurs. Out of these intuitions arises a more general view of critical performance than is available to the solitary scholar. Competition obscures this phenomenon. In a competition among critics, theories become machines of falsification used to refute the assumptions of rival critics. In a communal inquiry, however, theorizing is informed by intellectual compassion. It arises out of the urgency to end the pain associated with a specific problem. In that endeavor, performances must be made as effective as possible. Theorizing helps. Competing critical schools do not. But are schools of criticism necessary? Not if the warrants in literary arguments are intuitive. In communal inquiries, the concurrence of critics is more significant than their schooling.

Professing Literature in 2001

By way of conclusion to the preceding critique of the ideals of disciplinarity, I take a brief look at the universities of the future. For the most
part they will be electronic environments. As I mentioned in my discussion
of Gerald Graff's proposals for curricular change, the protocols governing
interactions with students will change dramatically. In ways unimaginable
now, the study of literature will be profoundly affected. Nonetheless, a pattern of development is beginning to emerge that suggests that Graff's
highly dialogical proposals are very well suited to the universities of the
future. In fact, taken together, they offer an architecture for those universities.

Already, in the academy, profound changes are taking place. For instance, virtual classrooms are now commonplace. In fact, virtual universities are already under construction. Alpha University, which goes beyond
the bulletin board services of MegaByte U or the Electronic College of
Theory, has been in development since November of 1991. David Downing
and I have been coordinating its activities from its inception. We believe
that proposals for future universities must be undertaken with virtual classrooms in mind. We live and work in a period of transition from print environments to electronic ones. As text-based learning, cultural study will be
deeply affected by this transformation.

Graff's proposals were influential in the building of Alpha U, since he
looks beyond the traditional classroom. "As long as it continues to be
taught in a privatized space," he writes, "even the best-taught course is
limited in its power to help students" ("Other Voices" 828).[1] He advocates
interrelated (networked) classrooms wherein teachers swap roles or organize the classes as symposia or conferences in ways that parallel work in

LAN (local area) or WAN (wide area) electronic networks. However, bringing classrooms into homes reconfigures them as "private spaces." Moreover, when not monitored by surveillance devices, interactions in cyberspace ("a parallel universe created and sustained by the world's computers and communication lines" [Benedikt 1]) are impenetrably private. There persons often do not know and cannot identify each other. (The virus problem is one unhappy instance of such networking privacy.) Indeed, since future classrooms will be in cybertime/space, those who wish to pursue Graff's proposals find themselves in a dilemma: Will cybertime/space make "classrooms" of the future even more privatized despite networking facilities? Will they, for instance, countermand academic ivory-towerism?

Graff's proposals for curriculum change, specifically, for foregrounding conflict, suit the virtual universities of the future. If we can break out of our self-imposed isolationism and connect with students, he argues, we can restore our transformative cultural role ("Other Voices" 831). At the outset of his project, Graff wrote that embracing "new methods is no answer in itself, for they too have been unable to create a usable cultural context for literary study. The close, concrete reading of literary works, which remains one of the primary tasks of criticism, is not likely to recover the sense of mission that once informed it as long as it takes place in a vacuum—separated from historical, philosophical and social contexts. Thus a fusing of cultural inquiry and the most scrupulous textual attention would begin to restore to criticism a constructive role in the literary culture" (*Professing Literature* 10–11).

Graff has set out to construct a university that is not an ivory tower. Since he tells us in detail what professing literature *could* be like in a reconstructed university, it seems appropriate to inquire what it can be like in a virtual university. First I describe those features of Graff's proposals most likely to be affected in virtual classrooms. His new university features (1) a *learning community* in which (2) students *collaborate* with their teachers (3) on *cultural texts* (4) to resolve *"real-time" problems.* Then I offer some recommendations as friendly amendments to Graff's recommendations.

Graff's University

Graff is the architect of a postmodern university. Whereas the modern university was organized on the basis of a consensus or conformity model, his is based on a conflict or difference model. He hopes "to reconceive educational coherence as a coherence of conflict rather than of consensus. Such a rethinking would mean moving from the consensus model which has governed educational philosophy in the past to a conflict model, in which we would start from the assumption that we do not need agreement on first principles in order to make humanities education more accessible" ("What Should We Be Teaching" 199). Such a fundamental change in the organizing principle of an institution radically alters it.

Graff's proposal reverses the bonds that usually hold the social relations in universities together. As he compellingly argues, consensus could be the principle underlying the "old college" because it was predetermined by religious affiliation. Although historians often describe the modern university as a democratic institution governed by consensus, Graff notes that consensus was never the norm ("Future of Theory" 260). After a century of illusory discourse about common principles and shared aims, we should not delude ourselves further by basing our curricular proposals on a consensus model. Instead we should restructure the university (or at least the humanities) on the basis of our differences. Graff focuses almost entirely on the pedagogical implications of this new order.

From a pedagogical perspective, a university is constituted by relations among teachers and students. The transmission of information (often called the "banking" theory of education) is an issue that has engaged educators since Paulo Freire wrote his influential *Pedagogy of the Oppressed* (1970) and has been vigorously renewed in our information era. Graff rivets his attention on the connectivity issue in this debate. In "Colleges Are Depriving Students of a Connected View of Scholarship," Graff remarks that, when students are not connected to the issues underlying faculty researches, courses are less "intellectually stimulating" (48). Without connectivity, students soon forget and forgo their learning. For Graff, connectivity is more likely when students take part in the conversations going on in the intellectual communities to which their teachers belong.

1. *Learning Communities.* In the same essay, Graff envisions the curriculum as a forum for discussion, a "learning community" (48). Gabelnick, MacGregor, Matthews, and Smith, the authors of *Learning Communities: Creating Connections among Students, Faculty, and Disciplines,* define a learning community as

> any one of a variety of curricular structures that link together several existing courses—or actually restructure the curricular material entirely—so that students have opportunities for deeper understanding and integration of the material they are learning, and more interaction with one another and their teachers as fellow participants in the learning enterprise. . . . In learning communities, students and faculty members experience courses and disciplines not as arbitrary or isolated offerings but rather as a complementary and connected whole. These interwoven, reinforcing curricular arrangements make it possible, then, for faculty and students to work with each other in less distant, routinized ways and to discover a new kind of enriched intellectual and social ground. (19)

They see Graff's proposal as one of many variants: "One solution, offered by Gerald Graff, suggests that we 'teach the debate' over the canon instead of trying to resolve it through narrow definitions" (8). To perceive Graff's proposals as "one of many variants" fits their taxonomy of learning communities. But this is misleading. Their five basic models of learning communities dovetail more easily with the modern university than with a postmodern one. From a postdisciplinary perspective, their view of learning communities, wherein methods are consensual matters, is at its core modern. Graff's view of learning and his view of community are more distinctively postmodern in their tolerance of difference and dissent. He writes: "As the disciplines have moved away from the positivism of the nineteenth century, knowledge has come increasingly to be visualized not as a unified structure, a pyramid of building blocks, but as a set of social practices, a conversation. Whether this spells the death of the concept of the disciplines as a 'body of knowledge' is still very much open to debate—the kind of debate that I have been recommending we put in the forefront of education" ("Teach the Conflicts" 66). Gabelnick et al. have a less supple sense of a discourse community than Graff (see discussion of Swales below).

In Graff's postmodern university, teachers and students discuss texts that have cultural significance. Neither the persons nor the texts are construed in patterned isolation from each other. However, this discourse community does not take a *united* front on the rationales of its own existence. Nor is it a discourse community in the sense John Swales developed in *Genre Analysis,* which takes as its defining characteristic that the members have "a broadly agreed set of common public goals" (24–25). It comes closer to Swales's recent redefinition, in which he proposes that discourse communities have only "a discoverable set of goals":[2]

1. A discourse community [d.c.] has a discoverable set of goals. These may be publicly and explicitly formulated and either generally or partially assented to by the members; they may be consensual; or they may be separate but contiguous (Old Guard and Young Turks; researchers and practitioners, as in the just-holding-together American Psychological Association).
2. A d. c. has mechanisms of intercommunication among members. There is no change here. Without mechanisms there is no community.
3. A d. c. uses its participatory mechanisms for a range of purposes: to provide performance-enhancing information and feedback; to channel innovation; to maintain the value and belief systems of the community; and to enhance its professional space.
4. A d. c. utilizes an evolving selection of genres in the furtherance of its set of goals and as instantiation of its participatory mechanisms.
5. A d. c. has acquired and continues to search for d.c.-specific terminology.

6. A d. c. has an explicit or implicit hierarchical structure which manages the processes of entry into and advancement within the discourse community. (lecture handout)

Item five in Swales's definition of a discourse community matches an important point in Graff's view of the role of theory in the conflict model.

2. *Collaborative Arguments.* Graff recommends that students learn theorizing by "living the language" in a way that parallels the learning process of normal language acquisition—by living in the country in which the language is spoken. The living conversation of theory is, for Graff, debate. This is the work on which teachers and students of cultural studies collaborate. Writings and readings in cultural studies are structured by debate. In its most rudimentary form, cultural study is constituted by cycles of arguments.

To collaborate is to work together. Thus, teachers and students work on cultural issues together by writing out their readings of them. Agreeing or disagreeing about the social and cultural effects of readings is the work of collaboration. Hence, in Graff's proposals the crucial issue is how to disagree constructively. As he often points out, critics do not know how to disagree. For him, *debate is a constructive form of disagreement.*

To many this seems counterintuitive. Debates are often rationalized quarrels. In a postmodern critical climate wherein there are no grounds for refutation, debating would seem little more than a competition for truth.[3] It is not competition for Graff; it is "dialogical." He writes: "To me, the bottom line in analyzing the institutional processes I discuss in *Professing Literature* is the results these processes produce at the student's end, not whether a culture of 'argument' is or isn't maintained. More specifically, what matters to me is the extent to which educational institutions help students to see what is at issue in the political and cultural conflicts that they have a stake in" ("Response" 91).[4]

3. *Cultural Texts.* In Graff's recent essays, he construes conflict as dialogical:

> In a dialogical curriculum, questions that challenge or redefine the premises of the discussion would not arise in one class only to be abruptly dropped in the next, as tends to be the case now. Since such questions would have a chance to become part of other conversations besides the one taking place in the privacy of a single course, the more pertinent ones would figure to be sustained and reinforced. This is the case if only because the inevitable inequalities of authority in the pedagogical situation mean that questions like "So what?" "Who cares?" "Could you clarify that?" "How is that point relevant?" and "Why are we going on about this issue to the exclusion of that one?" are more likely to come from other faculty than from students, at least for the moment. ("Other Voices" 831–32)

In "Teach the Conflicts," Graff concludes that there is no alternative to consensus but to "agree to disagree." However, he is well aware that any group working together on a problem will sometimes agree and sometimes disagree. Agreement and disagreement are dialogical relations. Disciplinary discourse communities can be distinguished from other kinds of discourse communities—concurrences, for instance (see below). A disciplinary community wherein consensus is achieved by argumentation (akin to Swales's original definition of a discourse community) is organized on agreement-to-disagree protocols, to which agreements to agree are secondary. By contrast, a concurrence (akin to Swales's redefinition) is based on agreement-to-agree protocols, which take priority over agreements to disagree. Protocols shape the various relations of agreement and disagreement in dialogical situations.

Yet how can a policy of conflict be a productive form of work? Debate in a postmodern climate is far more likely to encourage an ever-widening range of diversity. As Graff notes, we have rarely if ever depended on consensus in the humanities. For him, cultural studies provides ways of embracing diversity ("What Should We Be Teaching" 192; "Future of Theory" 266). The recommendations of Terry Eagleton (*Literary Theory*) and William Cain (*The Crisis in Criticism*) for changes in the conduct of literary criticism, combined with Raymond Williams's exemplary practice, delineate for Graff a viable cultural studies. How is it, then, that cultural studies can offer us a productive way of handling increasing diversity where other attempts have failed?

Reading Graff's work, one is tempted to think that the answer is that cultural studies can admit a diversity of conflicting methods. But Graff's analysis does not easily allow that inference. Theory has come under the sway of the field-coverage principle. The schools-and-movements curricular scheme, which presupposes a pluralism of unified methodologies or approaches, is thereby governed by both a consensus principle and a field-coverage principle. A school is an interpretive community that appears to achieve consensus about its methods of reading. In his remarks about Fish's conception of interpretative communities, Graff expresses doubt that consensus exists even at this level of our curricular system ("Co-optation" 179). His analysis invites distrust of the schools-and-methods view of literary study as a microscopic version of field coverage. Is applying a method the "work" Graff would have students do? Is this what they are trained for? In such a view, students are destined to be future disciples (or should we say clones?). Though it has seemed so to some of his critics, this is not the outcome Graff anticipates. What is the alternative?

Throughout his writings Graff insists that students should be actively engaged in, rather than passive spectators of, academic disputes. In "Cultural Studies, Postmodernism, and Composition," John Schilb sees students as potential collaborators, a view he deems consonant with Graff's proposals. Schilb writes that "*a composition program would therefore be a research program* examining various theories of 'cultural studies' and 'postmodernism,' as well as how they diverge or mesh." He explains this remark by saying that

> this agenda might appear to threaten the field's current pluralism, the range of scholarly concerns and methodological approaches it now exhibits. But they could be productively juxtaposed even as faculty undertake the collective study I have in mind. It could actually help writing teachers avoid the fragmentation that Gerald Graff has found plaguing literary scholars because they fail to admit and work through their conflicts. And just as Graff has proposed that literary studies foreground conflict in a way productive and involving for students, so *they should be enlisted in the project I am suggesting for composition,* not conceived as mere recipients of its fruits. (174–75; emphases mine)

Following Schilb's version of Graff's conflict model, let me stipulate that the activity in which students engage is, in principle, collaborative; they are potential co-researchers. Understanding students as potential coworkers in research fits future classrooms. A different structure of authority governs education's electronic environments. In computer labs students handle virtual learning community situations more adeptly than their teachers do. Even so, assuming that collaboration is the wave of the future, why *debate* together?

4. *Problems That Derive from Real-Time Experiences.* Where does debate lead us? The conflicts Graff offers as instances of his model are derived not only from texts but also from extratextual concerns. As I have already noted, he writes that "the close, concrete reading of literary works, which remains one of the primary tasks of criticism, is not likely to recover the sense of mission that once informed it *as long as it takes place in a vacuum*—separated from historical, philosophical and social contexts" (*Professing Literature* 10–11; emphasis mine). The problems texts presuppose "live" outside the discussion, namely, our social or cultural experiences. Texts are, in Kenneth Burke's famous phrase, "equipment for living."

Graff's university is a *learning community* in which students *collaborate* with their teachers on *cultural* problems that derive from *real-time experiences.* With these parameters in mind, let us consider what happens when Graff's university becomes a virtual university.

Graff's University and Alpha University

Alpha U is a virtual university. It exists in a virtual space/time continuum, not in real space or time. In *The Computer Glossary* Alan Freedman defines "virtual" as "a simulated or conceptual environment." Through the aid of computers, for instance, scientists simulate weather patterns in order to understand real weather patterns in what has become known as "chaos theory" (Gleick). Architects test the design of buildings by computer simulations of stress factors. In addition, they can show prospective clients exactly what their new environments will look like. Virtuality has become a standard aspect of marketing, even in hairdressing. There is, however, a dark side to this phenomenon—for instance, virtual news, wherein images and voices in databases are restructured to serve as virtual reality scenarios for events that have transpired but for which there was no immediate coverage. Nonetheless, we can expect the rapid development of virtual classrooms. Will Graff's recommendations (e.g., develop learning communities as the sites of cultural debates) work in virtual classrooms?

The problem Graff hopes to solve (classrooms as privatized spaces) is exaggerated in virtual environments. Cyberspace is a highly privatized space. As any subscriber to a computer listserv knows, writing and reading expand at a rapid pace in the differing tempo of cybertime. Placing your name on a listserv commits you to a deluge of mail because messages arriving at its site are sent to everyone on the list. Each morning your e-mail box is crammed with messages. The difficulties of reading available materials are amplified tenfold in cyberspace. Thus an emphasis on disagreement would be likely to produce not only diversity but also endless controversy.

That productive work is accomplished by listservs is questionable—persons are so swamped with scattered "talk" that they cancel their subscriptions. Downloading material sent by a listserv parallels tape-recording telephone conversations on party lines. This form of networking is not collaborative. It is not an instance of an exemplary learning community. The level at which assumptions and conceptions are shared is indeed minimal. Moreover, as Graff notes, the assumption that humanists share assumptions does not hold up even in real time.

Debates on computer party lines tend toward a chaotic state. Everyone is talking at the same time to no one in particular but to everyone in general. This propagates pandemonium. In such an environment, the pre-existing tendency for critics to behave as schools unto themselves is magnified. In virtual classrooms, "conversations" tend toward solipsistic cybercism or critical self-envelopment because they lack the constraints of real-time dialogue (e.g., a listener's bored countenance). If Graff's aim is not "to bring conflicts to a consensual resolution, but to exploit the conflicts themselves as an organizing principle" ("Future of Theory" 261), we have to ask, Is such an aim feasible in cyberspace?

To avoid the listserv problem, we developed *Cycles,* a set of research protocols that form "a cooperative document editing tool," for Alpha University. The model was inspired by a 1988 review of Lotus Corporation's *Notes,* a major business networking software. In his "Top of the News," Mike Hogan writes that Lotus Corp's new program *Notes* is a

> group productivity tool that lets co-workers share documents and graphics across local area and wide area networks. *Notes* is intended as a vehicle to enable a wide range of knowledge workers to share their ideas and comments on projects. The package acts as a cooperative document editing tool that records all input. Several large companies and about 200 Lotus employees have put *Notes* to a variety of uses, including tracking the product's own development. The software gathers and archives input from multiple departments, pulling together material for large-scale brainstorming. Action items are suggested and then tested against the reactions of corporate reviewers. Project members don't have to meet as often when they can interact this way. (14)

Cycles, the database that stores the various cycles in Alpha U, merges the protocols of classrooms, research projects, and journals into cycles of dialogues linked by cross-references and indexes so that they can be searched and reassembled productively. Taking Graff's view of the classroom as a dialogical site of debate, we record the ongoing dialogue among the co-researchers in a journal-like circular comprised of "letters to the editor" through which projects are negotiated at every stage (see below).

Like Lotus's *Notes, Cycles* functions as a cooperative group project that records its communications in a collaborative document that is continuously edited with the aim of publication. It takes the complex process individuals undertake in their research and makes every step collaborative. All the researchers enter their "notes" into the same database. Through a series of editing protocols, these notes are revised toward making recommendations for specific actions. *Cycles* participants communicate with each other while tracking the communication as an electronic exchange interfaced with editing programs that record it in journal-like formats. Many of the traditional protocols and techniques of scholarly communication merge with each other. *Cycles* has some of the characteristics of a journal, an edition, a conference, a phone call, a video tape, a computer instruction program, and a classroom.

We construe classes in Alpha U as research projects in which students are co-researchers with their teachers, lending their skills to its aims. Each class project starts with the shared perception of a problem and discusses various ways of handling it. Since these discussions are recorded and edited, the "conversations" and "debates" teachers and students enjoy become a "journal" of their research activity. Let me offer three examples of the *Cycles* model.

David Downing, who has been collaborating with me on Alpha U, gave students registered for his Theory and Pedagogy course in the fall of 1992 the option of writing letters to me, as the editor of *Cycles,* describing problems they had as teachers who were at the same time students. Ann Ott wrote a letter about "the awful graduate course" she had taken at another university in which she was asked to accomplish more than was physically possible in a semester. Shortly afterward, Bill Thelin wrote me about student apathy. His letter was followed by one from Karrie Szatek about student resistance. I wrote back, pointing out the connections among their observations. They decided to form a cycle to discuss the problem of student apathy and resistance. Bennis Lathan, Cathy Haskell, Laura French, and Celene Seymour, all of whom had written to me about other problems, found themselves more interested in the issues Ann, Bill, and Karrie had initially articulated and joined their cycle. As a part of an ongoing class, this cycle constituted itself as a research group focused on the problem of student apathy and resistance. David Downing and I are co-researchers in the project. Moreover, in response to their e-mail letters, I referred them to Graff's "Other Voices, Other Rooms," which argues that student apathy is related to the lack of connectivity in our curricula.

One of the precursors to *Cycles* was a collaboration between four graduate students (Kathy Burkland, Terry Cooper, Kim Gannon, and Les Epstein) and myself on the dilemma of being "taught teachers." As students, an expressive pedagogy was *prescribed* to them in a graduate seminar. They experienced this prescriptive pedagogy as a contradictory restraint. They had no voice in the classroom of their professor, who insisted they give voice to freshmen in their own classrooms. When they approached me I suggested that we take their dilemma as a research project and organize a symposium, inviting well-known scholars and our own graduate faculty to join us in a discussion of the problem. At the time I did not understand my pedagogy to be in line with Graff's proposals. In retrospect, I do.

Two years later, Marian Sciachitano and Rory Ong approached me about teaching a seminar on theory. I agreed on the premise that the seminar would be organized not on the principle that we would cover theory as a field (again, this is a retrospective realization) but along the lines of the "taught teachers" research group. They agreed, and we formed the Miami University Theory and Pedagogy Research Group. The course began with the seminar participants (now including Bob Broad, Holly Roberts, Dan Dawson, Cher Uhl, and Don Armstrong) articulating their problems in dealing with theory. Theory had important consequences in their graduate training and in their teaching, but these situations did not always match up well. This research group has its counterpart in Alpha U, where Steven Horvath, Jennifer Gehrman, Margery Vagt, and Peter Naruscewicz have discussed the same problem. (I might add that Craig Frey and Don Paul Palutis formed another cycle concerned with graduate students who were not teaching assistants.) Once problems are on the table, we work with their connections. Sometimes these function extramurally. For instance, David Downing invited the Miami University Theory and Pedagogy Research Group to visit his theory and pedagogy seminar. We presented our seminar papers to David's class and interested faculty. Eventually, four papers from this research group were published in the fall 1990 issue of *Works and Days,* edited by Mark Hurlbert.

These research groups are instances of the learning community for which Graff calls. Moreover, because it is an electronic medium, *Cycles* is also an instance of "multicourse conferencing," in Graff's sense, as the Lotus *Notes* analogy makes clear. It is also an electronic form of teacher swapping. In addition, it enjoys some of the features of teleconferencing. Though I have visited the Indiana University of Pennsylvania campus, which was the site of the student apathy and resistance project, most of our dialogue took place in cyberspace. And, as the project continues, we expect other teachers and students at different universities to join in.

Cycles is not a privatized classroom, even though we work in an electronic environment. Without going into the complex details of the database and how the materials are collected, stored, retrieved, indexed, and edited, I will simply mention that we have made adjustments to Graff's delineation of intellectual communities in order to circumvent the problems cyberspace/time introduces, in particular the problem of the privatization of learning. There are two interrelated cyberspace problems that are connected to privatization—solipsism and discursive violence. Let me take up the problem of violence first.

Anyone who has taught in a computer classroom is likely to be familiar with the discursive violence known as "flaming." Since cyberspace is opaque, speakers can remain anonymous. Anonymity lends itself to discursive violence. Insults, crude jokes, mean-spirited criticisms, anger, resentment, and other negative interpersonal emotions are often vented in cyberspace. The problem is an exaggeration of the more familiar one in which the anonymous reviewers of essays, books, and tenure and promotion documents use their anonymity to level hurtful critiques at colleagues. Such practices, known euphemistically as refutation, destroy open dialogue. This issue is intensified in cyberspace and raises the question, How can we create productive disagreement in electronic environments?

If the disagreeing parties in a controversy take as their starting point the mutual recognition of a problem, they can be productive. However, unless all the parties involved care about the resolution of the problem more than about their own stake in how the problem is conceived or approached, the conflicts lapse into quarrels about terms and methods. There has to be a willingness to let one's own conceptual frameworks be changed by negotiation.

In Alpha U, care rather than rejection is the key to overcoming the "resistance to conflict" syndrome to which Graff often alludes. Alpha U offers its registrants a safe space, inspired by the phenomenology of caring Milton Mayeroff presents in *On Caring*. At its core is the premise that "in caring as helping the other grow, I experience what I care for (a person, an ideal, an idea) as an extension of myself and at the same time as something separate from me that I respect in its own right" (5). Mayeroff goes on to contrast care to "dogmatically clinging to a belief" (5) as a state wherein we are unable to experience others as having worth in their own right. He writes that in caring "I experience the other as having potentialities and the need to grow; I experience an idea, for instance, as seminal, vital, or promising" (7); and he contrasts this experience of "trust" to one that gives a feeling of power and provides "something to dominate." Conflicts of interest that occur in Alpha U are negotiated through protocols of care.

By introducing an ethos of caring, we emend Graff's proposals by shifting from a text-oriented view of literary study to a person-oriented view:

> Alpha University has as its aim the creation of an environment conducive to the understanding of other human beings. It is governed by a protocol of caring. As a consequence, all of its projects, including *Cycles,* are organized on the principle of care for others. Alpha U is dedicated to building a more caring environment in which to live. The strategy involved in its design is simple. Once the building of such an environment is deemed feasible, the hope is that it will spread by imitation. If persons involved in Alpha U find this environment fulfilling, hopefully they will not only maintain it but help it grow and encourage others to be involved. Alpha U is a self-selecting institution. Unlike a corporate institution, it is founded "not for profit" but for the benefit of its builders. Every person who works in this environment works to make it a more caring one. Thus all the members of Alpha U are its builders because the single task of Alpha U is to build a just and caring environment. Like persons who enjoy living in their homes and work hard to maintain, repair, and remodel them, so too, the inhabitants of Alpha U work to maintain, redesign and re-negotiate the interpersonal relations that constitute Alpha U because they enjoy being in its environs. (From the brochure "Starting a Cycle")

But this reorientation from texts to persons does not by itself make conflicts productive (socially transformative). As I mentioned earlier, there is a tendency toward intellectual solipsism in electronic educational environments, familiarly described as a tendency to "get lost in cyberspace." Once inside the privatized world of on-line databases in which the only interaction necessary involves concepts and keystrokes or clicks, persons can dwell within this simulated world as a private weltanschauung. In the study of texts located in cyberspace, reading can be highly solipsistic. To use Gregory Ulmer's term somewhat ironically, all stories become "mystories."

What is outside cyberspace? We could say real experiences. This answer would perturb many postmodern thinkers. They would persuasively argue that there is no metadiscursive grounding to thought. The realism invoked here, however, is not a logical or metadiscursive conception. It is simply a reference to persons in a physical world contrasted to their personae (roles) in virtual classrooms. The realism involved is not epistemological but practical. Yet, since virtuality is a conceptual environment in cyberspace, which is a simulacrum of the physical world, we need to maintain the distinction between physical and virtual.

Alpha U anchors itself in physical pain and joy. In electronic educational environments, we have to anchor problems outside of cyberspace, in persons. We cannot allow cybernetics to take over intellection. However difficult it may become to tell the difference between virtual reality and physical events, pain (if not joy) will demarcate that difference. Since these events occur in real time, they anchor our work and provide what Graff calls "coherence of conflict." Let me explain.

The three interrelated seminar/research groups I mentioned at the beginning of this section were grounded in concrete problems—the painful experiences of students were the starting points. Rather than begin with a pedagogical discourse, we made actual teaching experiences our point of departure. This move provoked further research. Moreover, our seminars were not organized according to the field-coverage principle, wherein a professor presents various schools and methods to graduate students as a transmission of the current state of theoretical knowledge. Rather, students started with concrete pedagogical problems and then used available theoretical formulations to understand them.

The problem-solving orientation of these research groups, which is maintained in Alpha U's cycles, grounds research in mutually recognized pains and joys, and this counters the tendency of electronic educational environments to privatize intellectual projects. From this perspective, pain and joy are the real problems underlying the debates in Alpha U's cycles. We name this way of organizing collaborative research "concurrence." We emend Graff's conflict model by introducing concurrence protocols.

A concurrence is an event in which several persons, because they mutually recognize a problem (or a joy), get together to change (or maintain) that situation. Concurrence is not based on consensus. It is not required that all those concurring agree on fundamental principles. On the contrary, the differences among those concurring *are* the values they bring to the collaboration. The paradox in this situation is that the more diverse the disagreement is, the more perspicuous the problem becomes because there are more perspectives involved. Rather than strive for conceptual agreement, persons are encouraged to look for coincidences in understanding amid their differences. Whereas in the procedures of disciplines anomalies are heuristic, in the protocols of concurrence coincidences are. When concurring, persons do not apply preconceived methods. Instead they allow events to break down the conceptual frameworks they bring to them. These articulations of the problem are negotiated. Agreement and disagreement are in continuous dialogical relation. Whereas at one moment several articulations exhibit striking coincidences and govern the group's plans for action, at another stage different views of the problem pertain, especially when the pressures of experience break down the *always temporary* frameworks in use. Even continuing disagreements help sharpen the perspectives of the persons to whom they are addressed if they are "careful" disagreements. Concurrence depends on *care* for the other members in the group who work to come to terms with mutually recognized pains and joys. Without such care, disagreements cripple research groups.

Controversies or conflicts that inspire debate in literary studies are rooted in experiences of pain and joy. In negotiating them, researchers build cultures. Concurrences, as intertextual relations, are nothing less than building blocks of cultures. We need to incorporate interactions that are not divorced from imagination and emotion into the design of future universities. Our link to the public is through their cultural pains and joys. Imagination and emotion are "fields" we all too often neglect in cultural studies. They are indispensable in electronic educational environments. The overintellectualized analyses that disciplinary mechanisms have occasioned in our work will only be exaggerated in electronic educational environments.

At this historical juncture, as Graff's work makes us aware, we are faced with a crucial choice—concurrence or conflict. There is another, related dilemma: Program or be reprogrammed!

Appendix
Notes
Works Cited
Indexes

The MURGE Experiment

There are four basic elements and two conditions of a logically adequate test. The four basic elements are (1) a hypothesis, (2) initial conditions—an occurrence of a state of affairs stipulated to be the occasion of the test, (3) auxiliary assumptions about the effect of the variables in the initial condition on the outcome of the prediction, and (4) a prediction. The prediction, of course, is the most important element. For a prediction to be valid it must describe beforehand the occurrence of a possible state other than that of the initial conditions in which any witness can observe that something has happened or failed to happen as the outcome of the initial conditions (Giere* 86–94). I followed these conditions in general during the MURGE experiment in the fall of 1980, when I directed a research group that undertook an exhaustive analysis of Joyce's "Araby" based on Seymour Chatman's model of texts as delineated in *Story and Discourse.* First I formulated each of Chatman's concepts as an instruction to select particular features from the sentences in Joyce's "Araby" and sequenced the instructions. Then nine readers followed these instructions and compared their results (see my "*Story and Discourse* and the Practice of Literary Criticism").

Our experiment tested the following hypotheses: (1) that trained readers learn to read texts as literature by selectively attending to groups of textual features as a result of acquiring the relevant literary concepts, and (2) that identifying their principles of selection would describe this process. These two stipulations could provide grounds for the possibility of replicating readings of texts as literature. Readers trained in the same way should read in the same way. In effect, they will replicate the readings of similarly trained readers on the basis of the same set of remembered instructions about reading canonical texts.

We were interested in our ability as readers to identify or recognize similar groups of textual features. We hypothesized that such identifications are a matter of selective attention to the sentences or parts of sentences in the text being read. Trained readers learn to recognize specific textual features as the result of acquiring the relevant framing concepts. In the case of literary critics, these concepts are acquired through professional training in university graduate schools.

Further, we assumed that critical readers' ability to identify relevant features of literary texts is part of their ability to process information. As cognitive psychologists suggest, groups of features selected for attention are perceived as patterns analogous to but not identical to those previously perceived in remembered texts. In addition, we assumed that students of literature ordinarily have read similar texts and have been trained to use literary concepts (plot, character trait, etc.—see my "On the Anvil of Theoretical Debate" and Prince's "What's the Story in Narratology?"). Thus, when these preconceptions of literary texts are activated by a specific text, certain features of that text stand out in relief. These assumptions can be summed up in the following hypothesis: if a reader of a text is to replicate another reader's reading of that text, he or she has to be trained to recognize the same kinds of features and to draw similar kinds of inferences from them as the first reader. This is a key precondition of the possibility of replicating a reading.

When we turned our attention to the variables in the experiment, an insurmountable series of uncontrollable situations came to mind. For instance, similarly trained readers often do not replicate each other's readings because they have a vested interest in making specific claims about the texts in question or because they have different value systems. If we could find readers who had not read the text in question and who had no particular professional stake in interpreting the text, such readers would be ideal candidates to test a particular model of reading. There are, of course, no such ideal candidates. Moreover, every reader has gaps in his or her competence to read a text. Nor was it possible to assume that readers who have been trained in the same school of thought are in possession of the same store of information. Nonetheless, it seemed sensible to us to assume that if a reader is neither an excitable proponent nor an ardent critic of a particular model of criticism, then such a reader can reliably test that model.

Since testing other readers was impossible, we constituted ourselves as a research group made up of critical readers who agreed to analyze James Joyce's "Araby." Further, we agreed to follow a set of procedures for reading texts developed from Chatman's *Story and Discourse.* If we had taken a hard line, we would have had to assume that when instructed by the rule implicit in Chatman's concepts to select textual features, every reader in the group should select the same sentences or parts of sentences. Or, more to our point, when instructed to follow a specific procedure for identifying, say, the plot of "Araby," every reader should come up with virtually the same plot summary. Our expectations were far more modest. We hoped for a good degree of uniformity in our selection of features.

We conducted the experiment systematically to establish a statistical correlation between the learning of highly specified literary concepts of texts in general and the ability to recognize (select) the relevant textual features in the text being read. To increase the likelihood of replicability, we worked as an interpretive community, that is, in collaboration with each other, like a class studying a particular text. We first studied the interrelated concepts (not only plot, but character traits, point of view, etc.) in Chatman's *Story and Discourse.* Next we formulated procedures for selecting particular textual features from a group of sentences as a sequenced set of interrelated selection rules to be used in the experiment. Then we set about analyzing "Araby."

The results of the experiment did not confirm our hypotheses. Acquiring detailed concepts of common textual features did not automatically lead to common identifications of textual features. Most identifications of textual features had to be negotiated and then renegotiated. The circularity of our procedures became apparent. As Jonathan Culler pointed out in his commentary on the published analysis,

> When a group of people are working together to apply a theory, the importance of precise procedural or operational definitions becomes even greater, for each time the members of the group disagree about a identification this will be taken as evidence of the imprecision and even inapplicability of the model. As James Sosnoski notes in "On the Anvil of Theoretical Debate," members of the group will come to prefer definitions based on easily identifiable linguistic features and will come to feel that something is seriously lacking in definitions that can only be applied if the group has already agreed upon an interpretation of the story. ("The Application of Theory" 289)

In many instances, we could not identify the features of the text unless we had first agreed on an interpretation of the text through negotiation. The application of Chatman's theory went counter to our intuition as readers.

Shortly after the MURGE experiment, I developed a similar set of selection rules for Toulmin's theory of argumentation. This less formal pedagogical experiment proved a disaster. Outside the parameters of a collaboration, students, working in isolation, produced completely contradictory analyses of "Araby" essays while following the same set of selection rules. When I tried in class to adjudicate among the conflicting identifications of textual features (the same proposition identified alternately as a claim, as the grounds of a claim, and as the warrant for the inference), I found it impossible. At first I thought the rules were too vague, but later, after complaints that they were too scientific (a complaint made by Chatman about the MURGE analysis), I abandoned the project, persuaded that critical essays were more illogical than logical in their structure.

I then tried a final simple experiment. I turned to Gerald Prince's *A Grammar of Stories* and attempted to do a reading of "Araby" based on his exacting and detailed semiotic delineation of the structure of all stories. I came up with the following plot summary:

> "Araby" is the story of a boy who did not know how he could tell [his friend's sister] of his confused adoration. [At the time] he was thankful that he could "see so little" [of himself]. When she said she would love to go to a splendid bazaar, *Araby,* he [tells her] "If I go, I will bring you something." He asked for leave to go to the bazaar on Saturday, and reminded his uncle that he wished to go. When he came home to dinner, his uncle had not yet been home. [Finally] he heard his uncle's latchkey in the door. He asked his uncle, who had forgotten, to give him the money to go to the bazaar. His uncle was very sorry he had forgotten. [Then] he left the kitchen, took his seat in a train, passed out onto the road and found himself in a big hall. Remembering with difficulty why he had come, he went over to one of the stalls and examined porcelain vases and flowered tea-sets [while] he listened vaguely to the conversation [of a young lady and two men]. The young lady came over and asked him did he wish to buy anything. He looked humbly at the great jars at either side of the dark entrance to the stall and murmured, "No, thank you." He knew his stay was useless and, gazing up into the darkness, he saw himself as a creature driven and derided by vanity.

My first conclusion was that Prince's concept of plot differed from those of Freimarck and others (see chapter 7). In each case a different set of selection rules produced (not surprisingly) different plot summaries. Different readers employing different warrants produce different plots. At this point I asked myself, Can Prince's concept of "plot" be used to correct the plot summaries of the critics I quoted earlier?

To use the plot produced by Prince's theory as a corrective for the plots given by Mandel, Freimarck, Lyons, or Beck seems a dubious procedure. The concepts Joyce critics used all warrant comparisons of "Araby" to other texts. Freimarck, whom Mandel follows, compares "Araby" with the Grail quest romances; Lyons compares it with Chaucer's "Prioress' Tale"; and Beck compares it with other *Dubliners* stories. Though a descriptive model such as Prince's would seem a prerequisite for generic comparisons of stories, it was developed to explain how critics are able to summarize plots. Prince's model, by his own account, is continuously under revision and too limited to explain such critical activity. (In his work after *A Grammar of Stories* Prince abandoned his theory and adopted a much looser, more flexible model.) It seems unlikely that a theory of narrative based exclusively on linguistic markers in the text can account for the decisions readers make, since so many nontextual frames come into play. In short, it seems impossible to develop descriptive techniques that would provide the grounds for the refutation of critical claims.

Prologue

1. Following Cohen's careful scrutiny of the body of criticism on James Thomson's *The Seasons,* I undertook a similar analysis of criticism on James Joyce's *Portrait of the Artist as a Young Man.* The anomaly that surfaced in my study was that *Portrait* critics used identical passages to support conflicting claims. This disconcerting feature of criticism led me to investigate evidence in literary arguments. I adopted Steven Toulmin's account of informal arguments in *The Uses of Argument* to assess the *Portrait* essays as arguments. I soon realized my analysis should account for the logical function of every proposition in a critical essay, not merely sentences purporting to offer evidence for interpretive claims. The type of analysis I undertook is often called discourse analysis. At the time I was quite influenced by text grammars developed by Tuen van Dijk and Gerald Prince and attempted to develop a similar text grammar for critical arguments. I decided to concentrate on the smaller body of "Araby" criticism so that I could do a detailed analysis of each sentence. Statements purporting to be evidence (quotes from Joyce's text or descriptions of it) remained focal. This focus soon led to a study of the relationships between the evidence offered in support of interpretive claims about Joyce's text and the sentences in "Araby" that were quoted, referred to, alluded to, or paraphrased. I concluded that the sentences that purportedly described the story actually described how differently its various critics read it. This brought clearly into view the significance of warranting assumptions used by differing schools of criticism. Readings of the text were often framed by different and sometimes incompatible assumptions about how texts were constructed. Regardless of the differences, every reading entailed a method of reading. See my "The Use of the Word 'Text' in Critical Discourse" and "Reading Acts and Reading Warrants" for an illustration of the ways in which warranting terms entail frameworks for reading acts characteristic of various schools of criticism.

2. We analyzed Joyce's short story "Araby" using Seymour Chatman's *Story and Discourse.* The correlation of our analyses, despite the specificity of the rules for describing texts, was about 50 percent and would have been less if the students had felt more independent of my understanding of Chatman. Shortly afterward I analyzed "Araby" using Gerald Prince's *Grammar of Stories* and showed it to Prince. By this time he was moving away from the descriptive techniques elaborated in *Grammar* because they were unfeasible. He was fascinated by my description of "Araby" but also surprised by my application of his theory—not that he thought it misguided but that its results were counterintuitive. During this period, together with students in my Introduction to Criticism seminars, I regularly analyzed "Araby" criticism using Stephen Toulmin's model of argumentation. Again, despite the very high degree of specificity in the rules for describing the texts, the analyses were disconcertingly inconsistent.

Chapter 1: What Skeletons?

1. Postmodern thinkers customarily reject the notion of a coherent self. Thus the notion that persons had past "selves" different from their present ones would be regarded as a fiction. However, since many postmodern critics were educated through modern conceptions, they would once have thought they "had" a self. So it would be descriptive to speak of their "past selves." At the same time, the expression illustrates the difficulty many postmodern critics have of avoiding modern conceptions. I treat such terminological difficulties in "The Theory Junkyard."

2. I prefer to use the term "tactic," but in this passage I use "strategic" as a synonym.

3. C. Barry Chabot expresses such skepticism in "The Problem of the Postmodern."

4. In "Students as Theorists: Collaborative Hypertextbooks" I offer a detailed example of such a modern use of hypertext proposed by its author as a fulfillment of postmodern theory.

Chapter 2: Changing Arguments

1. De Man's public celebrity hinges on the scandal of his wartime journalism even more than on his literary analyses.

2. It was rejected by that committee, according to de Man, because he did not "define" literary theory. Rather, he argued that literary theory resists its own definition by definition. This point was at that time deemed unsuitable for an introduction to literary theory. I have commented on the irony of this situation in "Why Theory?"

3. The development of cultural studies suffers from exclusive comparisons with other university disciplines. However amusing it might seem, comparisons between what we and cooks do are not unenlightening. Do we, for instance, work from recipes? Or, we might ask, are methods recipes? More to

the point, would we bother to defend ourselves because our recipes included many variables?

4. Throughout this work I use the term "refutation" in its technical sense, pertaining to argumentation wherein a person offers counterevidence or a counterwarrant to disprove his or her opponent's claim by showing it to be illogical or miscontructed (see chapter 7).

5. Though many critics think of de Man as a postmodern critic, for him "the 'postmodern approach' seems a somewhat naively historical approach" (*Resistance to Theory* 119–20). However, in this remark de Man is responding to Stefano Rosso's question about the concept of "postmodern" as applied to literary works. In the sense in which I am using the term "postmodern" in this work, the term applies to de Man.

6. The obvious objection is that many issues are political and many opponents are duplicitous and hostile. In the cultural wars, for instance, debates over artifacts often presuppose homophobia, xenophobia, sexism, and racism. In such circumstances, opponents are not functioning "rationally" and may even use violence as a means to achieve their ends. However, from a rhetorical point of view, writers/speakers attempt to persuade the audience that their opponent's view is suspect. Convincing the opponent is not a necessary condition of the success of an argument. When debates are conducted in public forums and several persons in the audience take on the role of speakers, the success of the arguments still depends on a negotiation *with the audience.* This is the premise of democracy.

Another objection is that contemporary audiences are not persuaded by rational means but by advertising. This raises the question of whether a democracy can exist in a culture dominated by the media. Though Graff does not limit persuasion to rational outcomes and does entertain the use of media in debates, I take his view of argument further toward a media orientation in my advocacy of configurative arguments (see chapter 6).

7. On some issues concurrence is not possible. This does not necessitate that the protocol be abandoned. In matters of etiquette, the protocol of politeness does not have to be abandoned because situations occur that do not call for it. Protocols are always contextualized. Persons have to be willing to debate before they can agree to a protocol of concurrence. When hostilities break out into violence, the context for debate dissolves.

Chapter 3: Disciplining

1. These six senses of the word "discipline" are taken from *Webster's New World Dictionary.*

2. Unfortunately, my categories may need to be revised in the light of publications too recent to be taken into account, especially those in the series edited by Ellen Messer-Davidow, David Shumway, and David Sylvan, of which this volume is a part. However, since this study was conceived against the background of discussion of the issue of disciplinarity that I do describe, my limited scheme may still be helpful to readers.

3. Zavarzadeh and Morton suggest that their theory of transdisciplinarity

is "historico-political, rather than merely logical" (*Texts for Change* 10), which sounds similar to what I am saying about Graff. The difference between the two views is discernible in that they call their view a theory, that is, a conceptual construct often formulated as a method. By contrast, Graff offers not so much a theory as a set of protocols, which are based on his research into the history of literary study given in *Professing Literature.*

4. For a delineation of her postmodern sophistry see Harkin and Sosnoski, "Barbara Herrnstein Smith: A Contemporary Sophist."

5. See Shumway, "Symposium on Crossdisciplinarity"; Messer-Davidow and Shumway, "Disciplinarity: An Introduction"; and Messer-Davidow, Shumway, and Sylvan, *Knowledges.* Messer-Davidow and Shumway also annually direct a meeting of GRIP (the Group for Research into the Institutionalization and Professionalization of Literary Studies).

6. This thesis is based on the historical conjuncture of the rise of professionalism (Bledstein) and the advent of departments (Veysey) formed to house autonomous disciplines understood as the collective use of conceptual frameworks or paradigms (Kuhn; Toulmin, *Human Understanding*).

7. I do not deny that it can be said to govern much of poststructuralist criticism. As I have argued in *Token Professionals and Master Critics* (146–50) (an earlier version of which was published as "Why Theory?") as well as in the previous chapter, Paul de Man's version of deconstruction is surprisingly disciplinary in its orientation. However, I distinguish between poststructuralist endeavors and a postmodern ethos. The former is a specific critique of structuralism by thinkers, parts of whose work have become popular in our postmodern era, that is, in the information age, which begins roughly with the electronic revolution and the invention of the microchip. For a fuller delineation of postmodern, see chapter 12.

8. Earlier I suggested that at least two senses of disciplinarity can be found in contemporary literary studies: a strong sense (à la Toulmin) and a weak sense (à la Vattimo or Barbara Herrnstein Smith). The correlative professional aspects of a discipline that Toulmin identifies come closer to the sense of discipline proffered by Smith and (if we understand procedures primarily as constraints) Foucault. My interest here is in the modern (Toulmin) rather than the postmodern (Foucault) concept of discipline. In both senses literary arguments appeal to evidence, proof, fact, and so on. The strong sense of discipline requires not only evidential criteria but also testability. The weak sense requires the constitution of evidential criteria by an interpretive community. Both senses require the condition of inferential consequence: if you do *x,* then *y* results; thus if you find *y,* then you can assume *x.* This is the condition of refutability. It is not possible to refute someone unless some inferential pattern has been accepted as the standard of judgment. These are criteria taken from the domain of logic. So disciplinarity in my sense entails a form of reasoning that can be construed as logical. For instance, would a literary critic committed to "discipline" be willing to admit that his judgments were "illogical"?

9. As Graff has pointed out (*Professing Literature* 2–3), such claims are logically implausible because it is not possible to make sound arguments without inferential warrants, and all warrants are theorems belonging to the conceptual

framework of the discipline in question. Therefore one cannot claim to be working in a theory-free discipline.

10. In *Literary Knowledge,* Paisley Livingston argues forcefully that a theory in one discipline is viable only to the extent that it coordinates with theories in other disciplines. In this view, disciplines are not autonomous.

11. I have made this case in detail in *Token Professionals and Master Critics.* See, in particular, "Theories Need Not Be Methods" and "Theoretical Lore" (159–78).

12. I discuss this problem at length in "Theories Need Not Be Methods" in *Token Professionals and Master Critics,* 159–67.

13. Literary criticism is informed by the rhetorical structure of an argument. Critics persuade other readers of the meanings of texts by offering evidence. (Evidential criteria for argument is the key here—a motif in this study. The institutional structure that exhibits this preoccupation is the exam.) The warranting assumptions critics use establish that evidence—presumably by establishing inferential links between the reading and the text. The warrants used are invariably concepts derived from theories employed in other disciplines. Though there are a large number of formal warrants (conceptions of rhetorical tropes and devices) endemic to the study of literature, the bulk of literary criticism goes beyond such formalisms by borrowing heuristic conceptions of texts (or other signifying systems) from neighboring disciplines. Such arguments are identified with critical schools and usually associated with major thinkers in nonliterary studies. Most of these disciplines operate inferentially. Critical schools are the afterimage of scientific paradigms. In each school, conceptual models of texts are offered as warrants for literary projects and justify research methodologies, *even though literary study does not depend on inferential logic and its warrants disguise intuitions.* As I argue in chapter 10, the field of literature is not a set of facts. Nonetheless, we have inherited the practice of borrowing successful methods (warranting principles) from more rigorous disciplines in an effort to legitimate our reading activities. When our arguments are based on inferential warrants (i.e., on the informal logic used in the sources from which we borrow), they tend to ally themselves with methods governed by scientific or disciplinary ideals in the strict sense.

Chapter 4: Disciplined Isolation

1. Theoretically, I do not subscribe to the idea that we live in a single culture. I am persuaded that, in a postmodern era, we live in a plurality of cultures. However, since the use of the plural noun is not idiomatic in English, please understand my use of the word "culture" to imply an aggregate of cultures.

2. I intend this distinction to be heuristic, not essentialist. Further, to the objection that persons can extrapolate from the uses of buttons on one machine to their parallel uses on another, I would respond that this is a relative matter. To the extent that they *do* understand the buttons in relation to each other, they can extrapolate. To use a button designated on/off on one machine in the same way as a button designated on/off on another machine does not require the ability to extrapolate. Extrapolation in these cases would pertain to the extent to which the

persons involved come to understand the generic character of the machines in use. Extrapolation takes place when a person apprehends that the interface on a newly encountered machine has generic affinities to the interface of other machines in its genre.

3. This condition (the requirement that understanding be converted to information) imposed on us by modern institutions of learning is itself exacerbated by the publishing industry. Anything published has the de facto status of information. But although disciplinary knowledge is, in principle, convertible to information, not all information has, in principle, the status of knowledge. Nonetheless, the referee system of academic publishing is mandated to ensure that only knowledge, only the result of scholarly inquiry, gets published. However, academic publishers have marketing concerns and tend to publish what can be sold. Thus information that has market value tends to get published and often takes publishing precedence over knowledge governed by inquiry. Ironically, Graff's account of the successes of attacks against the university illustrates this pattern. The attacks are not inquiries into the structure of the modern university, but rather make available "interesting information." The best example of this phenomenon is an essay attacking Eve Sedgwick's *title* for a paper, "Jane Austen and the Masturbating Girl," which appeared before she wrote the paper. As Graff remarks, "Mere nonexistence did not prevent Sedgwick's essay from becoming a central exhibit in countless subsequent anti-PC articles, and it still remains largely unread now that it has been published" (*Culture Wars* 157). Here the information that the paper was about masturbation was separated from the inquiry that produced her understanding.

4. I describe this orientation in detail in *Token Professionals and Master Critics*. See especially chapter 3, "*Homo Criticus Americanus*."

5. This tendency is exacerbated by the institutional reward system. Institutional practices of cost accounting led to evaluations of staff on the basis of their productivity. Hence the search for *rewardable* knowledge invariably leads to the production of information because of the store-to-retrieve syndrome in the *account*ability factor. Generally speaking, publication is not related to inquiry in administrative judgments about reward-ability, merely to certain criteria of merit-ability.

6. Considering that shared inquiries require renegotiation through argumentation, Graff's use of the term "debate" is almost synonymous with the term "collaborate."

7. Liz McMillen, in "Literature's Jeremiah Leaps into the Fray," writes, "After years of fuming quietly in his one-man department at Yale University, Harold Bloom has eagerly leaped bayonet sharpened, into the canon wars," referring to the publication of his *The Western Canon* (September 7, 1994, A11).

8. This remark is quoted by Graff from an unpublished manuscript of Waller's.

9. By ordinary language I mean the usage recorded in standard dictionaries.

10. As Graff has persuasively argued, our curricula are expanding and thus intensifying the problem of connectivity—where once conformity reigned (in the religious college), now diversity does (in its successor—the modern university). This shift in orientation (from religious to secular values) is one condition of the cafeteria-curricula syndrome, but not the only one. That conformity to a par-

ticular set of beliefs is no longer required is surely a reason we now have more diverse studies available to us. On the other hand, we need to consider that conformity of beliefs is not synonymous with uniformity in practices. Wearing a uniform does not ensure conformity to the beliefs for which the uniform stands. Sometimes a uniform only testifies to the powerlessness of individuals in the face of the institution that governs their conduct. The fact that conformity may no longer be required does not entail that uniformity is also not required. The shift from religious to secular values is also a shift from regulated conformity of beliefs to regulated uniformity in practices. Graff's analysis attends to the former but not the latter.

11. David Downing and I develop this notion in "A Multivalent Pedagogy for a Multicultural Time: A Diary of a Course." As the title suggests, our term for it is "multivalence," whose primary meaning is "the capacity of an element or part of a structure or system to combine with other elements or parts in more than one way" (*Webster's New World Dictionary*) and by which we mean "the ability of social structures or organizations to allow for their members to combine in more than one group" (311). This is a vital element of courses conducted through telecommunications and one we encouraged in a telecommunications seminar we taught in the winter semester of 1993 entitled "Cultural Turns," which took as its problematic the culture wars then prevalent. Graff's *Beyond the Culture Wars* was one of the texts much discussed in the course.

12. This does not mean that by reaching our students we reach the general public. It suggests that we should direct our attention outward rather than inward. In such a reorientation, students are the most proximate link we have to the general public because they are a part of it.

13. What do we have to say about those persons in the room who want to forget the social issues in the film and concentrate on its meaning as a cultural text? What do we say about critics who maintain that detachment (rather than identification) and disinterest (rather than engagement) are the primary critical protocols? Clearly these are some of the disciplinarians in the group. They are the persons whose credo is "Just read the text!" (*Culture Wars* 71). Disciplinary critics who would have us just read the text (and its contexts) with a detached and objective attitude have faith that the discovery of the meanings of those texts will produce knowledge. However, those meanings have to be stored and retrieved as ideas or themes or conceptual descriptions of the texts. In my view, which I believe is consonant with Graff's, readers cannot "just read the text." Reading is inescapably interested. On the other hand, method reading is hardly something we should impose on our students.

Moreover, the results of such disciplinary readings have produced (if not knowledge nonetheless) a vast database of criticism stored in libraries. How much of the accumulated information about literary texts that is presently stored in libraries is likely to be of interest either to our students or to the general public? And further, in its present state, is it interconnected as a coherent body of knowledge? And, most importantly, when it is transported into classrooms, can students in one classroom easily extrapolate the connections?

14. This is my articulation, not Graff's, but I believe it to be an accurate reflection of the presuppositions in his proposals.

Chapter 5: Shifting Status

1. Graff devotes two chapters to this conflict in *Professing Literature* and dates it from 1915 to 1965.

2. In this chapter I conflate the terms "traditional" and "modern" in a sense that combines Foucault's delineation of the period of our history dominated by discipline and Lyotard's suggestion that we are postmodern because the conditions of knowledge production have radically changed. In this context, the reliance on various kinds of warranting in informal logic, which Toulmin sees as the defining characteristic of university studies called "disciplines," fits well into the notion of modern as the logocentric worldview under critique by postmoderns. In my account, the university system Laurence Veysey describes in *The Emergence of the American University* is still in place and remains modern.

3. In chapter 6 I describe the shift as a movement away from arguments intended to convince their audiences and toward arguments intended to sway their audiences.

4. My career spans the same years as Graff's. The history of the writing of this book is a history of the shift I describe (see Prologue).

5. It also reflects the emendation I have already made to Graff's notion of the field-coverage principle, adding the proliferation of methods as co-villain.

6. Willard put the matter succinctly in the following sentence: "If epistemic guarantors are impersonal, they have this status because they are residua of traditions of human practices" (4).

7. Nominally defined, critics are those persons who have been *named* critics by persons who call themselves critics and their work criticism.

8. The work of Stephen Toulmin and Chaim Perelman seems to have the corner on the literary market. Statistically speaking, Toulmin's texts probably dominate. For this reason and, more significantly, because of the link between Toulmin's theory of argumentation and his theory of disciplinarity, I use Toulmin as my reference point.

9. I follow Perelman's distinction here between convincing and swaying. See chapter 6 for a fuller account.

10. Nimis's essay, which is written in English, is ironically entitled "Fussnoten: Der Fundament der Wissenshaft." A further irony is that he is a classicist and his examples are taken from journal articles in the most footnoted area of literary study.

11. In remarks such as this I use the term "disciplinary" in the strict sense that Toulmin employs in *Human Understanding*. See chapter 3.

12. Freimarck's essay is used here as an example because it was extensively analyzed in the seminars to which I referred in the Prologue. Despite its age, it remains a rather typical literary argument. Whether Freimarck's conclusions are acceptable or unacceptable is less important here than the format he follows in presenting them.

13. See my "Reading Acts and Reading Warrants."

14. This assumes that texts are not objects, because in reading acts they have a virtual existence dependent on readers' selection strategies. Though tradi-

tional critics may disagree with this premise, postmodern critics generally accept some version of it.

15. Let me add a speculative note. Although not the subject of this work, the format of critical discourse may take quite a different turn in the twenty-first century. As George Landow, David Bolter, Richard Lanham, and many other critics working in electronic environments have repeatedly suggested, much of the way we format our discourses in print will change dramatically in the coming years as more and more of our communication is formatted as hypertext. In this electronic format, the relations between passages are readable in various ways, each with a distinct structure or pathway. It is not difficult to envision a history of criticism, for example, in which the various data customarily found in our present histories are entered into a database and given any number of potential patterns, each narrating a somewhat different history. It would be like reading the history of criticism through the eyes of all of its historians in one text. This would, of course, alter the perception of those relations.

Similarly, the texts of any literary artist can be made available together with the entire corpus of known critical readings. Those readings, structured as a hypertext, would be organized as an argument in only one instance of the database. In other instances, passages from the various essays would be organized in a variety of relations to gloss the text for a novice reader, changing their function from parts of an argument discourse to parts of an expository or hortatory or imaginative discourse. One wonders if critics will continue to formulate arguments as the principal means of communicating their readings of texts when those communications are hypertextual. However, such speculations require another volume.

Chapter 6: Explaining, Justifying, Configuring

1. We can transfer this contrast to a difference in modes of argumentation. On the one hand, metonymic arguments (so to speak) depend on inferential warrants: if p, then q. This line of argument might easily be understood as linear or syntagmatic and therefore be associated with metonymy. On the other hand, metaphoric arguments (so to speak) depend on resemblance warrants, on the perception of similarities: $p::q$ as $x::y$. This type of insight might easily be understood as nonlinear and, perhaps, even paradigmatic. I do not wish to take this any further. My point is that some arguments—for example, explanations—depend on a relation of entailment: q is entailed in p. Whenever we have p we also have q because q is a part of p. Justifications also depend on entailment, but the entailments result from shared definitions. Freimarck's argument works with this type of logic: "Araby" is a romance because it contains a quest and quest stories are romances, so that whenever you have quests you have romances. Other arguments do not depend on this type of relation. If boats are like cars in that they both are vehicles, that does not mean that every time you have a car you also have a boat. No one would recommend that you use a car as the vehicle to transport you across a lake. Robyn's point is not that every time you have a factory you have a hell but that although hellishness is not entailed in factories, this one is a hell.

It should be noted that the efficacy of a metonymic argument over a metaphoric one in one context does not entail the efficacy of the former over the latter in another context. Nor does this difference in their effectiveness entail that one must always be preferred to the other. Further, that Robyn turns from one style of argument to the other does not mean that the latter is a critique of the former nor that one is superior to the other (see Lodge's *Modes of Modern Writing*).

2. I say "fiction" because I take the postmodern view that discourse is inescapably intertextual. See Foucault's "What Is an Author?"

3. An equally likely answer is that critics need to maintain copyright in order to advance their careers in a climate wherein coauthored essays in literary studies are not looked on favorably by administrators.

4. The tendency to refer to literary analysis as an explanation of the text belongs, I believe, to a disciplinary attitude. It claims similarity between literary and scientific explanations.

5. Many persons read and understand arguments about texts without ever reading the texts in question. If they accept the claims made by the argument, it is not because they have been persuaded of them but rather because they trust the author or wish his or her views to be valid.

6. It is interesting to note how dependent literary criticism has been on other disciplines for its warranting assumptions. It is difficult to think of a literary school of thought whose founder was a literary critic. The two best candidates would be reader-oriented criticism (I. A. Richards) and New Criticism (John Crowe Ransom), but even in these instances the founders drew so heavily from philosophy and, in Richards's case, from linguistics and psychology that an argument for them as literary forebears of critical schools of thought could be challenged.

Chapter 7: Pretending to Refute

1. There are several senses in which the verb "refute" (or "refuting") is used. In general, its use is situational. The context of its use requires that some argument has been presented or is commonly believed. A second or subsequent speaker/writer then offers a counterargument or counterevidence (which implies an argument) in the course of reworking similar investigations. In *A Theory of Discourse,* James Kinneavy observes that although Aristotle included refutation as one of the parts of an argument, he did not give it much importance. Quintillian, in contrast, regarded it as a necessary part of any argument. In support of Quintillian's view of refutation, Kinneavy offers Kenneth Burke's observation that persuasion would not be needed at all unless some disagreement existed. However, few theorists pay much attention to refutation. Here I offer several of the standard remarks about refutation:

a. re·fute vt. -fut·ed, -fut'ing 1. to prove (a person) to be wrong; confute; 2. to prove (an argument or statement) to be false or wrong, by argument or evidence disprove —re·fut'a·ble adj. —re·fut'a·bly adv. —re·fut·er n. (*Webster's New World Dictionary*)

b. "Latin rhetoricians . . . further refined [Aristotle's] divisions [of an argument], recognizing six parts: (1) the introduction (*exordium*); (2) the statement or exposition of the case under discussion (*narratio*); (3) the outline of the points or steps in the argument (*divisio*); (4) the proof of the case (*confirmatio*); (5) the refutation of the opposing arguments (*confutatio*); (6) the conclusion (*peroratio*)" (Corbett 36). Corbett distinguishes four kinds of refutation: (1) by appeal to reason, (2) by emotional appeals, (3) by ethical appeals, and (4) by wit (323–28).

c. refute: strictly, not only to deny but also to provide sufficient reason for believing that what is denied is in fact false. If you say that somebody refuted something you thereby associate yourself with both parts of this claim and must expect to be challenged to make good the more disputatious second. In general usage the word is frequently employed as a mere synonym of "deny" (see under "refutation" in Flew).

d. refutation: a denial. Usually a formal disproof of an argument or statement, showing its falsity or error. Sometimes involves showing that some assertion has not been supported correctly or proved true (see under "counterexample, method of" in Angeles).

e. refutation: "The basic task in refutation is to minimize the believability and importance of your opponent's arguments. Certain types of argument . . . —the dilemma and the *reductio*—are particularly suited for weakening the force of an opponent's claim. . . . Three major methods of refutation are to deny an argument, to diminish an argument, and to dismiss an argument. The strategy of diminishing an argument usually takes the form of challenging the qualifier that is asserted by an opponent. One supplies counterargument and counterevidence, using these as a basis for asserting that the opponent's claim is overstated. . . . In contrast to the refutation strategies of denial and diminishment, the dismissal technique does not represent an assault on the argument itself. Rather, to dismiss an argument is to claim that it is irrelevant" (Sproule 428–29).

(Note: The terms "refute," "refuting," and "refutation" are not found in any of the common dictionaries of literary terms. Consult Abrams, *Glossary of Literary Terms;* Baldick; Barnet et al.; Beckson and Ganz; Ducrot and Todorov; Fowler; Grogan and Kreiswirth; Hawthorn; Holman and Harmon; Lentricchia and McLaughlin; Makaryk; Morner and Rausch; Preminger; and Williams, *Keywords.*)

f. rebuttal: Steven Toulmin refers to refutation only briefly in *The Uses of Argument,* preferring to call it "rebuttal." In *An Introduction to Reasoning,* a short chapter is devoted to rebuttal. In it, the authors speak mostly of the "*extraordinary or exceptional circumstances that might undermine the force* of the supporting arguments" (95).

2. Even when the refutation may be abbreviated to the mention of some counterexamples that diminish the force of someone's earlier argument, such countering implies a fuller argument that could be made explicit.

3. Thus we might say that refutations are dialogical in character. However, this would be somewhat misleading. In speech situations, especially those we think of as debates, refutations are offered as rebuttals of the previous speaker's argument or they anticipate an argument one might make in turn and hence do have a dialogical character. However, in written discourse refutation often universalizes its opponents. At other times, rival arguments are presented by the writer in the absence of their authors and then refuted. Neither of these last two instances

deserves the designation "dialogical." Graff's notion of debate requires a dialogical aspect. And, for the most part, Graff does not encourage refutation as the appropriate means of the negotiation of disagreements.

4. If a used-car salesperson said, "This wagon is analogous to a car," the client would be likely to respond, "Yes, but it's not the same as a car." For the same reason, if a literary critic said, "This text is analogous to a dream," a psychoanalyst might well respond, "Yes, but it's not the same as a dream."

5. I treated disciplinarity as a modern trait in chapter 3.

6. A reminder seems in order here. Recall my analysis of de Man. A critic who is a poststructuralist is not necessarily a postmodern.

7. To readers it may seem that I am refuting such thinkers in this passage. It is true that I am expressing disagreement with the position that the practice of refutation is a viable postmodern practice. Technically, though, I not refuting anyone's position; that is, I am not making a counterargument to another critic's argument in the hope of falsifying its claims or warrants. Disagreeing with a generalized position ascribed to no one in particular is not a refutation of someone's argument. To object to the practice of refutation in scholarly matters does not require forgoing the expression of disagreement. Attempts to refute arguments authored by individuals in the absence of grounds for refutation injure the author and are conceptually inconsistent with postmodern notions of meaning and textuality.

8. That is, any methodology deemed by the majority of practitioners in a given field to be appropriate to the investigation.

9. As Gerald Graff points out, deconstruction assumes that the same premises can, and usually do, justify opposing conclusions. I agree. This makes de Man's attempts to refute Bate seem to be an instance of a modern skeleton in a postmodern closet.

10. For an account of *Portrait* criticism as a set of arguments, see my "Reading Acts and Reading Warrants" and "The Use of the Word 'Text' in Critical Discourse."

11. Although "Araby" and *Portrait* criticism are a small body of critical discourse relative to the history of critical discourse, I believe they can represent critical discourse in general considering the work done by various metacritics such as Ralph Cohen, Morris Weitz, Siegfried Schmidt, and others, including Toulmin and his associates.

12. For a discussion of the inconsistencies among these commentators see Barney et al., "Analyzing 'Araby' as Story and Discourse."

13. On this point see Siegfried Schmidt's "Literary Science as a Science of Argument."

14. For an account of the problem of replicability in relation to Chatman's model, see my "On the Anvil of Theoretical Debate"; Gerald Prince's "What's the Story in Narratology?"; and Jonathan Culler's "The Application of Theory." Chatman objects to selection rules as a search for "perfect replicability" in "Analogorithm."

15. This description of literary-critical argumentation differs slightly from Toulmin's in *An Introduction to Reasoning* and is based on detailed analyses of

"Araby" criticism as well as *Portrait* criticism developed over four years in seminars on literary criticism in which we thoroughly examined "Araby" criticism.

16. By "reliable knowledge" I refer to statements that can be used purposefully in some customary activity. For example, statements of weather forecasters count as knowledge only to the extent that they are reliable. Were their statements like those of alchemists, they would not be considered reliable. Hence reliability always carries with it the suggestion of predictability. In this sense, scientific statements are the model of reliable knowledge.

Chapter 8: Examining Exams

1. Earlier versions of this exam appeared in my "The Use of the Word 'Text' in Critical Discourse" and in Messer-Davidow, Shumway, and Sylvan, *Knowledges.*

2. Intuitions are usually understood to be uninferred insights into experience (see Angeles's *Dictionary of Philosophy* or Flew's *A Dictionary of Philosophy*). Kant's pure or formal (a priori) intuition "structures what is given by the empirical intuition into sensations that have the quality of being in space and time" (Angeles). By intuition I mean an insight (uninferred relation) between an immediate experience (as in reading a text) and past experiences that loosely resemble it which gives persons a way of patterning the experiences they are undergoing. Intuitions organize masses of sense data impinging on a person by recognizing ways in which the confusing array of impressions resembles a previous experience whose organization is familiar. For instance, managing hypertexts is like organizing note cards in file drawers. Although this analogy is now well known to those interested in computers, at some point it was some person's intuitive apprehension of a resemblance between the activity at hand (working with a new software) and a previous experience (indexing note cards).

Chapter 9: Constructing Intellectuality

1. The term "implied author" is usually associated with Wayne Booth's use of it in *The Rhetoric of Fiction.* I do not use it in exactly his sense. As I use the term, it is synonymous with the phrase "the shared set of beliefs implied by a text."

2. In my analysis of the phenomenon of orthodoxy in *Token Professionals and Master Critics,* orthodoxy is understood to be an institutional, self-regulating mechanism. Thus there is a deconstructive orthodoxy as well as a New Critical orthodoxy. However, when the two schools are housed in the same department, one tends to be regarded as the departmental orthodoxy and the other as its heterodoxy. In other words, the term refers to those beliefs that were taken for granted and, on the arrival of a rival school, had to be defended. In this sense, New Criticism can be considered the prevailing orthodox school of criticism during the forties and fifties. At the same time, at the University of Chicago, for instance, it was not the orthodox position.

3. I use the expression "normal study" to suggest that there is an analogy between the function of textbooks in literary study and the function Thomas Kuhn identifies with respect to scientific textbooks without seeming to suggest that it can be characterized in exactly that way. See *The Structure of Scientific Revolutions*, 10–51, and Toulmin's *The Uses of Argument*, 97–102, for an explanation of "warrant"; see also my "Reading Acts and Reading Warrants."

4. See my "The Use of the Word 'Text' in Critical Discourse."

5. See my "The Role of Selection Strategies in Reading(s)."

6. Once a reading performance has to be measured, there has to be some kind of disclosure of it because it is virtual. Hence critical self-disclosure is usually tantamount to publication. Knowing they are to be measured, critics measure themselves in preparation. Thus comparison is inescapable, and, since performances are rewarded, competition for prizes is inevitable.

7. See my "The Role of Selections Strategies in Reading(s)," 18–19, 25–27.

8. See Parenti's *Power and the Powerless,* 5, for a conventional view of the power relation. More germane to an analysis of discursive formations is a more Foucauldian view of power: "We have argued that power is not a property of individuals *per se,* but a relation, and that its directionality depends both on the particular discourse in operation and the positioning of individuals within that discourse" (Urwin in Henriques et al. 84).

9. Bourdieu and Passeron, *Reproduction in Education, Society and Culture,* 22–23, 107–30.

10. I no longer accept at face value the distinction I just invoked. I invoke it here in somewhat different terms, borrowed in large measure from Michael Oakeshott. My distinction between attitude and competence (which I parallel in this passage to the distinction between professional and disciplinary attributes) reflects Oakeshott's distinction between self-enactment and self-disclosure. I retain this distinction to account for the difference between a detached, impersonal style and an emotional, personal style of arguing.

Also, in the preceding sentence I used the expression "disciplined" rather than "disciplinary" to avoid seeming to suggest that I construe literary study as a discipline.

11. See Foucault's *Discipline and Punish,* 170–94. One of Foucault's most interesting remarks is that "the formation of a whole series of codes of disciplinary individuality . . . made it possible to transcribe, by means of homogenization the individual features established by the examinations: the physical code of signaling, the medical code of symptoms, the educational or military code of conduct or performance. These codes were still very crude, both in quality and quantity, but they marked a first stage in the 'formalization' of the individual within power relations" (189–90). This remark is especially significant to our concerns. Examinations individualize literary critics. By "scoring" differently within a possible range of scores you simultaneously "distinguish" yourself from others and establish yourself as the "disciple of another."

12. This remark does not presuppose that Brooks's practice was invariably New Critical. As I point out in *Token Professionals and Master Critics,* it is easier to establish that Brooks violated New Critical premises than that he consistently

adhered to them. This circumstance, however ironic, does not prevent him from being referred to as the exemplary New Critic.

13. I draw my five axioms from the following sources: Lyotard's *The Postmodern Condition;* Veysey's *The Rise of the American University;* Bledstein's *The Culture of Professionalism;* Touraine's *The Academic System in American Society;* Jencks and Riesman's *The Academic Revolution;* and Parsons and Platt's *The American University.*

14. They define knowledge on page 17 and link it with money as symbolic on pages 23, 25, and especially 77, reminding us of Bourdieu's discussion of symbolic capital in *Outline of a Theory of Practice.*

15. Wayne Booth's "defense" of rationality in *Now Don't Try to Reason with Me,* written about the sixties university, is an excellent instance of this belief. See also his *Modern Dogma and the Rhetoric of Assent.*

16. See Foucault's comments on exams in *Discipline and Punish.*

17. See ibid. and also Althusser's "Ideology and Ideological State Apparatuses."

18. In *Theory of Literature,* Wellek and Warren argue that certain questions, especially extrinsic ones, are unanswerable due to a lack of evidence and therefore should not be a part of critical inquiry.

19. "*Unity:* The sense of oneness—of having a total and final meaning. See 'fiction,' 11–12" (917).

20. See the "Discussions" after many of the selections—for example, to "My Last Duchess" (294).

21. There are exercises after virtually every selection; some are answered by the authors in their "Discussions," a number of which are derived from published answers to "research" questions, most of which are listed for students to answer in imitation of the "Discussions" and can be construed as "pedagogic."

22. Note the expression "intended effect." As I remarked earlier, New Criticism as an orthodoxy is best understood as a historical/formal school of thought. Only in its extreme form does it bracket historical study. Brooks, for instance, often worked historically—for example, in his editorial work and in his studies of Faulkner.

23. These definitions remain unchanged through the various editions of *An Approach to Literature* and vary relatively little from Brooks's other textbook glossaries.

24. That Brooks and Warren define their terms does not necessarily mean that their definitions are sound warrants. For parallel definitions of literary terms see Holman, *Handbook to Literature,* and Barnet, Berman, and Barto, *A Dictionary of Literary Terms.*

Chapter 10: Academic Subjects

1. In this phrase, it should be understood that a "subject" is both a grammatical and a psychological category, both a "topic" and an "object of discourse" (Ducrot & Todorov 83, 210, 271).

2. In *Technologies of Gender,* Teresa de Lauretis broaches the same terrain when she discusses Wendy Holloway's notion of "investments" in "Gender Differ-

ence and the Production of Subjectivity." What Paul Smith argues about the individual, namely, that "'The individual' . . . be understood . . . as simply the illusion of whole and coherent personal organization, or as the misleading description of the imaginary ground on which different subject-positions are colligated" (xxxv), can be applied to a concept of "the world." See also chapters 1 and 2 of Silverman and Torode, *The Material World.*

3. In this context, Toulmin's *Human Understanding* and Kuhn's *The Structure of Scientific Revolutions* are the main points of reference. For a view counter to mine see Shumway's *Creating American Civilization* and Barnes's *Interests and the Growth of Knowledge.*

4. As I remarked in chapter 1, the phrase "traditional literary criticism" refers to a multitude of critics who differ widely among themselves but share a common form of argumentation, specifically, the mode of informal logic delineated by Toulmin in *The Uses of Argument.*

5. Though many critics pay lip service to postmodern theory, their practices are traditional and depend on these assumptions. Moreover, textual scholars, whose work is in some sense fundamental to literary criticism, are quite traditional, and their roles within the profession are yet to be challenged. In the spring of 1987, the Society for Critical Exchange held a symposium on the relationship between contemporary critical theory and textual scholarship and invited well-known participants from both areas of literary study. The responses of the textual scholars to postmodern issues left little doubt of their conservative posture toward the text. This is surely an important index of the conservative nature of the institution of criticism.

6. See *The GRIP Report,* volumes 1 and 2.

7. By "traditional view" I refer to the view of the text that has reigned since Dryden and has only recently been challenged by poststructuralist thought. New Criticism is in this sense as traditional as neo-Aristotelianism.

8. Said, *Orientalism.* See also articles by H. Schmidt, P. Franklin, and D. Shumway in *The GRIP Report,* volume 1, for analyses of the ways in which social demands channeled through the university have dictated the formation of literary disciplines.

9. In "The *Magister Implicatus* as an Institutionalized Authority Figure" I describe this process in detail.

10. See my "The Use of the Word 'Text' in Critical Discourse."

Chapter 11: Truth Wars

1. Postmodern criticism is inconceivable without feminism. Though at the newsworthy surface of our profession it seems that deconstruction reigns, postmodern critics only make use of deconstruction. I believe that the kind of political criticism that rejects logocentrism while maintaining phallocentrism is not intellectually viable. In this regard, the work of postmodern feminists suggests what seems to me the prevailing pattern, namely, that the politicization of literary study is more fundamental than the deconstruction of literary texts. In this respect, feminists have led the way.

2. See Miner and Longino, *Competition: A Feminist Taboo,* for a comprehensive collection of essays on competition from a feminist point of view.

3. I borrow this phrase from Toril Moi's *Sexual/Textual Politics: Feminist Literary Theory.*

4. In this section I take an admittedly general look at some aspects of our collective past that can be understood as the historical conditions of the career profile of the literary scholar-critic. Most of my remarks are based on research conducted by the Society for Critical Exchange's Group for Research into the Institutionalization and Professionalization of Literary Studies (GRIP). Many of the papers published in *The GRIP Report* involve brief historical accounts of exemplary academic figures: George Marsh, Francis March, Francis Child, Ulrich von Wilamowitz-Moellendorf, Gustave Lanson, Cleanth Brooks, and others.

5. In *Token Professionals and Master Critics* I analyze the role the notion of a career has played in the development of literary criticism.

6. This paragraph summarizes an essay entitled "The *Magister Implicatus* as an Institutional Authority Figure," originally published in *The GRIP Report.* That essay was the seminal work for *Token Professionals and Master Critics.*

7. For detailed discussions of competition and women, see Miner and Longino's *Competition: A Feminist Taboo.*

8. Cixous's distinction between the "proper" and the "gift" is in my mind as I make this suggestion because it succinctly captures the relationship between knowledge and social institutions.

9. Earlier, for rhetorical reasons, I used the term "insight" in place of the term "intuition." Also, for reasons that will be apparent later, I define intuition not in the traditional way as "the immediate knowing of something without the conscious use of reasoning" (*Webster's New World Dictionary*) but as the instantaneous accommodation of unspecifiable differences.

10. I use "intuition" in roughly Michael Polanyi's sense of "insight." In his account of intelligence, he focuses on "tacit knowledge," which is so complex that it cannot be articulated because the particulars are unspecifiable.

Chapter 12: Through a Postmodern Lens

1. I borrow this anecdote from Clifford Geertz's *Interpretation of Cultures* (26).

2. Though knowledge might seem to displace belief (moving us out of states of ignorance into states of enlightenment), it increases the need for belief. Knowledge is thought to be inversely proportionate to belief—the greater our store of knowledge, the less our need for beliefs—but knowledge precipitates desire and desire, belief.

3. Understanding might be construed an English equivalent for "the 'drifting' movement of desire. This movement has available a 'natural knowledge' (*savoir* in French, *Wissen* in German) bound to human needs; but the subject still does not know where the current is going and so does not have what is called *connaissance* in French or *Kenntnis* in German" (Benvenuto & Kennedy 173).

4. The question of the formation of cultural subjects, so much the con-

cern of Althusser's and Foucault's work, can only be mentioned here as an important issue. As a kind of shorthand, we might say that textbooks interpellate students as New Critical subjects.

5. If we stop reading critically but go on reading, our vested interests go unexamined because the beliefs that inspire our desires remain unconscious. Contemporary students, for example (in both radical and conservative accounts), are notoriously uncritical of their own desires. They cannot recognize them when they encounter them.

6. To some extent, I beg the question "Why this aim?" Specifically, why the formation of cultural subjects? My answer is that intellectuals should show persons how to become agents of their cultural formation in order to create a culture with a greater tolerance for difference. I wish to open a door to research groups whose aim it is to intervene in deleterious cultural formations. At the moment, because of its scientistic character, the study of literature can only reinforce cultural norms. I want to work for a style of cultural study that plays a part in the formation of the culture. Whereas the current disciplinary mode of literary study is moribund, a postmodern cultural study returns a vital role to the critic, namely, his or her status as intellectual. I opt for the role of an intellectual who intervenes in cultural formations rather than the role presently assigned to me as the guardian and disseminator of current cultural norms, because I believe cultures that produce painful effects in their members must change. Though not everyone may identify as damaging the particular cultural effects I identify, the formation of the culture should be a site of contestation rather than a field that reproduces itself. Though I do not describe specific ill effects of cultural formations in this study, I am envisioning another in which I describe a range of them.

7. In "Rhetoric and Suffering," chapter 17 of *Token Professionals and Master Critics,* I develop this line of reflection in detail.

8. William Cain distinguishes between intellectuals and "intellectual workers" (his term, 160–61) on the grounds that the activities of the latter are necessarily constrained by the institutional aspects of universities. Anyone working in a university, then, can only be an intellectual worker. I would argue that this is the effect of organizing our work as a discipline.

9. My notion of public spheres is influenced by Foucault's idea of a "specific intellectual." For me, colleagues are a "public sphere," and students in my literary criticism and Introduction to Literature classes are "public spheres." Is this a "light one little candle" approach? No—by addressing these audiences as public spheres, I set the conditions for enlarging my audience. I understand "public sphere" as a rhetorical notion. I have little control over the impact of my work. My aim is to address the culture. I have no control over what part of the culture will actually become my audience. The political act is in choosing my rhetoric. This constitutes a stand. It has its consequences.

10. A new way of conceiving the humanities not only as cultural study but as the formation of cultural subjects is to consider that what is learned is lived. The imaginative construction of a subject through fiction is a story whose testability is the extent to which it can be lived, that is, the extent to which it is a viable personal history. One of the problems with literary study has been that what is studied is not a part of one's life; it remains a part of a conceptual system.

11. See Lyotard's *The Postmodern Condition* (124–26) on "stores" of knowledge. Also see Patricia Harkin, "The Post-Disciplinary Politics of Lore."

12. Throughout *Discerning the Subject,* Paul Smith makes a strong case for this agenda.

13. The premise of my counterdisciplinary critique is that literary study is not the discovery of cultural artifacts, as we once thought. Rather, it is an important part of the constitution of our culture as a discursive environment. It concerns subjects in possible worlds. In other words, in its concern for the constitution of our culture it concerns the future, a matter no less germane to the daily life of the public. The conclusion I would draw from my analysis is that the modern institutional rationale for literary study must now give way to a postmodern one.

14. Dispositions have positive and negative valences, and myths usually encompass both.

Chapter 13: Alternative Cultures

1. What I suggest here is not intended to replace Graff's model but to be seen as another area where the potential for engagement with our work is considerable.

2. I borrow the phrase "emotional curve" from Kenneth Burke.

3. In some accounts of arguments by analogy, the link between the warranting premise and the conclusion is described as a *weak* inference. In this account, the link is not in any sense weak. Since the conclusion of the type of analogical argument I describe is the understanding of possibility, the intuition of a connection between an experience and previous analogous experiences based on the perception of some similarities is not a weak link if it results in the apprehension of what is possible. Configurations are arguments about possibilities, not probabilities. The circumstances under which such arguments are used differ from those under which justificatory arguments about probabilities are used. Imagine, for instance, persons trapped in a burning building. When those persons know that certain exits to the building exist, they may then decide which one is probably safest. However, when they know all the probable exits are blocked, then possible exits can be imagined by analogy with experiences of exiting from fires—for example, a bedsheet twisted into a rope to convert a window into an exit. In the circumstances, there is nothing intellectually weak about intuiting this possible avenue of escape. We rarely give sufficient credit to the significant role the perception of virtual scenarios plays in our lives. Recently the use of images (in place of conceptions) in the development of such scenarios has become an important aspect of planning for the future.

4. As in the previous two chapters, I am not using the word "analogy" to imply an inferential logic.

5. As Ellen Messer-Davidow has pointed out to me, Burke's pentad is an inadequate theory of agency. I quite agree. I think this limits its efficacy in the study of social agents, but it does help us here to understand how we express agency in our fictions and thus in our cultures. Though I am using Burke because

his views are well known, I hope my notion of a configuration introduces a social dimension to this discussion.

6. In her reading of this manuscript, Ellen Messer-Davidow noted that Kenny's and Burke's models of agency are individualistic rather than collaborative. I agree, and this needs to be corrected. However, I offer their schemes here to clarify what happens to individuals but I presuppose they are acting in concert with other individuals in a dialectic that has the net effect of creating a history for the group.

7. See Nicholas Meyer's *The Seven-Percent Solution.*

Chapter 14: Critical Concurrence

1. The parts of this essay that follow were drafted with David Shumway for the MLA annual convention in 1983 in New York as a paper entitled "Critical Protocols." This version is indebted to that collaboration.

2. It is important to make a distinction between difference as it may apply to persons (the agency they have constituted from their subjection and individuation) and the difference that applies to individuals (as a result of individuation). In the first case difference is marked by its heterodoxy; in the second it is marked by its orthodoxy. The clearest mark of the difference spawned by orthodoxy, that is, by unexamined individuation, is its aversion to collaboration. One might argue that an orthodox person willing to collaborate shows a willingness to be heterodox.

3. See Chessman and Southgate, *Heritage and Promise,* 78, 18, 31.

4. Henriques et al. in *Changing the Subject* argue that the individual/social dualism is a founding concept in the social sciences that must be deconstructed (12–13).

5. See Lugones and Spelman's essay for a detailed discussion of compassion. My use of the term, suggested to me by their essay, differs from theirs.

6. It is not enough to say that critics should play a role in changing culture. It is not enough to say that by configuring experiences critics may get their audiences to change their beliefs. The question is always, Why? The answer is, to alleviate pain. The fundamental assumption behind this work is that culture must constantly change. A second assumption is that cultural institutions consistently resist change in the sense that they are self-regulating systems that maintain themselves as they are. Although these institutions do not work perfectly—despite resistance to change, they do change—they do actively impede change. A crucial corollary to the first assumption is that cultures must change because all cultures induce pain (as well as pleasure). As a consequence, cultures require criticism.

7. The tolerance of difference is healthy. Independence, according to Fairbairn, is marked by "an ability to tolerate difference" (Cashdan 10). Henriques's essay on "Social Psychology and the Politics of Racism" considers the tolerance of difference in the light of changes in the conception of the subject, and so on.

8. Unlike scientific theories, literary theories are not paradigms for research. Whereas in paradigmatic research theories govern the formulation of ques-

tions in the search for sameness, in literary research groups many, even contradictory, theorems can be used in search of differences that might precipitate concurrences.

9. I agree with Lugones and Spelman that competition has its political usefulness and support their contention that groups competing collectively for the welfare of the public can be beneficial. As they point out, while competition is akin to excelling, communal excelling is not destructive in the way that an individual's competing in self-interested ways is. For them, the crucial difference is that in communal excelling, self-interest is regulated by the interests of the group.

10. Concurrences do not form orthodox communities in which there is an underlying pressure to achieve uniformity. Said's notion of affiliation (vs. filiation in *World*) is especially significant here. If affiliations, through social institutions, replace filiations, then critical communities are affiliations that replace older social communities such as neighborhoods, church groups, and so on.

11. One of the topics in Ernesto Laclau and Chantal Mouffe's *Hegemony and Socialist Strategy* is the possibility of differences in political action.

12. Assimilation (gap in schema) produces a sense of error, whereas accommodation produces a sense of difference. It is like the contrast between suspense and surprise: the former depends on maintaining a consistent framework of belief and the latter on allowing it to dissolve.

13. Without a strong relationship to public spheres, intellectuals are vulnerable to elitism. This is as true of an intellectual who works in a university as it is of any other.

Chapter 15: Professing Literature in 2001

1. Ellen Messer-Davidow points out that classrooms are not so much privatized spaces as they are localized ones. I agree yet believe that Graff's point pertains to both private and local contexts.

2. In a lecture entitled "The Concept of Discourse Community: Dog, Cash Cow, Problem Child or Star?" at the 1992 University of Toledo Rhetoric Symposium, Swales distributed a handout. The passage I quote is from that handout.

3. See Patricia Harkin's comments on this problem in her "Arguing a History: Gerald Graff's *Professing Literature*."

4. See David Downing's "The Cultural Politics of Graff's History of Literary Studies" for an excellent account of the potential for social transformation in Graff's work. Written in 1987, it anticipates many of the emendations Graff has made to his initial articulation of the conflict model.

WORKS CITED

Abrams, M. H. *A Glossary of Literary Terms*. New York: Holt, Rinehart and Winston, 1957.

———. *The Mirror and the Lamp*. New York: Norton, 1953.

Althusser, Louis. "Ideology and the Ideological State Apparatuses." In *Lenin and Philosophy and Other Essays,* translated by Ben Brewster. New York: Monthly Review Press, 1971.

Angeles, Peter A. *Dictionary of Philosophy*. New York: Barnes and Noble, 1981.

Applebee, Arthur N. *Tradition and Reform in the Teaching of English: A History*. Urbana, Ill.: National Council of Teachers of English, 1974.

Arac, Jonathan. *After Foucault: Humanistic Knowledge, Postmodern Challenges*. New Brunswick, N.J.: Rutgers Univ. Press, 1988.

———. *Critical Genealogies: Historical Situations for Postmodern Literary Studies*. New York: Columbia Univ. Press, 1987.

———. "Is 'History' of Scholarship a Counter-Disciplinary Practice?" In *The GRIP Report,* vol. 2, edited by James Sosnoski. Oxford, Ohio: Society for Critical Exchange, 1984.

Bakhtin, Mikhail. *The Dialogic Imagination*. Translated by Michael Holquist and Caryl Emerson. Edited by Michael Holquist. Austin: Univ. of Texas Press, 1981.

Baldick, Chris. *The Concise Oxford Dictionary of Literary Terms*. New York: Oxford Univ. Press, 1990.

Barnes, Barry. *Interests and the Growth of Knowledge and His T. S. Kuhn and Social Science.*

Barnet, Sulvan, Morton Berman, and William Burto. *The Study of Literature: A Handbook of Critical Essays and Terms*. Boston: Little, Brown, 1960.

Barthes, Roland. *The Pleasure of the Text*. Translated by Richard Miller. New York: Hill, 1975.

———. *S/Z*. Translated by Richard Miller. New York: Hill and Wang, 1974.

—————. *Writing Degree Zero and Elements of Semiology.* Translated by Annette Laves and Colin Smith. Boston: Beacon Press, 1970.

Beck, Warren. *Joyce's* Dubliners: *Substance, Vision, and Art.* Durham, N.C.: Duke Univ. Press, 1969.

Beckson, Karl, and Arthur Ganz. *Literary Terms: A Dictionary.* New York: Noonday Press, 1990.

Belenky, Mary Field, Blythe McVicker Clinchy, Nancy Rule Goldberger, and Jill Mattuck Tarule. *Women's Ways of Knowing: The Development of Self, Voice, and Mind.* New York: Basic Books, 1969.

Belsey, Catherine. *Critical Practice.* London: Methuen, 1980.

Benedikt, Michael, ed. *Cyberspace: First Steps.* Cambridge, Mass.: MIT Press, 1991.

Benvenuto, Bice, and Roger Kennedy. *The Works of Jacques Lacan: An Introduction.* New York: St. Martin's Press, 1986.

Berlin, James A. "Contemporary Composition: The Major Pedagogical Theories." *College English* 44 (December 1982): 765–77.

—————. "Rhetoric and Ideology in the Writing Class." *College English* 50 (September 1988): 477–94.

—————. *Rhetoric and Reality: Writing Instruction in American Colleges, 1900–1985.* Carbondale: Southern Illinois Univ. Press, 1987.

—————. *Rhetorics, Poetics, and Cultures: Refiguring College English Studies.* Urbana, Ill.: National Council of Teachers of English, forthcoming.

Bialostosky, Don H. "Dialogics as an Art of Discourse in Literary Criticism." *PMLA* 101 (1986): 788–97.

—————. "The English Professor in the Age of Theory: Scapegoating Theory." *Novel* 19, no. 2 (1986): 165–70.

—————. "Liberal Education, Writing, and the Dialogic Self." In *Contending with Words: Composition and Rhetoric in a Postmodern Age,* edited by Patricia Harkin and John Schilb. New York: MLA, 1991.

Bledstein, Burton. *The Culture of Professionalism.* New York: Norton, 1976.

Bleich, David. *Readings and Feelings: An Introduction to Subjective Criticism.* Urbana, Ill.: National Council of Teachers of English, 1975.

—————. *Subjective Criticism.* Baltimore: Johns Hopkins Univ. Press, 1978.

Bolter, David J. *Turing's Man: Western Culture in the Computer Age.* Chapel Hill: Univ. of North Carolina Press, 1984.

Booth, Wayne. *Critical Understanding: The Powers and Limits of Pluralism.* Chicago: Univ. of Chicago Press, 1979.

—————. *Modern Dogma and the Rhetoric of Assent.* Chicago: Univ. of Chicago Press, 1974.

—————. *Now Don't Try to Reason with Me.* Chicago: Univ. of Chicago Press, 1970.

—————. *The Rhetoric of Fiction.* Chicago: Univ. of Chicago Press, 1961.

Borklund, Elmer. *Contemporary Literary Critics.* New York: St. Martin's Press, 1977.

Bourdieu, Pierre. *Distinction: A Social Critique of the Judgment of Taste.* Translated by Richard Nice. Cambridge: Harvard Univ. Press, 1984.

—————. *Homo Academicus.* Translated by Peter Collier. Stanford, Calif.: Stanford Univ. Press, 1988.

—————. *Outline of a Theory of Practice.* Translated by Richard Nice. Edited by Jack Goody. Cambridge: Cambridge Univ. Press, 1979.

Bourdieu, Pierre, and Claude Passeron. *Reproduction in Education, Society and Culture.* Translated by Richard Nice. London: Sage, 1977.

Bové, Paul A. *Intellectuals in Power: A Genealogy of Critical Humanism.* New York: Columbia Univ. Press, 1986.

Bowman, James Cloyd, ed. *Contemporary American Criticism.* New York: Henry Holt, 1926.

Brand, Stewart. *The Media Lab: Inventing the Future at MIT.* New York: Penguin, 1987.

Brooks, Cleanth. *Modern Poetry and the Tradition.* Chapel Hill: Univ. of North Carolina Press, 1939, 1967.

————. *The Well Wrought Urn: Studies in the Structure of Poetry.* New York: Harcourt Brace, 1947; London: Dobson, 1949.

Brooks, Cleanth, and Robert Heilman, eds. *Understanding Drama.* New York: Holt, 1960.

Brooks, Cleanth, and Robert Penn Warren, eds. *Understanding Fiction.* New York: Holt, 1945; revised edition 1960.

————. *Understanding Poetry.* New York: Holt, 1950.

Brooks, Cleanth, Robert Penn Warren, and John Thibaut Purser, eds. *An Approach to Literature.* New York: Appleton-Century Crofts, 1938; revised editions 1952, 1964, 1975.

Brooks, Cleanth, and William K. Wimsatt Jr. *Literary Criticism: A Short History.* New York: Knopf, 1965.

Brooks, Peter. *Reading for the Plot: Design and Intention in Narrative.* New York: Vintage, 1984.

Burke, Kenneth. *Attitudes toward History.* Boston: Beacon Press, 1937.

————. *Counter-Statement.* Chicago: Univ. of Chicago Press, 1931, 1957.

————. *A Grammar of Motives and a Rhetoric of Motives.* Cleveland: Meridian, 1962.

————. *Language as Symbolic Action: Essays on Life, Literature, and Method.* Berkeley: Univ. of California Press, 1966.

————. *Permanence and Change.* Indianapolis: Bobbs-Merrill, 1954.

————. *The Philosophy of Literary Form: Studies in Symbolic Action.* Los Angeles: Univ. of California Press, 1973.

————. *The Rhetoric of Religion: Studies in Logology.* Boston: Beacon Press, 1961.

Cain, William E. *The Crisis in Criticism: Theory, Literature, and Reform in English Studies.* Baltimore: Johns Hopkins Univ. Press, 1984.

————. *"Literature against Itself* Briefly Revisited." *Critical Exchange* 23 (Summer 1987): 31–36.

————. "Notes toward a History of Anti-Criticism." *New Literary History* 20 (Autumn 1988): 33–48.

Cashdan, Sheldon. *Object Relations Therapy: Using the Relationship.* New York: Norton, 1988.

Certeau, Michel de. *Heterologies: Discourse on the Other.* Translated by Brian Massumi. Minneapolis: Univ. of Minnesota Press, 1985.

Chabot, C. Barry. "The Problem of the Postmodern." In *Zeitgeist in Babel: The Post-Modernist Controversy,* edited by Ingeborg Hoesterey. Bloomington: Indiana Univ. Press, 1991.

Chambers, Ross. *Story and Situation: Narrative Seduction and the Power of Fiction.* Minneapolis: Univ. of Minnesota Press, 1984.

Chatman, Seymour. "Analogorithm." *James Joyce Quarterly* 18 (Spring 1981): 293–99.

———. *Story and Discourse: Narrative Structure in Fiction and Film.* Ithaca: Cornell Univ. Press, 1978.

Chessman, G. Wallace, and Wyndham M. Southgate. *Heritage and Promise: Denison 1831–1981.* Granville, Ohio: Denison University Sesquicentennial Publication, 1981.

Cixous, Hélène. "Castration or Decapitation?" *Signs* 7.I:41–55.

Clifford, John. "The Subject in Discourse." In *Contending with Words: Composition and Rhetoric in a Postmodern Age,* edited by Patricia Harkin and John Schilb. New York: MLA, 1991.

Cohen, Ralph. *The Art of Discrimination: Thomson's* The Seasons *and the Language of Criticism.* London: Routledge and Kegan Paul, 1964.

———. "Literary Theory as Genre." *Centrum* 31 (1978): 45–64.

Corbett, Edward P. J. *Classical Rhetoric for the Modern Student.* New York: Oxford Univ. Press, 1971.

Courtivron, Isabelle de, and Elaine Marks, eds. *New French Feminisms: An Anthology.* Boston: Routledge and Kegan Paul, 1983.

Crane, Ronald. *The Idea of the Humanities.* 2 vols. Chicago: Univ. of Chicago Press, 1967.

———. *The Languages of Criticism and the Structure of Poetry.* Toronto: Univ. of Toronto Press, 1953.

Culler, Jonathan. "The Application of Theory." *James Joyce Quarterly* 18 (Spring 1981): 287–92.

———. "Problems in the 'History' of Contemporary Criticism." *JMMLA* 17 (Spring 1984): 3–15.

———. *Structuralist Poetics: Structuralism, Linguistics and the Study of Literature.* London: Routledge and Kegan Paul, 1975.

Dadufulza, Concepcion D. "The Quest of the Chalice-Bearer in James Joyce's 'Araby.'" *Diliman Review* 7 (1959): 256–73.

Danto, Arthur. *Narration and Knowledge.* New York: Columbia Univ. Press, 1985.

de Beaugrande, Robert. *Critical Discourse: A Survey of Literary Theorists.* Norwood, N.J.: Ablex, 1988.

de Lauretis, Teresa. *Technologies of Gender: Essays on Theory, Film, and Fiction.* Bloomington: Indiana Univ. Press, 1987.

Deleuze, Gilles, and Felix Guattari. *Anti-Oedipus.* Minneapolis: Univ. of Minnesota Press, 1983.

de Man, Paul. *Allegories of Reading.* New Haven: Yale Univ. Press, 1979.

———. *Blindness and Insight: Essays in the Rhetoric of Contemporary Criticism.* New York: Oxford Univ. Press, 1971.

———. *The Resistance to Theory.* Minneapolis: Univ. of Minnesota Press, 1986.

Derrida, Jacques. *Of Grammatology.* Translated by Gayatri Chakravorty Spivak. Baltimore: Johns Hopkins Univ. Press, 1976.

———. *Positions.* Translated by Allan Bass. Chicago: Univ. of Chicago Press, 1981.

Downing, David. "The Cultural Politics of Graff's History of Literary Studies." *Critical Exchange* 23 (Summer 1987): 31–36.

————, ed. *Changing Classroom Practices: Resources for Literary and Cultural Studies.* Urbana, Ill.: National Council of Teachers of English, 1994.

Downing, David, and James M. Cahalan, eds. *Practicing Theory in Introductory College Literature Courses.* Urbana, Ill.: National Council of Teachers of English, 1991.

Downing, David, Patricia Harkin, and James Sosnoski. "Configurations of Lore: Changing Relations of Theory, Research, and Pedagogy." In *Changing Classroom Practices: Resources for Literary and Cultural Studies,* edited by David Downing. Urbana, Ill.: National Council of Teachers of English, 1994.

Downing, David and James Sosnoski. "A Multivalent Pedagogy for a Multicultural Time: A Diary of a Course." *PRE/TEXT* 14 (Fall-Winter 1993): 307–40.

————. "The Protocol of Care in the Cycles Project." *JMMLA* 27 (Spring 1994): 75–84.

Dreyfus, Hubert L., and Paul Rabinow. *Michel Foucault: Beyond Structuralism and Hermeneutics.* Chicago: Univ. of Chicago Press, 1982.

Ducrot, Oswald, and Tzvetan Todorov, eds. *Encyclopedic Dictionary of the Sciences of Language.* Translated by Catherine Porter. Baltimore: Johns Hopkins Univ. Press, 1979.

Eagleton, Terry. *The Function of Criticism: From the Spectator to Post-Structuralism.* London: Verso, 1984.

————. *Literary Theory: An Introduction.* Minneapolis: Univ. of Minnesota Press, 1983.

Eco, Umberto. *The Role of the Reader: Explorations in the Semiotics of Texts.* Bloomington: Indiana Univ. Press, 1979.

————. *A Theory of Semiotics.* Bloomington: Indiana Univ. Press, 1976.

Fasteau, Marc Feigen. *The Male Machine.* New York: Delta, 1975.

Fekete, John. *The Critical Twilight: Explorations in the Ideology of Anglo-American Literary Theory from Eliot to McLuhan.* London: Routledge and Kegan Paul, 1977.

Feyerabend, Paul. *Against Method: Outline of an Anarchistic Theory of Knowledge.* London: Verso, 1975.

Fish, Stanley. "Anti-Foundationalism, Theory Hope, and the Teaching of Composition" and "Interview with Stanley Fish." In *The Current in Criticism,* edited by Clayton Koelb and Vergil Lokke. West Lafayette, Ind.: Purdue Univ. Press, 1987.

————. "Anti-Professionalism." *New Literary History* 17 (Autumn 1985): 89–108.

————. "Consequences." In *Against Theory,* edited by W. J. T. Mitchell. Chicago: Univ. of Chicago Press, 1985.

————. *Doing What Comes Naturally: Change, Rhetoric and the Practice of Theory in Literary and Legal Studies.* Durham: Duke Univ. Press, 1989.

————. *Is There a Text in This Class? The Authority of Interpretive Communities.* Cambridge: Harvard Univ. Press, 1980.

————. "Profession Despise Thyself: Fear and Self-Loathing in Literary Studies." *Critical Inquiry* 10, no. 2 (1983): 349–64.

Fisher, Walter R. *Human Communication as Narration: Toward a Philosophy of Reason.* Columbia: Univ. of South Carolina Press, 1987.

Flew, Antony. *A Dictionary of Philosophy.* New York: St. Martin's Press, 1979.

Foucault, Michel. *The Archaeology of Knowledge and The Discourse on Language.* Translated by A. M. Sheridan Smith. New York: Harper, 1972.

———. *Discipline and Punish: The Birth of the Prison.* Translated by Alan Sheridan. New York: Pantheon, 1977.

———. *The History of Sexuality: An Introduction.* Translated by Robert Hurley. New York: Pantheon, 1978.

———. *Language, Counter-Memory, Practice.* Translated by Donald F. Bouchard and Sherry Simon. Edited by Donald F. Bouchard. Ithaca: Cornell Univ. Press, 1977.

———. *Politics, Philosophy, and Culture: Interviews and Other Writings. 1977–84.* Edited by Lawrence Krintzman. New York: Routledge and Kegan Paul, 1988.

———. *Power/Knowledge: Selected Interviews and Other Writings, 1972–1977.* Edited by Colin Gordon. New York: Pantheon, 1980.

———. "The Subject and Power." In *Michel Foucault: Beyond Structuralism and Hermeneutics,* edited by Hubert L. Dreyfus and Paul Rabinow. Chicago: Univ. of Chicago Press, 1982.

———. *The Uses of Pleasure.* Vol. 2 of *The History of Sexuality.* Translated by Robert Hurley. New York: Pantheon, 1985.

———. "What Is an Author?" In *Language, Counter-Memory, Practice,* translated by Donald F. Bouchard and Sherry Simon, edited by Donald F. Bouchard. Ithaca: Cornell Univ. Press, 1977.

Fowler, Roger. *A Dictionary of Modern Critical Terms.* London: Routledge and Kegan Paul, 1987.

Franklin, Phyllis. "English Studies: The World of Scholarship in 1883." *PMLA* 99 (1984): 356–70.

Freedman, Alan. *The Computer Glossary.* New York: AMACOM, 1981.

Freimarck, John. "'Araby': A Quest for Meaning." *James Joyce Quarterly* 7, no. 1 (1970): 366–68.

Freire, Paulo. *Pedagogy of the Oppressed.* Translated by Myra Bergman Ramos. New York: Continuum, 1970.

Freud, Sigmund. *The Interpretation of Dreams.* Translated by A. A. Brill. New York: Modern Library, 1950.

Friend, Christy. "The Excluded Conflict: The Marginalization of Composition and Rhetoric Studies in Graff's *Professing Literature.*" *College English* 54, no. 3 (1992): 276–86.

Frye, Northrop. *Anatomy of Criticism: Four Essays.* Princeton: Princeton Univ. Press, 1957.

Gabelnick, Faith, Jean MacGregor, Roberta S. Matthews, and Barbara Leigh Smith. *Learning Communities: Creating Connections Among Students, Faculty, and Disciplines.* New Directions for Teaching and Learning, no. 41. San Francisco: Jossey-Bass, 1990.

Gardner, Howard. *Frames of Mind: The Theory of Multiple Intelligences.* New York: Harper, 1985.

Geertz, Clifford. *The Interpretation of Cultures.* New York: Basic Books, 1973.
————. *Local Knowledge.* New York: Basic Books, 1983.
Giroux, Henry. *Theory and Resistance in Education: A Pedagogy for the Opposition.* South Hadley, Mass.: Edward Arnold, 1978.
Giroux, Henry, David Shumway, Paul Smith, and James Sosnoski. "The Need for Cultural Studies: Resisting Intellectuals and Oppositional Public Spheres." *Dalhousie Review* 64 (Summer 1984): 472–86.
————. *Teachers as Intellectuals: Toward a Critical Pedagogy of Learning.* Mass.: Bergin and Garvey, 1988.
Gleick, James. *Chaos: Making a New Science.* New York: Penguin, 1987.
Godzich, Wlad. "The Tiger on the Paper Mat." Foreword to *The Resistance to Theory,* by Paul de Man. Minneapolis: Univ. of Minnesota Press, 1986.
Goffman, Erving. *Forms of Talk.* Philadelphia: Univ. of Pennsylvania Press, 1983.
————. *Frame Analysis: An Essay on the Organization of Experience.* New York: Harper and Row, 1974.
————. *Strategic Interaction.* Philadelphia: Univ. of Pennsylvania Press, 1969.
Goldstein, Philip. *The Politics of Literary Theory: An Introduction to Neo-Marxist Theory.* Tallahassee: Florida State Univ. Press, 1990.
Graff, Gerald. *Beyond the Culture Wars: How Teaching the Conflicts Can Revitalize American Education.* New York: Norton, 1992.
————. "Co-optation." In *The New Historicism,* edited by H. Aram Veeser. New York: Routledge and Kegan Paul, 1989.
————. "Colleges Are Depriving Students of a Connected View of Scholarship." *Chronicle of Higher Education,* February 13, 1991, A48.
————. "The Future of Theory in the Teaching of Literature." In *The Future of Literary Theory,* edited by Ralph Cohen. New York: Routledge and Kegan Paul, 1989.
————. *Literature against Itself: Literary Ideas in Modern Society.* Chicago: Univ. of Chicago Press, 1979.
————. "Other Voices, Other Rooms: Organizing and Teaching the Humanities Conflict." *New Literary History* 21 (Autumn 1990): 817–39.
————. *Poetic Statement and Critical Dogma.* Chicago: Univ. of Chicago Press, 1970, 1980.
————. *Professing Literature: An Institutional History.* Chicago: Univ. of Chicago Press, 1987.
————. "Response to His Critics." *Critical Exchange* 23 (Summer 1987): 91.
————. "Taking Cover in Coverage." *Profession* 86 (1986): 41–45.
————. "Teach the Conflicts." *South Atlantic Quarterly* 89, no. 1 (1990): 51–67.
————. "The University and the Prevention of Culture." In *Criticism in the University,* edited by Gerald Graff and Reginald Gibbons. Evanston: Northwestern Univ. Press, 1985.
————. "What Has Literary Theory Wrought?" *Chronicle of Higher Education,* February 12, 1992, A48.
————. "What Should We Be Teaching—When There's No 'We'?" *Yale Journal of Criticism: Interpretation in the Humanities* 1, no. 1 (1988): 189–211.
Graff, Gerald, and Reginald Gibbons, eds. *Criticism in the University.* Evanston: Northwestern Univ. Press, 1985.

Graff, Gerald, and Michael Warner, eds. *The Origins of Literary Study in America.* New York: Routledge and Kegan Paul, 1989.

Gramsci, Antonio. *Selections from the Prison Notebooks.* Edited and translated by W. Hoare and G. Nowell Smith. New York: International, 1971.

Greenblatt, Stephen. "Towards a Poetics of Culture." In *The New Historicism,* edited by H. Aram Veeser. New York: Routledge and Kegan Paul, 1989.

Greene, Gayle, and Coppelia Kahn, eds. *Making a Difference: Feminist Literary Criticism.* New Accents. London: Methuen, 1985.

Grogan, Michael, and Martin Kreiswirth, eds. *The Johns Hopkins Guide to Literary Criticism and Theory.* Baltimore: Johns Hopkins Univ. Press, 1994.

Halliday, Michael. *Language as Social Semiotic: The Social Interpretation of Language and Meaning.* London: Edward Arnold, 1978.

Harkin, Patricia. "Arguing a History: Gerald Graff's *Professing Literature.*" *Critical Exchange* 23 (Summer 1987): 77–90.

———. "Bringing Lore to Light." *PRE/TEXT* 10, nos. 1–2 (1989): 55–67.

———. "The Post-Disciplinary Politics of Lore." In *Contending with Words: Composition and Rhetoric in a Postmodern Age,* edited by Patricia Harkin and John Schilb. New York: MLA, 1991.

———, ed. "Special Issue on the Work of Gerald Graff." *Critical Exchange* 23 (Summer 1987).

Harkin, Patricia, David Downing, and James Sosnoski. "Configurations of Lore: Changing Relations of Theory, Research, and Pedagogy." In *Changing Classroom Practices: Resources for Literary and Cultural Studies,* edited by David Downing. Urbana, Ill.: National Council of Teachers of English, 1994.

Harkin, Patricia, and James Sosnoski. "Barbara Herrnstein Smith: A Contemporary Sophist." *PRE/TEXT* 10, nos. 3–4 (1989): 135–40.

———. "The Case for Hyper-Gradesheets: A Modest Proposal." *College English* 54, no. 1 (1992): 22–30.

Harner, James L. *Literary Research Guide: A Guide to Reference Sources in the Study of Literatures in English and Related Topics.* New York: MLA, 1989.

Hassan, Ihab. *The Postmodern Turn: Essays in Postmodern Theory and Culture.* Columbus: Ohio State Univ. Press, 1987.

Hawthorn, Jeremy. *A Glossary of Contemporary Literary Theory.* New York: Edward Arnold, 1992.

Henriques, Julian. "Social Psychology and the Politics of Racism." In *Changing the Subject: Psychology, Social Regulation and Subjectivity,* edited by Julian Henriques, Wendy Holloway, Cathy Urwin, Couze Venn, and Valerie Walkerdine. London: Methuen, 1984.

Henriques, Julian, Wendy Holloway, Cathy Urwin, Couze Venn, and Valerie Walkerdine, eds. *Changing the Subject: Psychology, Social Regulation and Subjectivity.* London: Methuen, 1984.

Hirsch, E. D., Jr. *Cultural Literacy: What Every American Needs to Know.* Boston: Houghton Mifflin, 1987.

———. *Validity in Interpretation.* New Haven: Yale Univ. Press, 1967.

Hobsbawm, Eric, and Terence Ranger, eds. *The Invention of Tradition.* Cambridge: Cambridge Univ. Press, 1983.

Hogan, Mike. "Top of the News." *PC World* 6 (May 1988): 14.

Hohendahl, Peter Uwe. *The Institution of Criticism.* Ithaca: Cornell Univ. Press, 1982.

Holloway, Wendy. "Gender Difference and the Production of Subjectivity." In *Changing the Subject: Psychology, Social Regulation and Subjectivity,* edited by Julian Henriques, Wendy Holloway, Cathy Urwin, Couze Venn, and Valerie Walkerdine. London: Methuen, 1984.

Holman, C. Hugh, ed. *Handbook to Literature.* Based on the original by William Thrall and Addison Hibbard. New York: Odyssey Press, 1972.

Holman, C. Hugh, and William Harmon. *A Handbook to Literature.* New York: Macmillan, 1992.

Hyman, Stanley Edgar. *The Armed Vision.* New York: Knopf, 1948.

Iser, Wolfgang. *The Act of Reading: A Theory of Aesthetic Response.* Baltimore: Johns Hopkins Univ. Press, 1978.

Jameson, Fredric. *The Political Unconscious: Narrative as a Socially Symbolic Act.* Ithaca: Cornell Univ. Press, 1981.

———. *Postmodernism, or the Cultural Logic of Late Capitalism.* Durham, N.C.: Duke Univ. Press, 1991.

Jardine, Alice, and Paul Smith, eds. *Men in Feminism.* London: Methuen, 1987.

Jarratt, Susan C. "Feminism and Composition: The Case for Conflict." In *Contending with Words: Composition and Rhetoric in a Postmodern Age,* edited by Patricia Harkin and John Schilb. New York: MLA, 1991.

———. *Rereading the Sophists: Classical Rhetoric Refigured.* Carbondale: Southern Illinois Univ. Press, 1993.

Jay, Gregory S. *Modern American Critics since 1955. Dictionary of Literary Biography,* vol. 67. Detroit: Gale Research Co., 1988.

Jencks, Christopher, and David Riesman. *The Academic Revolution.* New York: Doubleday, 1968.

Johnson, Richard. "What Is Cultural Studies Anyway?" *Social Text* 6, no. 1 (1986–87): 38–80.

Kenner, Hugh. "The Pedagogue as Critic." In *The New Criticism and After,* edited by Thomas Daniel Young. Charlottesville: Univ. Press of Virginia, 1976.

Kenny, Anthony. *Action, Emotion and Will.* London: Routledge and Kegan Paul, 1963.

Kinneavy, James. *A Theory of Discourse* Englewood Cliffs, N.J.: Prentice-Hall, 1971.

Knapp, Steven, and Walter Benn Michaels. "Against Theory." In *Against Theory: Literary Studies and the New Pragmatism,* edited by W. J. T. Mitchell. Chicago: Univ. of Chicago Press, 1982.

Knoblauch, C. H., and Lil Brannon. *Rhetorical Traditions and the Teaching of Writing.* Upper Montclair, N.J.: Boynton/Cook, 1984.

Knox, George. *Critical Moments: Kenneth Burke's Categories and Critiques.* Seattle: Univ. of Washington Press, 1957.

Kolodny, Annette. "Dancing through the Minefield: Some Observations on the Theory, Practice, and Politics of a Feminist Literary Criticism." In *Feminisms: An Anthology of Literary Theory and Criticism,* edited by Robyn R. Worhol and Diane Price Herndl. New Brunswick, N.J.: Rutgers Univ. Press, 1991.

Krieger, Murray. *The New Apologists for Poetry.* Bloomington: Indiana Univ. Press, 1956.

Kuhn, Thomas. *The Structure of Scientific Revolutions.* Chicago: Univ. of Chicago Press, 1965.

Lacan, Jacques. *Ecrits: A Selection.* Translated by Alan Sheridan. New York: Norton, 1977.

Laclau, Ernesto, and Chantal Mouffe. *Hegemony and Socialist Strategy: Towards a Radical Democratic Politics.* Translated by Winston Moore and Paul Cammack. London: Verso, 1985.

Lakatos, I., and A. Musgrave. *Criticism and the Growth of Knowledge.* New York: Cambridge Univ. Press, 1970.

Lakoff, George, and Mark Johnson. *Metaphors We Live By.* Chicago: Univ. of Chicago Press, 1980.

Landow, George P. *Hypertext: The Convergence of Contemporary Critical Theory and Technology.* Baltimore: Johns Hopkins Univ. Press, 1992.

Langer, Susanne. *Philosophy in a New Key.* Cambridge: Harvard Univ. Press, 1957.

Larson, Magali Sarfatti. *The Rise of Professionalism: A Sociological Analysis.* Berkeley: Univ. of California Press, 1977.

Leitch, Vincent B. *American Literary Criticism from the Thirties to the Eighties.* New York: Columbia Univ. Press, 1988.

———. *Cultural Criticism, Literary Theory, Poststructuralism.* New York: Columbia Univ. Press, 1992.

Lentricchia, Frank. *After the New Criticism.* Chicago: Univ. of Chicago Press, 1980.

———. *Criticism and Social Change.* Chicago: Univ. of Chicago Press, 1983.

Lentricchia, Frank, and Thomas McLaughlin. *Critical Terms for Literary Study.* Chicago: Univ. of Chicago Press, 1990.

Lévi-Strauss, Claude. *Structural Anthropology.* New York: Basic Books, 1963.

Lichtman, Richard. *The Production of Desire: The Integration of Psychoanalysis into Marxist Theory.* New York: The Free Press, 1982.

Livingston, Paisley. *Literary Knowledge: Humanistic Inquiry and the Philosophy of Science.* Ithaca: Cornell Univ. Press, 1988.

Lodge, David. *The Modes of Modern Writing: Metaphor, Metonymy, and the Typology of Modern Literature,* Chicago: Univ. of Chicago Press, 1977.

———. *Nice Work.* New York: Penguin, 1988.

———, ed. *Modern Criticism and Theory: A Reader.* London: Longman, 1988.

Longino, Helen E. "The Ideology of Competition." In *Competition: A Feminist Taboo,* edited by Valerie Miner and Helen E. Longino. New York: Feminist Press, 1987.

Lugones, Maria C., and Elizabeth V. Spelman. "Competition, Compassion, and Community: Models for a Feminist Ethos." In *Competition: A Feminist Taboo,* edited by Valerie Miner and Helen E. Longino. New York: Feminist Press, 1987.

Lyons, John O. "James Joyce and Chaucer's Prioress." *English Language Notes* 2 (1964): 127–32.

Lyotard, Jean-François. *The Postmodern Condition: A Report on Knowledge.* Translated by Geoff Bennigton and Brian Massumi. Minneapolis: Univ. of Minnesota Press, 1984.

MacCabe, Colin, ed. *High Theory/Low Culture: Analyzing Popular Television and Film.* New York: St. Martin's Press, 1986.

Macksey, Richard, and Eugenio Donato, eds. *The Structuralist Controversy: The Languages of Criticism and the Sciences of Man.* Baltimore: Johns Hopkins Univ. Press, 1970.

Mailloux, Steven. *Interpretive Conventions: The Reader in the Study of American Fiction.* Ithaca: Cornell Univ. Press, 1982.

Makaryk, Irena R., ed. and comp. *Encyclopedia of Contemporary Literary Theory: Approaches, Scholars, Terms.* Toronto: Univ. of Toronto Press, 1993.

Mandel, Jerome. "Medieval Romance and the Structure of 'Araby.'" *James Joyce Quarterly* 13, no. 2 (1976): 234–37.

Martin, Wallace. *Recent Theories of Narrative.* Ithaca: Cornell Univ. Press, 1986.

Mayeroff, Milton. *On Caring.* New York: Harper, 1971.

McGowan, John. *Postmodernism and Its Critics.* Ithaca: Cornell Univ. Press, 1991.

McLaren, Peter. *Schooling as a Ritual Performance: Towards a Political Economy of Educational Symbols and Gestures.* London: Routledge and Kegan Paul, 1986.

McMillen, Liz. "Literature's Jeremiah Leaps into the Fray." *Chronicle of Higher Education,* September 7, 1994, A11.

Messer-Davidow, Ellen. "The Philosophic Bases of Feminist Literary Criticisms." *New Literary History* 19 (Autumn 1987): 63–104.

Messer-Davidow, Ellen, and David Shumway. "Disciplinarity: An Introduction." *Poetics Today* 12, no. 2 (1991): 201–25.

Messer-Davidow, Ellen, David R. Shumway, and David J. Sylvan, eds. *Knowledges: Historical and Critical Studies in Disciplinarity.* Charlottesville: Univ. of Virginia Press, 1993.

Meyer, Nicholas. *The Seven-Percent Solution.* New York: Norton, 1993.

Miller, Nancy K. *Getting Personal: Feminist Occasions and Other Autobiographical Acts.* New York: Routledge and Kegan Paul, 1991.

Miner, Valerie, and Helen E. Longino, eds. *Competition: A Feminist Taboo.* New York: Feminist Press, 1987.

Mitchell, W. J. T., ed. *Against Theory.* Chicago: Univ. of Chicago Press, 1985.

Moi, Toril. "Feminism, Postmodernism, and Style: Recent Feminist Criticism in the United States." *Cultural Critique* 9, no. 1 (1988): 3–22.

———. *Sexual/Textual Politics: Feminist Literary Theory.* London and New York: Methuen, 1985.

Morner, Kathleen, and Ralph Rausch. *NTC's Dictionary of Literary Terms.* Lincolnwood, Ill.: National Textbook Company, 1992.

Natoli, Joseph, ed. *Tracing Literary Theory.* Urbana: Univ. of Illinois Press, 1987.

Nelson, Cary, ed. *Theory in the Classroom.* Urbana: Univ. of Illinois Press, 1986.

Nimis, Stephen. "Fussnoten: Der Fundament der Wissenshaft." In *The GRIP Report,* vol. 1, edited by James Sosnoski. Oxford, Ohio: Society for Critical Exchange, 1983.

North, Stephen M. *The Making of Knowledge in Composition: Portrait of an Emerging Field.* Upper Montclair, N.J.: Boynton/Cook, 1987.

Oakeshott, Michael. *On Human Conduct.* Oxford: Clarendon Press, 1975.

Ohmann, Richard. *English in America: A Radical View of the Profession.* New York: Oxford Univ. Press, 1976.

————. *Politics of Letters.* Middletown, Conn.: Wesleyan Univ. Press, 1987.

Parenti, Michael. *Power and the Powerless.* New York: St. Martin's Press, 1978.

Parsons, Talcott, and Gerald M. Platt. *The American University.* Cambridge: Harvard Univ. Press, 1973.

Pears, David. *Ludwig Wittgenstein.* New York: Viking, 1970.

Perelman, Chaim. *The Realm of Rhetoric.* Notre Dame: Univ. of Notre Dame Press, 1982.

Phelan, James. *Life after Tenure.* Columbus: Ohio State Univ. Press, 1991.

Phelps, Louise Wetherbee. *Composition as a Human Science: Contributions to the Self-Understanding of a Discipline.* New York: Oxford Univ. Press, 1988.

Piaget, Jean. *The Psychology of Intelligence.* Paterson, N.J.: Littlefield, Adams and Co., 1963.

Polanyi, Michael. *Personal Knowledge: Towards a Post-Critical Philosophy.* Chicago: Univ. of Chicago Press, 1958.

Popper, Karl. *The Logic of Scientific Discovery.* Translated by Karl Popper, with the assistance of Julius and Lan Freed. New York: Harper and Row, 1968.

Poster, Mark. *Critical Theory and Poststructuralism.* Ithaca: Cornell Univ. Press, 1989.

————. *The Mode of Information: Poststructuralism and Social Context.* Chicago: Univ. of Chicago Press, 1990.

Pratt, Mary Louise. "Arts of the Contact Zone." *Profession 91* (1991): 33–40.

Preminger, Alex. *Princeton Encyclopedia of Poetry and Poetics.* Princeton, N.J.: Princeton Univ. Press, 1974.

Prince, Gerald. *A Dictionary of Narratology.* Lincoln: Univ. of Nebraska Press, 1987.

————. *A Grammar of Stories.* The Hague: Mouton, 1973.

————. "What's the Story in Narratology?" *James Joyce Quarterly* 18 (Spring 1981): 277–85.

Propp, Vladimir. *Morphology of the Folktale.* Translated and edited by Laurence Scott. Austin: Univ. of Texas Press, 1968.

Quine, W. V., and J. S. Ullian. *The Web of Belief.* New York: Random House, 1970.

Racevskis, Karlis. *Michel Foucault and the Subversion of Intellect.* Ithaca: Cornell Univ. Press, 1983.

Ransom, John Crowe. "Criticism Inc." In *The World's Body.* Baton Rouge: Louisiana State Univ. Press, 1968.

Richards, I. A. *The Philosophy of Rhetoric.* New York: Oxford Univ. Press, 1965.

————. *Poetries and Sciences.* New York: Norton, 1926, 1970.

————. *Practical Criticism: A Study of Literary Judgment.* New York: Harcourt, Brace and World, 1929.

————. *The Principles of Literary Criticism.* New York: Harcourt, Brace and World, 1925.

Rooney, Ellen Frances. *Seductive Reasoning: Pluralism as the Problematic of Contemporary Literary Theory.* Ithaca: Cornell Univ. Press, 1989.

Rorty, Richard. *Objectivity, Relativism, and Truth.* Vol. 1 of *Philosophical Papers.* New York: Cambridge Univ. Press, 1991.

Roszak, Theodore. *The Cult of Information.* New York: Pantheon, 1986.

Rueckert, William H. *Kenneth Burke and the Drama of Human Relations.* Minneapolis: Univ. of Minnesota Press, 1963.

Russell, David R. *Writing in the Academic Disciplines, 1870–1990: A Curricular History.* Carbondale and Edwardsville: Southern Illinois Univ. Press, 1991.

Said, Edward. *Beginnings: Intention and Method.* Baltimore: Johns Hopkins Univ. Press, 1975.

———. *Orientalism.* New York: Vintage, 1978.

———. "Response to Stanley Fish." *Critical Inquiry* 10, no. 2 (1983): 371–82.

———. *The World, the Text, and the Critic.* Cambridge: Harvard Univ. Press, 1983.

Saussure, Ferdinand de. *Course in General Linguistics.* Translated by Wade Baskin. New York: Philosophical Library, 1959.

Schilb, John. "Cultural Studies, Postmodernism, and Composition." In *Contending with Words: Composition and Rhetoric in a Postmodern Age,* edited by Patricia Harkin and John Schilb. New York: MLA, 1991.

Schmidt, Henry. "The Rhetoric of Survival: The Germanist in America from 1900–1925." In *The GRIP Report,* vol. 1, edited by James Sosnoski. Oxford, Ohio: Society for Critical Exchange, 1983.

Schmidt, Siegfried. "Literary Science as a Science of Argument." *New Literary History* 7, no. 3 (1976): 467–82.

Shor, Ira. *Critical Teaching and Everyday Life.* Boston: South End Press, 1980.

Shumway, David. *Creating American Civilization: A Genealogy of American Literature as an Academic Discipline.* Minneapolis: Univ. of Minnesota Press, 1994.

———. "Interdisciplinarity and Authority in American Studies." In *The GRIP Report,* vol. 2, edited by James J. Sosnoski. Oxford, Ohio: Society for Critical Exchange, 1984.

———. *Michel Foucault.* Charlottesville: Univ. of Virginia Press, 1989.

———. "Symposium on Crossdisciplinarity." *Social Epistemology* 4, no. 3 (1990):

———, ed. "Episodes in the History of Criticism and Theory: Papers from the Fourth Annual Meeting of the GRIP Project." *Poetics Today* (1988):

Shumway, David, and James Sosnoski. "Critical Protocols." In *The GRIP Report,* vol. 2, edited by James Sosnoski. Oxford, Ohio: Society for Critical Exchange, 1984.

Silverman, David, and Brian Torode. *The Material World: Some Theories of Language and Its Limits.* London: Routledge and Kegan Paul, 1980.

Smith, Barbara Herrnstein. *Contingencies of Value: Alternative Perspectives for Critical Theory.* Cambridge: Harvard Univ. Press, 1988.

Smith, Barbara Herrnstein, Don Bialostosky, David Konstan, and James Sosnoski. "A Conversation with Barbara Herrnstein Smith." PRE/TEXT 10, nos. 3–4 (1989): 143–63.

Smith, Frank. *Understanding Reading: A Psycholinguistic Analysis of Reading and Learning to Read.* New York: Holt, Rinehart and Winston, 1971.

Smith, Paul. *Discerning the Subject.* Minneapolis: Univ. of Minnesota Press, 1988.

Sosnoski, James J. "Analyzing 'Araby' as Story and Discourse: A Summary of the MURGE Project." *James Joyce Quarterly* 18 (Spring 1981): 237–54.

———. "Cleanth Brooks." In *Modern American Critics, 1920–1955,* edited by Gregory S. Jay. Detroit: Gale Research Co., 1988.

———. "Edward Said." In *The Johns Hopkins Guide to Literary Criticism and Theory,* edited by Michael Grogan and Martin Kreiswirth. Baltimore: Johns Hopkins Univ. Press, 1994.

————. "Examining Exams." In *Knowledges: Historical and Critical Studies in Disciplinarity,* edited by Ellen Messer-Davidow, David R. Shumway, and David J. Sylvan. Charlottesville: Univ. of Virginia Press, 1993.

————. "The GRIP Project: An Alternative to Traditional Research Practices in the Humanities." *Federation Reports: The Journal of the State Humanities Councils* 4 (April-May 1984): 7.

————. "Interpretive Force." *Critical Exchange* 24 (Winter 1988): 63–64.

————. "The Invention of the Literary Scholar." *North Dakota Quarterly* 55, no. 3 (1987): 40–48.

————. "Literary Study as a Field of Inquiry." *Boundary 2* 13 (Winter-Spring 1985): 91–104.

————. "Literary Study in a Post-Modern Era: Rereading Its History." *Works and Days* 9, no. 1 (1987): 7–33.

————. "The *Magister Implicatus* as an Institutional Authority Figure." In *The GRIP Report,* vol. 1, edited by James Sosnoski. Oxford, Ohio: Society for Critical Exchange, 1983.

————. "A Mindless, Man-Driven Theory Machine: Intellectuality, Sexuality, and the Institution of Criticism." In *Feminism and Institutions: Dialogues on Feminist Theory,* edited by Linda Kaufmann. London: Basil Blackwell, 1989; reprinted in *Feminisms: An Anthology of Literary Theory and Criticism.* edited by Robyn R. Worhol and Diane Price Herndl. New Brunswick, N.J.: Rutgers Univ. Press, 1991.

————. "On the Anvil of Theoretical Debate: *Story and Discourse* as Literary Theory." *James Joyce Quarterly* 18 (Spring 1981): 267–76.

————. "Postmodern Teachers in Their Postmodern Classrooms: Socrates Begone!" In *Contending with Words: Composition and Rhetoric in a Postmodern Age,* edited by Patricia Harkin and John Schilb. New York: MLA, 1991.

————. "The Psycho-Politics of Error." *PRE/TEXT* 10, nos. 1–2 (1989): 33–52.

————. "Reading Acts and Reading Warrants: Some Implications for Readers Responding to Joyce's Portrait of Stephen." *James Joyce Quarterly* 16 (Fall 1978–Winter 1979): 43–64.

————. "The Role of Selection Strategies in Reading(s)." *Reader* (Fall 1983): 10, 14–27.

————. "*Story and Discourse* and the Practice of Literary Criticism: 'Araby,' A Test Case." *James Joyce Quarterly* 18 (Spring 1981): 255–65.

————. "Students as Theorists: Collaborative Hypertextbooks." In *Practicing Theory in Introductory College Literature Courses,* edited by James M. Cahalan and David B. Downing. Urbana, Ill.: National Council of Teachers of English, 1991.

————. "The Theory Junkyard." *Minnesota Review* 41–42 (Fall 1993–Spring 1994): 80–94.

————. "The Token Professional." *JMMLA* 17 (Fall 1984): 1–12.

————. *Token Professionals and Master Critics: A Critique of Orthodoxy in Literary Studies.* Albany: State Universities of New York Press, 1994.

————. "The Use of the Word 'Text' in Critical Discourse." *College English* 39 (1977): 121–36.

————. "Why Theory? Rethinking Pedagogy." *Works and Days* 8, no. 2 (1990): 29–40.

Sosnoski, James J., K. Burkland, T. Cooper, L. Epstein, and K. Gannon. "Invisible Silences." *Works and Days* 8, no. 2 (1990): 41–47.

Sosnoski, James J., and David Downing. "The Protocol of Care in the Cycles Project." *JMMLA* 7 (Spring 1994): 75–84.

Sosnoski, James J., Henry Giroux, David Shumway, and Paul Smith. "The Need for Cultural Studies: Resisting Intellectuals and Oppositional Public Spheres." *Dalhousie Review* 64 (Summer 1984): 472–86.

Sosnoski, James J., and Patricia Harkin. "Barbara Herrnstein Smith: A Contemporary Sophist." *PRE/TEXT* 10, nos. 3–4 (1989): 135–40.

————. "The Case for Hyper-Gradesheets: A Modest Proposal." *College English* 54, no. 1 (1992): 22–30.

Sosnoski, James J., Patricia Harkin, and David Downing. "Configurations of Lore: Changing Relations of Theory, Research, and Pedagogy." In *Changing Classroom Practices: Resources for Literary and Cultural Studies,* edited by David Downing. Urbana, Ill.: National Council of Teachers of English, 1994.

Sosnoski, James J., and David Shumway. "Critical Protocols." In *The GRIP Report,* vol. 2, edited by James Sosnoski. Oxford, Ohio: Society for Cultural Exchange, 1984.

Sproule, J. Michael. *Argument: Language and Its Influence.* New York: McGraw-Hill, 1980.

Swales, John M. "The Concept of Discourse Community: Dog, Cash Cow, Problem Child or Star?" Lecture handout. Univ. of Toledo Rhetoric Symposium, 1992.

————. *Genre Analysis: English in Academic and Research Settings.* Cambridge: Cambridge Univ. Press, 1991.

Tamen, Miguel. *Manners of Interpretation: The Ends of Argument in Literary Studies.* Albany: State Univ. of New York Press, 1993.

Todorov, Tsvetan. *The Poetics of Prose.* Ithaca: Cornell Univ. Press, 1977.

Toulmin Stephen. *Human Understanding: The Collective Use and Evolution of Concepts.* Princeton: Princeton Univ. Press, 1972.

————. *The Uses of Argument.* Cambridge: Cambridge Univ. Press, 1976.

Toulmin, Stephen, Richard Rieke, and Allan Janik. *An Introduction to Reasoning.* New York: Macmillan, 1979.

Touraine, Alain. *The Academic System in American Society.* New York: McGraw-Hill, 1974.

Ulmer, Gregory. *Teletheory: Grammatology in the Age of Video.* New York: Routledge and Kegan Paul, 1989.

————. "Teletheory: A Mystory." In *The Current in Criticism: Essays on the Present and Future of Literary Theory,* edited by Clayton Koelb and Vergil Lokke. West Lafayette, Ind.: Purdue Univ. Press: 1987.

————. "Textshop for Post(e)pedagogy." In *Writing and Reading Differently: Deconstruction and the Teaching of Composition and Literature,* edited by G. Douglas Atkins and Michael Johnson. Lawrence: Univ. Press of Kansas, 1985.

Vallance, Elizabeth. "Hiding the Hidden Curriculum: An Interpretation of the Language of Justification in Nineteenth-Century Educational Reform." In *The Hidden Curriculum and Moral Education,* edited by Henry Giroux and David Purpel. Berkeley, Calif.: McCutchan, 1983.

Vattimo, Gianni. *The End of Modernity.* Translated and with an Introduction by Jon R. Snyder. Baltimore: Johns Hopkins Univ. Press, 1988.

Veeser, H. Aram. *The New Historicism.* New York: Routledge and Kegan Paul, 1989.

Veysey, Laurence R. *The Emergence of the American University.* Chicago: Univ. of Chicago Press, 1965.

Vitanza, Victor J. "'Notes' Towards Historiographies of Rhetorics; or The Rhetorics of the Histories of Rhetorics: Traditional, Revisionary, Sub/versive." *PRE/TEXT* 8, nos. 1–2 (1987): 63–125.

———. "Three Countertheses: Or, A Critical In(ter)vention into Composition Theories and Pedagogies." In *Contending with Words: Composition and Rhetoric in a Postmodern Age,* edited by Patricia Harkin and John Schilb. New York: MLA, 1991.

———, ed. "Special Issue on Kenneth Burke." *PRE/TEXT* 6, nos. 3–4 (1985).

Watkins, Evan. "Conflict and Consensus in the History of Recent Criticism." *New Literary History* 12 (Winter 1981): 345–65.

———. "Cultural Criticism and Literary Intellectuals." *Works and Days* 5 (Spring 1985): 11–31.

———. *Work Time: English Departments and the Circulation of Cultural Value.* Stanford, Calif.: Stanford Univ. Press, 1989.

Watson, George. *The Literary Critics: A Study of English Descriptive Crticism.* Baltimore: Penguin, 1962.

Watzlawick, Paul, Janet Helmick Beavin, and Don D. Jackson. *Pragmatics of Human Communication: A Study of Interactional Patterns, Pathologies, and Paradoxes.* New York: Norton, 1967.

Weber, Samuel. *Institution and Interpretation.* Minneapolis: Univ. of Minnesota Press, 1987.

———, ed. *Demarcating the Disciplines.* Minneapolis: Univ. of Minnesota Press, 1986.

Webster, Grant. *The Republic of Letters: A History of Postwar American Literary Opinion.* Baltimore: Johns Hopkins Univ. Press, 1979.

Wellek, René. *A History of Modern Criticism 1750–1950.* Vol. 6, *American Criticism 1900–1950.* Princeton, N.J.: Princeton Univ. Press, 1986.

———. "Literary Theory, Criticism, and History." In *Concepts of Criticism,* edited by Stephen G. Nichols Jr. New Haven: Yale Univ. Press, 1967.

Wellek, René, and Austin Warren. *Theory of Literature.* New York: Harcourt, 1956.

Widdowson, Peter, ed. *Re-Reading English.* London: Methuen, 1982.

Willard, Charles Arthur. *Argumentation and the Social Grounds of Knowledge.* Tuscaloosa: Univ. of Alabama Press, 1983.

Williams, Raymond. *Culture.* Glasgow: Fontana Press, 1981.

———. *Keywords.* New York: Oxford Univ. Press, 1976.

Wimsatt, W. K., Jr. *The Verbal Icon.* Lexington: Univ. of Kentucky Press, 1954.

Wimsatt, W. K., Jr., and Monroe Beardsley. "The Intentional Fallacy." In *The Verbal Icon.* Lexington: Univ. of Kentucky Press, 1954.

Winchester, C. T. *Some Principles of Literary Criticism.* New York: Macmillan, 1911.

Wittgenstein, Ludwig. *Philosophical Investigations.* Translated by G. E. M. Anscombe. Oxford: Basil Blackwell, 1953.

Zavarzadeh, Mas'ud, and Donald Morton. "Theory Pedagogy Politics: The Crisis of 'The Subject' in the Humanities." *Boundary 2* 15, nos. 1–2 (Fall 1986–Winter 1987): 1–22.

———, eds. *Texts for Change: Theory/Pedagogy/Politics.* Urbana: Univ. of Illinois Press, 1991.

Index of Names

Index of Concepts